D1648574

THE COLOGNE COMMUNIST TRIAL

ST. MARY'S COLLEGE OF MARYLAND
ST. MARY'S CITY, MARYLAND

055342

KARL MARX
AND
FREDERICK ENGELS

THE COLOGNE
COMMUNIST TRIAL

Revelations Concerning the Communist Trial in Cologne by Karl Marx,
Heroes of the Exile by Karl Marx and Frederick Engels, together with
other writings by Marx and Engels on the Cologne Trial

Translated with an Introduction and Notes
by
RODNEY LIVINGSTONE

INTERNATIONAL PUBLISHERS
NEW YORK

Copyright © Lawrence & Wishart, 1971

First U.S. Edition, 1971

All rights reserved

ISBN 0-7178-0240-X

Printed in England

CONTENTS

INTRODUCTION 9

ON THE HISTORY OF THE COMMUNIST LEAGUE—Frederick Engels 37
REVELATIONS CONCERNING THE COMMUNIST TRIAL IN COLOGNE
—Karl Marx 57
NOTES 118
THE COMMUNIST TRIAL IN COLOGNE (Appendix 4 to *Herr Vogt*,
1860)—Karl Marx 120
POSTSCRIPT (1875)—Karl Marx 131
HEROES OF THE EXILE—Karl Marx and Frederick Engels 135
NOTES 231

APPENDIX A
  I. Address of the Central Committee to the Communist
     League, March 1850—Karl Marx and Frederick Engels 237
 II. Address of the Central Committee to the Communist
     League, June 1850—Karl Marx and Frederick Engels 245
III. Minutes of the Meeting of the Central Committee of the
     Communist League of September 15, 1850—Hermann
     Wilhelm Haupt 250
 IV. Address of the Cologne Central Committee to the Com-
     munist League, December 1850 254
  V. Statutes of the Communist League 257

APPENDIX B
  I. Prussian Spies in London (*The Spectator*, June 14, 1850)—
     Karl Marx and Frederick Engels 263
 II. Prussian Spies in London: report published by the *Morning
     Advertiser*, October 26, 1852 265
III. The Cologne Trials: Declaration to the editors of the
     English Press (*The People's Paper*, October 30, 1852)—
     Karl Marx and Frederick Engels 266
 IV. Report of the Communist Trial in *The Times* (October 12,
     1852) 267
  V. The Trial of Cologne: Declaration to the Editor of the
     Morning Advertiser (November 2, 1852)—Karl Marx 268
 VI. A Final Declaration on the Late Cologne Trials (*Morning
     Advertiser*, November 29, 1852)—Karl Marx and Frederick
     Engels 269

VII. The Berlin Conspiracy (*New York Daily Tribune*, April 18, 1853)—Karl Marx   271

VIII. The Berlin Conspiracy (*New York Daily Tribune*, April 21, 1853)—Karl Marx   273

IX. Hirsch's Confessions—Karl Marx   275

X. Gottfried Kinkel—Charles Dickens   277

SELECT BIBLIOGRAPHY   286

INDEX OF NAMES   287

NOTE

The English translations of *On the History of the Communist League*, by Frederick Engels, and the *Address of the Central Committee of the Communist League* of March 1850, by Karl Marx and Frederick Engels, are taken from *Marx and Engels Selected Works*, two volumes, Lawrence & Wishart, London.

INTRODUCTION

The subject of the two pamphlets translated here is the revolution in defeat. The *Revelations concerning the Communist Trial in Cologne* by Marx and the *Heroes of the Exile* by Marx and Engels reflect different facets of the aftermath of the revolution of 1848. *Revelations* is a bitter attack on the triumphant reaction in Prussia. *Heroes of the Exile* is a no less bitter polemic against the political *émigrés* with whom Marx was forced to share his own exile. *Revelations* exposes the direct impact of the reaction on the working class in Germany, *Heroes of the Exile* shows the response of the *émigrés* to the indirect, but no less powerful pressures they were subjected to in exile. Written in 1852, the two pamphlets are satirical works of great power, despite the great difficulties in which *Revelations*, especially, was written.

The pamphlets are connected both in their outward fates and inner themes in a number of ways. The royal "plot" which set the machinery in motion that led to the trial of the Cologne members of the Communist League was itself provoked by the escape from prison of Gottfried Kinkel, the petit bourgeois revolutionary who figures so largely in *Heroes of the Exile*. The loss for over a century of the latter work was due to its theft by the Hungarian Colonel Bangya who was also one of the links in the chain that led to the arrest of the Cologne communists. There is a partial overlap in the dramatis personae of the two works and the ramifications of the intrigues, plots and counter-plots among the various *émigré* groups and governments are endless.

Above all, however, the two works reflect Marx's efforts to clarify his own position with regard to the strategy and tactics of revolution, to re-assess the situation in the light of the defeat of 1848 and to establish a firm demarcation line between his own views and those of the other revolutionaries in exile. His own position is based on the gradual recognition that the time was no longer ripe for revolution and that what was needed was a much more profound analysis of society and above all of its economic foundations. This insight distinguishes him from all the other *émigrés* who, still convinced that revolution was only just around the corner, were full of schemes for provoking and exploiting it. In the *Heroes of the Exile* he satirises the essentially romantic attitudes of the *émigrés*, attitudes that naturally give rise to innumerable crack-brained schemes for instant revolution. In the *Revelations*, this theoretical debate has a practical implication: he is concerned to prevent the police from attempting to secure a conviction

A*

by identifying his position with that of the conspiratorial tendencies of Willich and Schapper.

The background to both pamphlets is the development of the reaction after 1848. Specifically, the events leading up to the trial of the Cologne communists represent an important stage in that development. A brief account of the main events will therefore enable us to see the trial and hence Marx's pamphlet in its context.

I

The Prussian Reaction after 1848

The revolution collapsed in Prussia in the autumn of 1848. Encouraged by the storming of Vienna by Windischgrätz, the Prussian army under Wrangel entered Berlin. This led to the enforced withdrawal of the Prussian Assembly to Brandenburg and then to its dissolution. Then came a *coup d'état* by the King, Frederick William IV, who imposed a constitution, the so-called "dictated constitution", on his subjects on December 5, 1848. This meant that the old ruling classes were now more or less firmly back in the saddle. However, the reaction did not come all at once. What followed was a protracted battle lasting about five years between the principal ruling classes until they reached what was to them a satisfactory arrangement. Moreover, it was not possible simply to turn the clock back to the Metternich system. The new reaction that emerged was a synthesis between the old ruling classes—the Junkers, monarchy and bureaucracy—and the liberal bourgeoisie. The victims in this struggle were, of course, the peasantry, the artisans and the factory workers. The state that emerged set the pattern for the later Bismarckian state: a modern, ruthless and efficient industrial society, functioning within a revitalised framework of feudalism. Characteristic of it was the way in which the feudal aristocracy retained political hegemony, while ceding economic dominance to the middle classes. It was this compromise, achieved at the expense of the lower classes, that was worked out in the years following 1848. It is important to realise that even though the Communist Trial was directed at the industrial workers in the first instance, the working class was too small and undeveloped to become the true antagonist of the ruling class and that it takes second place to the emerging bourgeoisie. This is not to imply that its role in the struggle was insignificant or

lacking in consequences for the later history of the working class and of
Germany as a whole.

The Camarilla

Decisive though the defeat of the revolutionaries had been, the
aristocrary had not escaped unscathed. Their traditional bastions had
been gravely undermined by the liberals. In the army they could count
only on the officers; the civil service was badly infected by liberalism
and even the king had shown signs that, rather than rely exclusively
on the nobility, he might prefer to play the role of "Bürgerkönig"—
provided the conditions were right.

The Junkers rallied around a small group of nobles, headed by the
brothers Leopold and Ernst Ludwig von Gerlach, von Thadden-
Trieglaff and including Bismarck. It was this group that became known
as the Camarilla and it was their policies, in a modified form, that
came to dominate Prussia. Their ideals—the restoration of the absolutist corporate state of feudalism, were reactionary by any standards and
made even the king look almost liberal.

They succeeded in winning a twofold victory. Externally they
defeated the king, the liberal nobility and the bourgeoisie by preventing
a unification of Germany under Prussia. Internally they weathered an
agricultural revolution that enabled them to make the transition from
feudal to capitalist landownership.

Having rejected the offer of the German crown by the Frankfurt
Parliament, Frederick William IV was under pressure from Radowitz
and the so-called Gotha Party to bring about his own unification of
Germany, using the opportunity created by the continued weakness of
Austria. The Erfurt Union of March 20, 1850 attempted to bring the
smaller German states into line with this policy. However, Austria
was bound to be antagonistic, firstly because of its natural hostility to
Prussian hegemony in Germany and secondly because a unified
Germany contradicted the very idea of the supranational Austrian
state. That is to say the problems on which the Frankfurt Assembly had
foundered were still crucial. In May 1850 Austria revived the Bund,
the instrument of its own dominance of Germany under Metternich.
This led to a head-on collision between Austria and Prussia. It was
resolved externally by Nicholas I who opted for Austria and, within
Prussia, by the Camarilla. The Gerlachs naturally favoured the Czar
and Austria because the represented the traditional fuedal order. They
were suspicious of Frederick William IV and quite hostile towards

Radowitz. German unification under Prussia "smelled too much of the Paulskirche", i.e. of revolution. Hence they swung their support behind the Austrians and the Czar, Radowitz resigned and at Olmütz (November 19, 1859) Prussia agreed to abandon the Erfurt Union and to revive the Bund.

Thus Olmütz marked a decisive victory both for Austria and for the Camarilla, which controlled Prussia from then until 1858. As Leopold von Gerlach put it in his diary (1873): "Without Olmütz there would have been no period of reaction 1850–1858, no Bismarck . . . no victory over the enemies of the army from 1862 to 1866, no Sadowa, no Metz, no Sedan, no Paris, no German Empire."

The victory of Olmütz was followed by a change in government which introduced members of the Camarilla: Manteuffel, not himself in the Camarilla and regarded by them as a liberal, became Prime Minister, but other members were more acceptable, in particular Ferdinand von Westphalen, Marx's brother-in-law, who became Minister of the Interior, Hinckeldey the Police President of Berlin and Bismarck, who became Prussian representative at the Bundestag in Frankfurt.

The other issue on which the Camarilla joined battle with the Liberals was agriculture. The Camarilla had originally been formed to combat the liberal policy of ending the exemption of the nobility from taxation. The liberal policy on agriculture was in line with this: to end the police powers of the nobles, to commute feudal dues, to complete the emancipation of the serfs which had been initiated by Stein and Hardenberg but had languished since 1812.

The decrees of March 2, 1850, completed the process of emancipation. They were carried through despite opposition from the Gerlachs and had the effect of conciliating the peasantry. In fact, however, the Junkers were forced to make only a few political concessions in return for which they made very real economic gains. Servile obligations were abolished, as were the police powers of the nobles. The peasants were given the chance to buy the land they farmed at a price 18 times its annual value. Loan banks were established to advance long-term, low interest credit to the peasants. But here as elsewhere this largely meant that the peasants were thrown off their lands. Between 1850 and 1865 640,000 peasants freed themselves of their feudal obligations (three times as many as in the previous 35 years); in Pomerania and Silesia 13 per cent of the land under cultivation left peasant hands, the Junkers consolidated their estates in the east and thousands of peasants poured into the towns, becoming the "industrial reserve army". Even though the whole process enriched the Junkers enormously they felt badly done by because they were suffering from foreign competition. Many landowners saw their estates fall to the moneylenders and throughout the rest of the century impoverished nobles were only too happy to marry the rich daughters of businessmen to re-establish their fortunes. Others were more fortunate and were able to modernise their estates by farming them on a capitalist basis using cheap labour. To complete the Junker victory the privileges they had lost in 1850 were restored to them between 1852 (entails again legalised) and 1854 (rights of rural communities to govern themselves revoked and manorial police powers restored).

The Liberals

The bourgeoisie were badly defeated by the army and even more terrified of radicalism. After the War for the Imperial Constitution (1849) both they and the radicals suffered greatly at the hands of the military courts. Hence they were only too eager to achieve a merger with the ruling classes; they were happy to get what political concessions they could, however trivial, if only they could make real economic gains.

The dictated constitution of December 1848 and the revised constitution of December 1849 provided no more than the appearance of constitutional law. Admittedly a two-chamber system was set up, but the Three-Class Electoral Law of May 1849 ensured extremely conservative majorities. The constitution contained provisions guaranteeing basic rights such as freedom of worship, freedom of opinion and freedom of speech. Censorship was abolished and compulsory education and military service were introduced. But all these rights and duties were interpreted differently for the various classes. Thus the nobility had private schools, conscription for them meant one year's service as an officer. Freedom of opinion did not save theatrical plays from censorship because a play is not the expression of an opinion and therefore may be censored. By 1851 the whole book industry was put under state control, newspapers had to put up caution money, deposit copies with the police, and so on. Most of the "freedoms" thus obtained were undermined in practice. Nevertheless, unlike Franz Joseph, Frederick William IV could never do away with the constitution altogether.

These facts were unpalatable to the bourgeoisie, but the liberals nevertheless hastened to accept them. As early as the beginning of 1849 the old Revolutionaries Hansemann, Camphausen and Harkort were to be found supporting the government in the Chambers. They were in fact content to subordinate themselves to the nobility if only they could gain economic advantages. Their chief gain under the new system was control of the Ministry of Trade under Von der Heydt. This enabled them to pass measures that laid the foundation for the industrial revolution in Prussia.

The Prussian economy was of course backward compared to those of England and France. But like them it enjoyed the advantages of a boom after the collapse of the revolution. The years of depression had stimulated demand; the gold-rushes in California and Australia rapidly increased the supply of money and these two factors provided a stimulus to set up new factories. Germany recovered more slowly than France and England but even in its backward state of 1850 industrial profit was growing at a faster rate than Junker profit from land, so that weak though the bourgeoisie appeared, the future already belonged to them.

The first few years after the revolution saw the construction of the framework for the new industrial state. A decree was passed permitting the formation of share companies. A series of laws on the mines (which had hitherto either belonged to the Crown or were run under state direction) opened them up to capitalist development. The railway network which had been established for military purposes was now adapted to commercial ones. The first of the four great German banks was founded. These measures produced a boom in which new businesses proliferated, and if the economy developed so quickly in the latter half of the century, this was due in great measure to the great profits amassed in the early 1850s.

The compromise between the bourgeoisie and the old ruling classes was sealed symbolically by the establishment of the Royal Order of the House of Hohenzollern. This Order was available primarily to the aristocracy but it could also be purchased by members of the middle classes for 1,500 Talers, i.e. the king used this means to open up a road to the aristocracy for the bourgeoisie.

The Working Class

Germany was still predominantly rural at the end of the revolution. The working class was still quite small and within it there was an almost unbridgeable gulf between the traditional artisans and the modern factory workers. In 1849 about 541,000 people worked in factories while artisans and workers in the domestic industries were about five times as numerous. There were few large factories (in 1848 Borsig was one of the biggest with 1,200 employees) and a large number of factories were barely distinguishable from artisans' and manufacturing workshops.

Socially, however, the gulf between factory worker and artisan was deep and enduring. The artisans looked down on the factory workers. Factory produce was often imperfect and crude compared to handicraft and the artisan tended to think of himself as a craftsman. Among the factory workers were many women and children and the men were essentially transformed farm-labourers who had flocked to the city. Nevertheless, the factory workers earned more even at this time and the guilds were rapidly collapsing in the face of competition from the factories. The artisans tended to cling to their faith in the traditional system and their views were often reactionary. There was much hostility towards machines, and the masters put pressure on the government to restrict "Gewerbefreiheit", the freedom to exercise trade outside the guild system.

The conditions of the workers improved superficially in the early 1850s. Wages rose and prices remained stable until 1851, when they started to rise in an inflationary spiral that did not end until the crash at the end of the decade. But living standards were low and Reden's statistics (quoted by Herrnstadt) suggest that the wages of 90 per cent of the population were below subsistence level. In 1848 there had been serious outbreaks of cholera and typhoid and in addition unemployment was rife. In Breslau, for example, the second largest city in Prussia, 32,000 people depended on charity out of a total population of 104,000. Moreover, the flood of emigrants which had abated immediately after the revolution again began to rise, reaching its highpoint in 1854 when 252,000 people left the country.

The attitude of the government was inspired by conservatism of the public service. Radowitz, for example, had hoped to pursue a paternalistic policy designed to drive a wedge between the workers and socialism. Traces of this attitude can be found in the law of May 16, 1853, banning work for children under 12 and restricting the hours worked by children from 12 to 14 to 6 hours per day (at a time when 8 was the minimum age for child workers in England and France). Measures like this were passed by the conservatives in the face of bitter opposition by the liberals who regarded them as unduly restricting the right to work. The Camarilla, however, was mainly concerned to perpetuate the division between the artisans and factory workers by supporting the former and repressing the latter. A series of decrees were passed imposing restrictions on "Gewerbefreiheit" and under their influence the decline of the guilds was temporarily halted. Of course, in the long run their collapse could not be avoided but for the time being the alliance between the classes intent on reviving and strengthening privilege weakened working-class opposition.

The existence of such an "alliance" did not prevent the government from taking a repressive line with regard to all kinds of workers' organisations. The Constitution contained provisions guaranteeing the workers' right to form associations, but these were so hedged about with restrictions as to undermine the constitutional guarantees. Thus by a law of June 19, 1849, political associations were required to register and obtain official permission for public meetings "to prevent the abuse of the right to organise and associate in such a manner as to jeopardise public freedom and order". By a further law of March 11, 1850, meetings could only be held under police supervision. Women, children, schoolboys and apprentices were not allowed to attend. There was also a ban on all interclub committees or any form of centralised organisation. Again, all large outside meetings required police approval "except for funerals, weddings, church processions, pilgrimages, etc.". (Paradoxically, the restriction on central organisation did not apply to parties putting up candidates for election so that the reaction which was so repressive towards working-class organisations presided over the birth of the Prussian political parties.) A law of June 5, 1850, proclaimed a ban on the Berlin Workers Clubs and in general the police and minor officials were encouraged to show their zeal in putting down workers' organisations.

One contradiction in this policy is worthy of note. Anxious though the government was to disrupt political associations, it was nevertheless eager to retain organisational co-operation between workers. This was particularly important with respect to the so-called Wanderzeit of the journeymen training in the various trades. Thanks to this anomaly it was possible to make use of the journeymen to set up the system of emissaries which played such a significant part in the organisation of the Communist League.

The restrictions on working-class organisations could not fail to have their effect also on the Communist League. Of course, members of the League had been heavily involved in the revolution and this is particularly true of the Cologne branch. Cologne had been the centre of the activities of Marx and Engels and it was from here that they published the *Neue Rheinische Zeitung*. It is perhaps worth recalling that Cologne was the centre of the Rhine Province and as such of the most progressive part of Germany. It had the most advanced and varied industry, it was the most densely populated part of Prussia and Cologne was the third largest town in Prussia (after Berlin and Breslau). There was a sizeable proletariat and also a large, influential and in many respects progressive bourgeoisie. The traditions of the province were far more liberal than those of Prussia as a whole. This was reflected, for example, in the fact that the Code Napoleon was in force, political trials were held before juries and not professional judges and the trials were public and oral, not secret and written as in the rest of Prussia.

These facts are relevant to our assessment of the attack on the Cologne communists. Whereas all the ruling classes were agreed on the need to curb radicalism their motives were different. The Liberals were, of course, concerned to suppress radicalism among the workers and were even happy to put up with humiliations and persecution from the aristocracy if only this were done. The aristocracy, for their part (as Marx pointed out in the Postscript of 1875) were using the fear of radicalism as a stick with which to beat the Liberals. Thus the holding of the Trial in Cologne was, among other things, an attempt to beard the liberal bourgeoisie in their most important stronghold.

II

From the Royal "Plot" to the arrest of the Cologne Communists

By the end of 1850 the Reaction had achieved a preliminary consolidation of its position. With Olmütz something like the restoration of the Bund under Austrial hegemony had been established. The Revised Constitution of December 1849 concluded the preliminary series of political manoeuvres between the Junkers, the King and the liberal bourgeoisie. The process of placating the artisans and the peasantry, at least to the extent of reducing their militancy was well underway. Formal concessions had been made to revolutionary liberal demands while the reactionary forces had re-occupied positions of strength. The time was therefore ripe to eradicate the last vestiges of overt radicalism in the petite bourgeoisie and especially the working class. The "plot" following Kinkel's escape in November 1850 had this

function. Moreover, it was still possible to play on the fear of radicalism, of subversive activities by communists and others and thus make
more palatable the severe measures still to be enacted.

The final defeat of the revolutionaries at Rastatt in July 1849 brought
about also the collapse of the Cologne Workers' Club. In June 1849
there were no more than five local branches left (this rump was presided over by Röser). The end of July 1849 saw the Workers' Club
transformed into a Reading Circle or Educational Association (with
Röser, Reiff and Otto on the committee).

Meanwhile, Marx and Engels were making attempts to revive the
League from England. They sent Heinrich Bauer to Germany as an
emissary bringing the Address of March 1850 and by the early summer
the League had begun to revive; according to the June Address there
were centres at Frankfurt, Hanau, Mainz, Wiesbaden, Hamburg,
Schwerin and Berlin, in addition to Cologne. Thus despite the divisions
that developed in the League in the summer and autumn of 1850 (and
to which we shall return) some definite progress had been made by the
end of 1850. It was at this point however that the Prussian government
intensified its attack on the workers' movement.

The shock of Kinkel's escape from Spandau in November 1850 at
once raised the spectre of revolution in the muddled mind of Frederick
William IV. And not in his alone. One need only read the account given
by Dickens in *Household Words* of Kinkel languishing in gaol to see
what a romantic symbol he had become. Marx duly deflates the story
in *Heroes of the Exile*, but the echoes of Richard Coeur de Lion rescued
by his faithful Blondel are not fortuitous and the escape of such a
dangerous and intrepid revolutionary struck terror into the heart of the
Prussian monarch. Or perhaps he just saw his chance to tighten the
screw a little further. However that may be we are in possession of the
following curious document written by the king to his Prime Minister.

"My dear Manteuffel,
I have just finished reading the report of Kinkel's escape. It has
given me an idea which I would not exactly regard as honourable.
Namely, is it not so that Stieber would be an excellent person to
disentangle the knots of the conspiracy and at long last regale the
Prussian public with the long and justly awaited spectacle of the
discovery and (above all) the *punishment* of a plot? *Make all haste
therefore with Stieber's appointment* and let him show us a *specimen of
his talent.* I believe that this idea could be very fruitful and I attach
the very greatest importance to its *immediate implementation.* Niebuhr

reminds you in my name of the most vital task that faces us at present, namely of the projected alliance with England through Radowitz and Bunsen — Moses and Aaron. There is not a moment to lose. Burn this letter.

Vale! F.W."

The King's not exactly honourable idea was put into practice with all possible speed. On November 15, 1850, Stieber was installed as the head of the political police, i.e. as Hinckeldey's right-hand man. Hinckeldey was not entirely pleased with Stieber, who indeed succeeded in repelling almost everyone with whom he came into contact. He had begun his career by defending liberal revolutionaries, but as Marx makes clear, even at that time there were murky elements in his past. From the time of his appointment he develops into the very incarnation of a brutal and repressive police chief. In the Cologne Trial he becomes the chief enemy not only of the accused but by intimidation and corrupt practices he seeks to subdue the defence, the judges and even overrules the prosecution. In later years his methods came under attack and he was even put on trial and, though acquitted, was forced to retire prematurely (in 1860). Despite this he survived to become the head of Bismarck's secret police and was even involved in the preparatory investigations that eventually led to the banning of the Social Democrats.

The King's letter resulted in a flurry of activity among the Prussian authorities. On January 1, 1851, Westphalen announced that there would be a ruthless attack on democratic tendencies. Much of the attention of the police was focused on the coming Great Exhibition in London. From the police point of view London had developed into the centre of *émigré* activity. On March 9, 1851, Manteuffel and Westphalen attempted to persuade Bunsen (Prussian Ambassador to England) to induce the British government to expel all refugees. Westphalen had the idea that the British government might comply if proof of a treasonable plot could be brought. A greater and more immediate success in the Cologne Trial might have been used to achieve this. In the event Bunsen had no success, but this was by no means the end of police action. Westphalen encouraged the idea that the Great Exhibition might be used as a centre for a world-wide revolutionary plot. To counter this Hinckeldey sought firstly to enlarge the police network in London: in the spring of 1851 he organised the sending of informers to London. Alberts, an Embassy secretary in London, was put in charge of spies and agents. The enlarged police force was of course partly concealed from the British government and partly represented to them as being a harmless but necessary measure to control the inevitable influx of pickpockets and petty criminals during the Exhibition. Hinckeldey's second aim was to intensify co-operation with the other German governments. The abolition of manorial police meant the establishment for the first time of a modern centralised police system. Throughout this period Hinckeldey was anxious to expand and consolidate it, and the discovery of subversive activities would prove very helpful here. The police were convinced that workers would use the Exhibition as an excuse to emigrate to London. The various chiefs of police in the main German states were therefore requested to draw up a black list of people applying for passports to England or who travelled to England without passports and came to the notice of the police. Throughout the spring of 1851 there were frequent consultations between the various police chiefs, who formed an Association of Security Officials for the Maintenance of Public Order and Tranquility. At the beginning of April 1851 they received information from Brussels about the possibility of an uprising. On April 9th it was resolved to mount a strict watch on all travellers "especially Poles and Frenchmen—and to put difficulties in the way of workshy artisans and other vagrants". This meant a strict guard at the main railway stations and it was thus a police trap into which Nothjung, the emissary of the Cologne Communists, fell on May 10, 1851. The documents found on him—among them the March and June Addresses and the *Communist Manifesto*—were sufficient to persuade the police that they had uncovered a gigantic plot.

From the Arrest of Nothjung (May 10, 1851) to the Trial (October 4, 1852)

The arrest of Nothjung was followed by a massive police campaign. On June 4, 1851, the Minister of Justice Simons issued an instruction to the Chief Prosecutor in Cologne to use all possible means including "house-searchings, confiscations and precautionary arrests . . . with all energy and speed". This led at first only to the arrest of another member of the League, Wilhelm Haupt, who did not indeed reveal any evidence against the League, but did disclose the names of the prominent League members. He was induced to turn King's evidence, but disappeared to Brazil before the trial opened. However, his statements enabled the police to arrest the other League members: Röser, Bürgers, Becker, Daniels, Otto, Jacobi, Klein, Erhard, Reiff and Lessner. There was also a warrant out for the arrest of Ferdinand Freiligrath, the poet who had written for the *Neue Rheinische Zeitung*, but he had escaped to England. Of the accused, Daniels appears to have been the real leader; the hard core of the group consisted of Röser and Bürgers. Becker had ambitions outside the League on his own account and, despite his efforts to publish an edition of Marx's works, Marx's attitude towards him was not altogether free of suspicion. Of the others, Lessner should perhaps be mentioned as a future founder-member of the First International.

The investigation was opened on May 19, 1851. And from the start Hinckeldey and Westphalen by-passed the ordinary procedures. On June 16th Hinckeldey decided that the trial should take place in Cologne even though he had qualms about the reliability of a Cologne jury. He decided also that even those of the accused who were not Prussians should be tried in a Prussian court as they had conspired against Prussia. From the very start Hinckeldey was determined that the arrests should be used to strike a blow at the Workers' Clubs throughout the country, and Schulz, the Police Director of Cologne, was given special powers to investigate them. In addition, Hinckeldey sent copies of the documents found on Nothjung to Stieber in London to extend his investigations there.

By August 1851 the investigation which had been proceeding so briskly was languishing; Hinckeldey complained to Westphalen that no link had been established between the accused and the London Workers' Club or with the Workers' Brotherhoods (led by Stefan Born) recently established in North Germany, or with the workers' associations in Central and Southern Germany.

The only piece of evidence to turn up was the so-called Dietz Archive (See Chapter II of the *Revelations*) which Stieber together with Greif, a police officer, and Fleury, a police spy, managed to steal from the Willich/Schapper League. But this evidence proved insufficient and in October 1851 the Prosecution Council rejected the case and ordered a new investigation. That suggests that the Liberal Rhineland was not entirely willing to go along with the Prussian authorities and especially with Stieber, i.e. they had no objection to a communist witch hunt but were reluctant to subordinate themselves to the Prussian reaction.

The time between the original rejection of the police case and the beginning of the Trial in October 1852 was filled by ever more frantic efforts by Stieber and the police to discover, steal and finally to manufacture evidence against the accused. In order to understand the "proofs"

of conspiracy and treason finally produced at the Trial it is necessary to
look a little more closely at the history of the Communist League in 1850.

The split in the Communist League of September 1850

Although progress was made in reconstituting the League in the
spring of 1850, disagreements emerged during the summer between the
London Central Committee headed by Marx and Engels and the
majority of the League members with Willich and Schapper at their
head. The discord came to a crisis in September 1850 and resulted in a
split within the League.

The disagreements had their roots in different assessments of the
new situation that had emerged with the defeat of the revolutionary
forces. They also reflect a certain change in the thought of Marx and
Engels with regard to the function of the League. That is to say the
split reflected divisions of opinion and policy. This is important
because in the Trial the prosecution made light of the arguments in the
League, representing them as mere conflicts of personality. Their
purpose in so doing was to suggest that the policies of the two groups
were identical, that the "Marx Party" was just as capable of plot and
conspiracy as the "Willich/Schapper Party".

The first point at issue was whether an objectively revolutionary
situation still existed. In the March Address Marx still thought that
revolution was imminent (". . . the Central Committee considers it
extremely important that the emissary should leave precisely at this
moment when a new revolution is impending."). In the June Address
Marx is still sanguine even though the revolution seems now to be a
little more remote. (". . . All members are urged to make the greatest
possible efforts; these are especially vital at this moment when the
situation is so critical that the outbreak of a revolution can no longer
be very far away.") But in the course of the summer Marx and Engels
reviewed the situation again and came to the conclusion that no
revolution was imminent. They summarise the matter in the *Neue
Rheinische Zeitung, Politisch-Ökonomische Revue* of May to October
1850:

> "In view of this general prosperity, in which the productive
> forces of bourgeois society are flourishing as exuberantly as they
> possibly can under bourgeois conditions, there can be no talk of a
> real revolution. Such a revolution is only possible during periods
> when the two factors, modern forces of production and bourgeois

forms of production, come into conflict. The incessant squabbles in
which the representatives of the individual factions of the Continental Party of Order are now indulging and compromising one another
are remote from providing an opportunity for a new revolution.
On the contrary, they are possible only because conditions for the
time being are so secure and—what the Reaction does not know—so
bourgeois. All attempts of the Reaction to put a stop to bourgeois
development will recoil upon itself as certainly as all the moral
indignation and enthusiastic proclamations of the Democrats. A
new revolution is only possible as the result of a new crisis. But it is
just as inevitable as a new crisis."

It followed from this analysis that the League could not possibly
have the function of immediately instigating a revolution. Owing to
the circumstances prevailing in Prussia the League had to operate in
secret. But Marx never lost his dislike of secret organisations because
they attracted people who enjoyed the romantic attitudes of conspiracy. And this was the position here. Willich and the others refused
to accept the changed situation: their view was that revolution was
still imminent and that it could be triggered off by resolute and immediate action by the League. For Marx, however, the League had
but one task: the task of propaganda. He repudiated all conspiracies
and rash adventures. For a revolution two things were needed. There
must be an increase of class consciousness in the masses. And there
must be greater participation in actual processes—the acquisition of
civil rights, the organisation of trade unions, the fight for higher wages,
etc. This would eventually polarise the forces in society until the time
would be ripe for a new revolution. That is to say for Marx revolution
was the outcome of definite historical processes, whereas for Willich it
was something to be provoked by wilful acts of violence.

The whole issue was fought out at a meeting of the Central Committee on September 15, 1850 (see the Minutes of the meeting), and
resulted in a victory for Marx and Engels. It was resolved—as the
opposing sides proved irreconcilable—to transfer the leadership of the
League to Cologne and to split the London branch into two parts,
both subordinate to the Cologne Central Committee.

The majority decisions were given to Haupt to take to Cologne.
The Cologne members accepted them and rejected the account of the
meeting given by the Willich/Schapper faction. They produced their
own Address (of December 1850) together with new Statutes (both
printed here in the Appendix) which differed from earlier Statutes

chiefly in the article insisting on abstention from religious beliefs or membership of religious organisations.

The intention behind the move to Cologne was to preserve the unity of the League, but this proved impracticable. The Cologne Central Committee instructed Eccarius and Schapper to form two London branches. But Willich/Schapper sent an emissary to Cologne requesting them to expel Marx and Engels first. The Cologne CC refused and announced the self-expulsion of the Willich/Schapper group. The breach between the "men of action" and the "academic theorists" was now irreversible. Willich/Schapper set up three new communes in Paris and took part in every possible conspiratorial escapade (including the improbable scheme to float a loan to pay for the coming revolution—a scheme which Marx describes in *Heroes of the Exile*). The bitterness generated by the quarrel assumed the proportions of a longstanding feud, signs of which are very apparent in the *Revelations*.

It is evident then that the League hardly survived the split. Marx's attendance at the weekly meetings fell off and his only connection with it later arose out of the events leading up to the Trial. It is ironical therefore that the Prussian government should have conspired to destroy the League at the very moment when it was disintegrating under the impact of its own dissensions and the general pressures of the Reaction.

The Prosecution and the Willich/Schapper League

The evidence found on Nothjung no doubt sufficed to justify the investigation and arrest of the League members. But in the more liberal atmosphere of the Rhine Province with its established system of trial by jury it might have been difficult to secure a conviction. The defendants were charged with having, in the years 1848–51, conspired to overthrow the constitution and incite the populace to take up arms against the monarchy. The documents captured certainly demonstrated that the accused wished to see the state overthrown, but there was no evidence of an actual conspiracy, i.e. no specific plan to set a plot in motion. And after all, documents like the *Communist Manifesto*, which had been published, could hardly be regarded as evidence of an actual plot.

The solution adopted by Hinckeldey and Stieber was to ignore the facts of the split in the League and attempt to lay the harebrained schemes of the Willich/Schapper Party at the door of the Cologne Communists.

That the police were well aware of the true nature of the split is shown by one of Hinckeldey's regular reports (of April 6, 1852). "Schapper and Willich have done everything in their power to recruit supporters for their party. . . . Nevertheless, the Willich/Schapper Party has never been particularly notable for unity; its meetings were the occasion for the most unpleasant scenes; they hurled accusations at each other and the disreputable activities of their leaders as well as the wildness of their plans and ventures has gradually discredited them even among the supporters of communism so that more recently members of the League have tended to look more to the former leaders Marx and Engels who provided the League with its foundations and who are scientifically trained men . . . Their activity can be seen less in manifestoes and proclamations than in their undeniably greater concentration of intelligence—and this superiority will perhaps become even more apparent in the near future. . . . But even at this stage it can be said that the Marx Party stands head and shoulders above all the émigrés, agitators and Central Committees because it is indisputably in possession of much greater knowledge and qualities of mind. Marx himself is personally known and it is evident that he has more brains in his little finger than all the rest have in their heads."

Thus although the police were aware of the true state of affairs their tactics during the trial were to blur the distinction between the two parts of the League. Their first effort (as has been mentioned) was the theft of the Dietz Archive, which was the archive of the Willich/Schapper Party. They then attempted to drag in the so-called Franco-German Plot. This was an escapade in the course of which the Willich/Schapper Party had actually been lured by Cherval, an agent provocateur, into making a genuine conspiracy. The "plot" was discovered in September 1851 and the prisoners were sentenced for planning a conspiracy in February 1852. Cherval was allowed to escape to England. The *Red Catechism*, written by Moses Hess, was the next attempt to incriminate the Cologne Communists, by tarring them with the Willich/Schapper brush. Stieber finally abandoned all attempts to procure evidence and began simply to invent it. The fruit of his inventions was the original Minute Book: direct forgeries of the Minutes of the London Central Committee by Fleury and Hirsch.

The Trial (October 4–November 12, 1852)
The Trial itself opened in a blaze of publicity. Despite the unreliability of the evidence and the long delay the police were determined to make

it into a show trial. A second jury was kept in readiness in case it should last a long time. The sessions were held only in the morning because it was feared that friends of the accused might resort to violent measures under cover of the approaching darkness. The prosecution intended to call as many as fifty-two witnesses, although fewer appeared in the event.

The accused had been held, partly in solitary confinement, for a year and a half. Not all were in good health. Röser, for example, commenting on his failure to remember various details remarked at one point: "It is not at all surprising: 17 months in solitary confinement, an illness lasting a quarter of a year during which I was left alone to suffer the most excruciating pains and my request to be allowed to stay in hospital was refused on the grounds that no one felt it incumbent upon him to do anything for me. All these things were enough to break me physically and mentally and while in the past I could afford to be proud of my memory I feel now as if stones were pressing down on my head."

Lessner, too, has described his experiences during his detention. He spent most of the time in solitary confinement though he was fortunate enough to meet a girl who procured three meals a day for him. However, when he was transferred from Mainz to Cologne he had to walk the whole way (the journey lasted some eleven days) and along with 20–30 criminals. He was handcuffed throughout and at each stopping place he was put in solitary confinement as a particularly dangerous man.

With the exception of Daniels, however, who died in 1855, almost certainly as the indirect consequence of his experiences in prison, the accused were not broken by their privations. Certainly they were not intimidated by the police and stood their ground manfully in cross-examination. Thus Röser, for example, when asked about his denial of religion replied: "Alexander von Humboldt had proved in his *Cosmos* that the world came into being in quite a different manner from what religion had always taught and what Alexander von Humboldt can say may presumably be repeated by others. Moreover, I am only on trial here for high treason and not for my religious convictions."

In a sense, of course, it was Marx just as much as the Cologne Communists who was on trial. Indeed, the prosecution admitted as much on one occasion when they refused to allow a letter from Marx to be used as evidence on the grounds that if he were present in court he would himself be in the dock.

However that may be, Marx certainly came to the rescue of the defence. Throughout the trial he was occupied with feverish attempts to discredit the evidence brought by the prosecution. His main source of information was the *Kölnische Zeitung* which published detailed reports of the case. Having read the reports he had to get the refutations of crown evidence safely into the hands of the defence counsel Schneider II and von Hontheim. Jenny Marx gives a vivid picture of the way in which the whole Marx household was turned into a massive organisation for the defence:

"London, October 28, 1852

Dear Mr. Cluss,

You will, no doubt, have been following the monster trial of the Communists in the *Kölnische Zeitung*. The session of October 23 gave the whole thing an imposing and interesting turn, so favourable for the accused that we are all beginning to feel a little better. You can imagine how the 'Marx Party' is active day and night and has to work with head, hands and feet . . . . All the allegations of the police are lies. They steal, forge, break open desks, swear false oaths, perjure themselves, claiming they are privileged to do so against Communists, who are beyond the pale of society! It is truly hair-raising to see all this, and the manner in which the police, particularly their most villainous specimen, are taking over all the functions of the Ministry of Justice, pushing Sädt into the background, introducing unauthenticated slips of paper, mere rumours, reports and hearsay as actual, judicially proven facts, as evidence. All the proofs of forgery had to be submitted from here; thus my husband had to work all day at it, far into the night. Affidavits by the landlords duly acknowledged had to be procured and the handwritings of Liebknecht and Rings, the men alleged to have written the minutes, had to be officially certified to prove the forgery by the police. Then all the papers had to be sent in six to eight copies to Cologne by the most devious channels, via Frankfurt, Paris, etc., as all letters addressed to my husband, as well as all letters sent from here to Cologne, are opened and confiscated. The whole thing is now a struggle between the police and my husband, who is being blamed for everything: the whole revolution, even the conduct of the trial. . . . The struggle against this official power supplied with money and all the implements of combat is of course very interesting and the glory of it will be so much the greater, should we emerge victorious, since on the one side stand money and power and everything, while we often did not know where to get the paper for the letters that had to be written, etc., etc. . . . .

We have just received whole stacks of business addresses and fake business letters from Weerth and Engels for use in sending the documents, letters, etc. This very minute some issues of the *Kölnische Zeitung* have come in carrying the news of a fresh load of incredible outrages. Two despatches are going off at once to business addresses. A whole office has been established at our flat. Two or three write, others run errands, and still others scrape the pennies together to make it possible for the writers to continue their existence and furnish proof against the old official world of this most unprecedented outrage. In between, my three gleeful children sing and whistle and often get a good scolding from their papa. What a hubbub!

Good-bye, dear Mr. Cluss. Don't forget to write to your friends again soon.

With permission of the higher authorities,

Jenny Marx."

Marx had to postpone his own work during the trial as he remarks somewhat wryly in a covering letter to Weydemeyer, accompanying his MS of the *Revelations*: "You will appreciate the humour of our side of this pamphlet when you realise that its author is more or less imprisoned through his lack of adequate covering for his feet and posterior and moreover at any moment expects to see real misery overwhelming his family. The Trial is to blame for this as well, as I have been forced to spend five weeks working for the Party, against all the machinations of the government, instead of for my daily bread. To cap it all it has ruined my reputation with the German booksellers with whom I had hoped to come to terms for my book on economics." (To Weydemeyer, December 7, 1852.)

Exasperated though Marx undoubtedly was, and had a right to be, some of his statements about the defendants whom he worked so hard to defend nevertheless seem a little harsh. Here is one example: "If they are condemned they will only have their own statements to thank for it. These German workers must be the biggest asses in existence; Reiff's statements have been downright denunciations and a number of others have been just as stupid. This is what comes of getting mixed up with workers and organisations that have to remain secret. It is not surprising that they have treated them so badly; the longer they are kept in isolation the more beautiful are the confessions they make. Of course, there is no other factual evidence . . ." (To Engels, July 20, 1852.)

Marx's efforts were so successful that the liberal papers were prophesying acquittal towards the end of the Trial. Nevertheless, when the sentence was passed only Daniels, Klein and Erhardt were acquitted. Jacobi was acquitted but not freed as he was to be tried on another charge of high treason in Minden. Röser, Bürgers and Nothjung were given six years, Reiff, Otto and Becker received five and Lessner three years' imprisonment.

One immediate effect of the Trial was the dissolution of the Communist League on November 17, 1852 (see Marx's letter to Engels on November 19th) on the grounds that it was no longer "seasonable". Marx was never again to associate with secret societies.

No less important is the fact that the Trial ended the first chapter in the history of the German working class. This first chapter was distinguished by its revolutionary character, and Herrnstadt is right to emphasise that to neglect it (as is commonly the case in histories of the German workers' movement) is to underplay the revolutionary past for the benefit of the later reformist tradition.

The "Revelations"

Marx began to write the *Revelations* during the Trial itself. His motives in publishing it were essentially to expose the Prussian government's manipulations of its own legal system. "My pamphlet is not intended to defend any principles but to excoriate the Prussian government on the basis of a factual account of the events." (Marx to Engels, October 27, 1852.)

But also he was concerned to put the matter in its true light, in view perhaps of the misleading accounts in the press including no doubt the English press and especially *The Times*. "There will not be a more favourable opportunity in which to speak to the nation en large. Moreover, we must not put up with the appearance of the ridiculous which even the moral dignity and scientific depth of our gentle Heinrich (Bürgers) are unable to dispel." (To Engels, October 28, 1852.)

The MS was completed by early December. On December 6th a copy was sent to Schabelitz in Zurich and on the following day a second copy was dispatched to Cluss in the U.S. Schabelitz wrote on December 11th saying that he had prepared the first proofs "behind his father's back". In January 1853 the pamphlet appeared anonymously. But then in March there came the news from Schabelitz that almost the whole edition (2,000 copies) had been confiscated in the frontier village of Weill during an attempt to introduce it into Germany. Marx, undeterred, went ahead with an American edition. It appeared in instalments from March 1853 in Boston and then as a pamphlet. In May Engels received 440 copies of the Boston edition and Lassalle agreed to try and sell them in Germany.

The pamphlet was reprinted in thirteen articles in the *Volksstaat* in 1874 and here for the first time Marx was named as the author. A second book edition came out in 1875 with the Postscript and the Appendix from *Herr Vogt*. The third edition appeared in 1885 together with Engels' *History of the Communist League* and the March and June Addresses. Both of these editions appeared at a time when there was renewed pressure on the Social Democrats.

III

Heroes of the Exile

This pamphlet is one of Marx's most brilliant satirical achievements. Its excellence as satire stands out all the more clearly for the fact that, unlike many of his other works which have a satirical element, the prime purpose of the work is satirical: a polemic on the world of German *émigrés* with its venomous internecine struggles, its petty personality conflicts, complicated intrigues, pretentious political manoeuvres and sordid compromises with the realities of living in exile with "dubious sources of income".

It would be a mistake to suppose that the work was actuated by malice, that it was merely a series of personal attacks on people who irritated Marx. It is often supposed that Marx was essentially a heavy, humourless man and that if his works contain humour it is the expression only of a ponderous, "Germanic" predilection for sarcasm without true wit or feeling. His talent for polemic is then seen as springing from an almost obsessive compulsion to win, to be in the right, to beat down all opposition. That is to say, his scorn, often couched in scatological imagery, is held to be violent and authoritarian, and rooted in an emotionally impoverished psyche. Of course, it is thought permissible for him to inveigh against the evils of the capitalist system. It is when, as here, his heaviest cannon are summoned up to demolish unimportant, perhaps mistaken but often very sincere fellow revolutionaries, that his irony is called in question.

This view of Marx is perhaps more often felt than stated, more often stated than reasoned. I feel that it is based on a misunderstanding, often

wilful, on the part of his detractors. But even his admirers may in part
be responsible for the misconception in that their own practice on
occasion emulates this stereotype rather than Marx's own manner of
writing. Thus one often observes a sarcasm uttered in a tone of didactic
complacency, as if the speaker were somehow privileged always to be
in the right. Such complacency is, I feel, alien to Marx who is at once
too humorous and too passionate to have room for self-congratulation.
Moral feeling is certainly very powerful in him but it is prevented
from degenerating into dogmatism by the fact that his moral percep-
tions are bound up so completely with the dialectic with its ironies
and its "ruses of reason". Of course, there is anger and indignation in
the *Heroes*: the Kinkels and Ruges are not just figures of fun. They were
often irresponsible and dangerous enough to constitute a real threat in
the treacherous, spy-ridden emigration.

Thus the *Heroes* should not be regarded as an act of personal revenge.
If it were so it would have lost much of its interest for us if only because
the objects of Marx's polemic are now largely forgotten. Kinkel may
have been a "great man" in his day, but who knows of Kinkel now?
This situation is often met with in satire and here as everywhere we
must search for a deeper underlying theme. For there is no doubt that
the pamphlet still lives today and if that is true its survival must be due
to themes of greater permanence than their ostensible subjects.

One important underlying theme is the contradiction between the
views and the lives of revolutionaries on one level and the affinities
between them on another. Marx never made the mistake of assuming
that a revolutionary is merely the concrete incarnation of certain
abstract attitudes. A revolutionary's life-style is relevant to a judgement
of his views and actions. In summing up Struve, for example, it is not
enough to know his overt positions and his actions. To gain a real
understanding it is necessary also to take into consideration his cranki-
ness: his vegetarianism, his phrenology, his colony of renunciation, his
mania for founding papers entitled the *Deutscher Zuschauer*. All these
combine to give a portrait of a man dominated by a series of *idées fixes*.

Marx in fact asks the same kind of questions about revolutionaries as
elsewhere about actions and institutions: what are the real underlying
motives? What are the true springs of action? And even the most
intrepid revolutionary will need all his courage to withstand the force
of such questions.

Marx in fact provides a general answer for his age. Far too many
revolutionaries are impelled by ambition, by greed or by romantic

fantasies and delusions of grandeur. Thus he notes strange inversions of values: the Holy Grail of these revolutionaries is not the "kingdom of freedom" for all mankind, but the treasury of democratic party funds. Or again, whereas the defeat of the revolution should have meant the defeat of the revolutionaries, in reality it gave them their hour of glory. Now was the time for them to enjoy their martyrdom and to set themselves up as provisional governments in exile.

A related theme is that of Romanticism. Romanticism entered into the life of the people in a number of ways. The worship of great men, for example, had been at first the prerogative of exclusive circles of poets. After the second half of the nineteenth century with heroes like Garibaldi and Bismarck it became a significant political fact. Similarly, it was of great importance in inspiring people with the idea of total social revolution and there are all sorts of links between Romanticism and Marxism. But it is no less true that there was a revolutionary romanticism that stopped short at the symbols and attitudes of revolution. Inevitably, this trend was particularly pronounced after the failure of the 1848 revolution when it was easier to go on repeating the slogans than to rethink the situation. Thus Marx lays emphasis in his discussion of Kinkel on the Romantic fantasies that inhabit his mind. Kinkel as Heinrich von Ofterdingen, Mockel as the Blue Flower of Romanticism —such notions with their mixture of vanity and aestheticism are of the very essence of a debased Romanticism. Marx's use of Boiardo, his habitual designation of Willich as "ritterlich", i.e. chivalrous, is consonant with this. The romances of knighthood with their great swashbuckling heroes stand in vivid contrast to the achievements of the "heroes" of the Exile, while the pretensions of the latter yield in nothing to those of the Middle Ages.

The gulf between fantasy and reality which Marx exploits brilliantly is a variant of a common theme in German literature in the nineteenth century: that of the Philistine. Both Heine and Hoffman give the Philistine a crucial role in their works. For Heine the Philistine tends to be just the ordinary beer-drinking, money-grubbing German. He is characterised by the eternal attributes of his nightcap and dressing-gown, complacent and politically indifferent, unaware of any higher values, any beauty in nature, in art or in love. Marx was clearly writing in a satirical tradition strongly influenced, indeed created by Heine and Börne. Paradoxically, however, his attack on the Philistine is even closer to that of E. T. A. Hoffmann whose fairy tales and horror stories seem to come from a wholly different world. Yet Hoffmann's analysis of the Philistine has one thing in common with that of Marx: the Philistine is essentially a man who claims to have ideals while in reality his interest is quite earthly. In *Kater Murr* Hoffmann tells the tale of a highly sensitive and idealistic tom-cat. In his speech and his attitudes he is partly modelled on Goethe's Werther and the sentimental hero. Yet at the same time he is satirised: thus his longing for higher things is revealed as his irresistible tomcat's desire to go up and roam around the rooftops. Here too there are clear parallels with the whole story of the courtship of Kinkel and Mockel. Another instance can be seen in the brilliant description of the cosy scenes in the beer saloons where the heroes bask in the sunlight of the flattery of the German visitors to the Great Exhibition: i.e. the revolutionary Philistines worshipped by the paying Philistines.

These themes could be pursued much further, but suffice it to say here that the synthesis of political and theoretical insight with human and literary understanding make the *Heroes* a crucial work in Marx's total *oeuvre* and one that has suffered from a neglect explained, perhaps, but not justified by the circumstances attending its publication.

IV

The fate of the MS of the *Heroes* is even more unfortunate than that of the *Revelations* and worth telling because it throws light on the kind of situation that gave rise to the *Heroes*. Indeed, its substance would almost make it worthy of inclusion in that work, had it been at all feasible.

Having completed the work by July 1852 Marx entrusted it to a Colonel Bangya to take to a German bookseller. Bangya failed to do so and the work was not printed in Marx's lifetime. It first appeared in 1930 in Russian translation and it was not published in the original German until its inclusion in the *Werke* of 1960. Dr. Rosdolsky has researched into the background of the events leading up to the loss of the MS and I briefly summarise his findings here.

Johann Bangya was born in 1817. His early career was that of an officer in the Austrian army in which he rose to the rank of First Lieutenant before being compelled to leave the service by the pressure of his debts. The years between then and the revolution were spent working in a Vienna Chancellery and latterly as a journalist. Already at this time he seems to have performed confidential services for the Austrian government.

B

During the revolution he was in the Hungarian Revolutionary army and advanced to major and then colonel. He was involved in the occupation of the fortress of Komorn, but when it capitulated to the Austrian forces Bangya attempted to ingratiate himself with them by alleging that its surrender had been brought about by his treachery. He then offered his services to the Austrian government but it appears that his offer was not immediately accepted.

He then went to Hamburg with the intention of emigrating to the U.S. (in October 1849). Despite this he remained in Europe as a journalist and "politician" and became acquainted with the leaders of the Hungarian, German and Polish emigration in Paris and London. His extremely radical views endeared him to all, especially Struve and Schimmelpfennig. He again tried to enter the Austrian service but was expelled from Hamburg for his pains and went to London (April 1850), where he met Marx for the first time. Despite the expulsion he was by now in the confidence of the Austrian police. They now sent him to Paris where he joined the left-democratic faction of Szemere, one of the most radical *émigrés*. He used his position to spy on all the leaders of the German, French and Italian emigration.

From the middle of October 1850 he became a member of the *Filial-Komitee*, i.e. a branch committee associated with the Willich/Schapper League, whose membership, apart from Szemere and Schimmelpfennig (who soon resigned) consisted wholly of spies who instantly reported all the doings of the Willich/Schapper League back to Vienna. In addition he was in a position to report on the activities of Mazzini, Kinkel and the French societies. He even picked up some damaging information about Marx, and in particular there is some evidence that he wrote a report about Röser on February 22, 1851 (based on Schimmelpfennig's emissary reports from Cologne), and about Nothjung on March 12th. The latter report was passed on to the Prussian police and may have played a role in Nothjung's arrest.

After the German Revolutionary Loan was leaked suspicion (rightly) fell on Bangya (June/July 1851). But a breach came only with the Cherval plot in which he was arrested but released with such alacrity that it was obviously the result of connivance on the part of the French police. Following this Bangya's name was placed on Willich's list of government spies. Bangya naturally denied that he was a spy and, blaming Schimmelpfennig for his inclusion on the list, threatened to sue him. Schimmelpfennig challenged him to a duel in Belgium, and from this Bangya was saved by the timely intervention of the police who deported him back to England.

The deportation worked like magic to restore Bangya's credit; in particular he succeeded in persuading Kossuth to give him a clean bill of health. Kossuth even made him his "police president in partibus". With this recommendation he became acquainted with Marx who as might be expected treated him with the very greatest reserve. Nevertheless, it is evident that Bangya managed to win even his confidence. The very fact that Bangya was Kossuth's police chief explained his contacts with the governments, as a police chief would have to keep a line open to the government police. Moreover, Marx thought his knowledge of police activities might be of use on the eve of the Cologne Trial. Bangya further gained Marx's confidence by his unwillingness to discuss Marx's own political affairs and his refusal to join the Communist League at Marx's invitation. The acquaintance throve to the extent that it was at Bangya's invitation that Marx expanded his "Sketches" of the German leaders of the emigration written for the benefit of Szemere into a larger pamphlet, viz. the *Heroes*.

Having written the pamphlet Marx gave it to Bangya who claimed to know a bookseller who would publish it, but after many delays Marx finally realised in December 1852 that Bangya was deceiving him. By a public declaration in the *New-Yorker Criminal-Zeitung* of May 5, 1853, he denounced him as a spy and accused him of stealing the MS. Surprisingly even this did not finally discredit Bangya, for even though Szemere and the Germans would have nothing more to do with him, Kossuth continued to believe in his innocence. Marx gives his own account of their relations in Hirsch's *Confessions* (see Appendix B), maintaining *inter alia* that he did not cease to distrust Bangya and that in the final analysis he had risked nothing more than the copy of the MS of a pamphlet against the emigration which could hardly have been of great interest to the police. Marx was evidently not inconsolable at the loss of the MS., and unlike the *Revelations* did not take further steps to publish it, but we certainly have cause to regret the fact that the *Heroes* has come down to us in such an incomplete form.

Of Bangya's later history little need be added here above the fact that by the end of 1853 he was dropped by the Austrian police and so he went to Constantinople where he turned Moslem and became a colonel in the Turkish army. His habit of betrayal remained with him even here and nearly cost him his life. But he apparently survived even that and was restored to honour, dying a natural death in 1868.

R. L. LIVINGSTONE

Southampton, *December* 1970

ON THE HISTORY OF
THE COMMUNIST LEAGUE

FREDERICK ENGELS

ON THE HISTORY OF THE COMMUNIST LEAGUE

With the sentence of the Cologne Communists in 1852, the curtain falls on the first period of the independent German workers' movement. Today this period is almost forgotten. Yet it lasted from 1836 to 1852 and, with the spread of German workers abroad, the movement developed in almost all civilised countries. Nor is that all. The present-day international workers' movement is in substance a direct continuation of the German workers' movement of that time, which was the *first international workers' movement* of all time, and which brought forth many of those who took the leading role in the International Working Men's Association. And the theoretical principles that the Communist League had inscribed on its banner in the *Communist Manifesto* of 1847 constitute today the strongest international bond of the entire proletarian movement of both Europe and America.

Up to now there has been only one main source for a coherent history of that movement. This is the so-called Black Book, *The Communist Conspiracies of the Nineteenth Century*, by Wermuth and Stieber, Berlin, two parts, 1853 and 1854. This crude compilation, which bristles with deliberate falsifications, fabricated by two of the most contemptible police scoundrels of our century, today still serves as the final source for all non-communist writings about that period.

What I am able to give here is only a sketch, and even this only in so far as the League itself is concerned; only what is absolutely necessary to understand the *Revelations*. I hope that some day I shall have the opportunity to work up the rich material collected by Marx and myself on the history of that glorious period of the youth of the international workers' movement.

In 1836 the most extreme, chiefly proletarian elements of the secret democratic-republican Outlaws' League, which was founded by German refugees in Paris in 1834, split off and formed the new secret League of the Just. The parent League, in which only sleepy-headed elements à la Jakobus Venedey were left, soon fell asleep altogether; when in 1840 the police scented out a few sections in Germany, it was hardly even a shadow of its former self. The new League, on the contrary, developed comparatively rapidly. Originally it was a German outlier of the French worker-Communism, reminiscent of Babouvism and taking shape in Paris at about this time; community of goods was demanded as the necessary consequence of "equality". The aims were those of the Parisian secret societies of the time: half propaganda association, half conspiracy, Paris, however, being always regarded as the central point of revolutionary action, although the preparation of occasional *putsches* in Germany was by no means excluded. But as Paris remained the decisive battleground, the League was at that time actually not much more than the German branch of the French secret societies, especially the *Société des saisons* led by Blanqui and Barbès, with which a close connection was maintained. The French went into action on May 12, 1839; the sections of the League marched with them and thus were involved in the common defeat.

Among the Germans arrested were Karl Schapper and Heinrich Bauer; Louis Philippe's government contented itself with deporting them after a fairly long imprisonment. Both went to London. Schapper came from Weilburg in Nassau and while a student of forestry at Giessen in 1832 was a member of the conspiracy organised by Georg Büchner; he took part in the storming of the Frankfort constable station on April 3, 1833, escaped abroad and in February 1834 joined Mazzini's march on Savoy. Of gigantic stature, resolute and energetic, always ready to risk civil existence and life, he was a model of the professional revolutionist that played an important role in the thirties. In spite of a certain sluggishness of thought, he was by no means incapable of profound theoretical understanding, as is proved by his development from "demagogue" to Communist, and he held then all the more rigidly to what he had once come to recognise. Precisely on that account his revolutionary passion sometimes got the better of his understanding, but he always afterwards realised his mistake and openly acknowledged it. He was fully a man and what he did for the founding of the German workers' movement will not be forgotten.

Heinrich Bauer, from Franconia, was a shoemaker; a lively, alert, witty little fellow, whose little body, however, also contained much shrewdness and determination.

Arrived in London, where Schapper, who had been a compositor in Paris, now tried to earn his living as a teacher of languages, they both set to work gathering up the broken threads and made London the centre of the League. They were joined over here, if not already earlier in Paris, by Joseph Moll, a watchmaker from Cologne, a medium-sized Hercules—how often did Schapper and he victoriously defend the entrance to a hall against hundreds of onrushing opponents!—a man who was at least the equal of his two comrades in energy and determination, and intellectually superior to both of them. Not only was he a born diplomat, as the success of his numerous trips on various missions proved; he was also more capable of theoretical insight. I came to know all three of them in London in 1843. They were the first revolutionary proletarians whom I met, and however far apart our views were at that time in details—for I still owned, as against their narrow-minded equalitarian Communism*, a goodly dose of just as narrow-minded philosophical arrogance—I shall never forget the deep impression that these three real men made upon me, who was then still only wanting to become a man.

In London, as in a lesser degree in Switzerland, they had the benefit of freedom of association and assembly. As early as February 7, 1840, the legally functioning German Workers' Educational Association, which still exists, was founded. This Assocation served the League as a recruiting ground for new members, and since, as always, the Communists were the most active and intelligent members of the Association, it was a matter of course that its leadership lay entirely in the hands of the League. The League soon had several communities, or, as they were then still called, "lodges", in London. The same obvious tactics were followed in Switzerland and elsewhere. Where workers' associations could be founded, they were utilised in like manner. Where this was forbidden by law, one joined choral societies, athletic clubs, and the like. Connections were to a large extent maintained by members who were continually travelling back and forth; they also, when required, served as emissaries. In both respects the League obtained lively support through the wisdom of the governments which, by resorting to deportation, converted any objectionable worker—and in nine cases out of ten he was a member of the League— into an emissary.

The extent to which the restored League spread was considerable. Notably in Switzerland, Weitling, August Becker (a highly gifted man who, however, like so many Germans, came to grief because of innate instability of character) and others created a strong organisation more or less pledged to Weitling's communist system. This is not the place to criticise the Communism of Weitling. But as regards its significance as the first independent theoretical stirring of the German proletariat, I still today subscribe to Marx's words in the Paris *Vorwärts* of 1844: "Where could the (German) bourgeoisie—including its philosophers and learned scribes—point to a work relating to the emancipation of the

---

* By equalitarian Communism I understand, as stated, only that Communism which bases itself exclusively or predominantly on the demand for equality.

B*

bourgeoisie—its political emancipation—comparable to Weitlings'
Guarantees of Harmony and Freedom? If one compares the drab mealy-
mouthed mediocrity of German political literature with this im-
measurable and brilliant debut of the German workers, if one compares
these gigantic children's shoes of the proletariat with the dwarf proportions of the worn-out political shoes of the bourgeoisie, one must pro-
phesy an athlete's figure for this Cinderella." This athlete's figure
confronts us today, although still far from being fully grown.

Numerous sections existed also in Germany; in the nature of things they
were of a transient character, but those coming into existence more than
made up for those passing away. Only after seven years, at the end of 1846,
did the police discover traces of the League in Berlin (Mentel) and Magdeburg (Beck), without being in a position to follow them further.

In Paris, Weitling, who was still there in 1840, likewise gathered the
scattered elements together again before he left for Switzerland.

The tailors formed the central force of the League. German tailors
were everywhere: in Switzerland, in London, in Paris. In the last-
named city, German was so much the prevailing tongue in this trade
that I was acquainted there in 1846 with a Norwegian tailor who had
travelled directly by sea from Trondhjem to France and in the space of
eighteen months had learned hardly a word of French but had acquired
an excellent knowledge of German. Two of the Paris communities in
1847 consisted predominantly of tailors, one of cabinetmakers.

After the centre of gravity had shifted from Paris to London, a new
feature grew conspicuous: from being German, the League gradually
became *international*. In the workers' society there were to be found,
besides Germans and Swiss, also members of all those nationalities for
whom German served as the chief means of communication with
foreigners, notably, therefore, Scandinavians, Dutch, Hungarians,
Czechs, Southern Slavs, and also Russians and Alsatians. In 1847 the
regular frequenters included a British grenadier of the Guards in
uniform. The society soon called itself the *Communist* Workers'
Educational Association, and the membership cards bore the inscrip-
tion "All Men Are Brothers", in at least twenty languages, even if not
without mistakes here and there. Like the open Association, so also the
secret League soon took on a more international character; at first in a
restricted sense, practically through the varied nationalities of its
members, theoretically through the realisation that any revolution to
be victorious must be a European one. One did not go any further as
yet; but the foundations were there.

Close connections were maintained with the French revolutionists through the London refugees, comrades-in-arms of May 12, 1839. Similarly with the more radical Poles. The official Polish *émigrés*, as also Mazzini, were, of course, opponents rather than allies. The English Chartists, on account of the specific English character of their movement, were disregarded as not revolutionary. The London leaders of the League came in touch with them only later, through me.

In other ways, too, the character of the League had altered with events. Although Paris was still—and at that time quite rightly— looked upon as the mother city of the revolution, one had nevertheless emerged from the state of dependence on the Paris conspirators. The spread of the League raised its self-consciousness. It was felt that roots were being struck more and more in the German working class and that these German workers were historically called upon to be the standard-bearers of the workers of the North and East of Europe. In Weitling was to be found a communist theoretician who could be boldly placed at the side of his contemporary French rivals. Finally, the experience of May 12th had taught us that for the time being there was nothing to be gained by attempts at *putsches*. And if one still continued to explain every event as a sign of the approaching storm, if one still preserved intact the old, semi-conspiratorial rules, that was mainly the fault of the old revolutionary defiance, which had already begun to collide with the sounder views that were gaining headway.

However, the social doctrine of the League, indefinite as it was, contained a very great defect, but one that had its roots in the conditions themselves. The members, in so far as they were workers at all, were almost exclusively artisans. Even in the big metropolises, the man who exploited them was usually only a small master. The exploitation of tailoring on a large scale, what is now called the manufacture of ready-made clothes, by the conversion of handicraft tailoring into a domestic industry working for a big capitalist, was at that time even in London only just making its appearance. On the one hand, the exploiter of these artisans was a small master; on the other hand, they all hoped ultimately to become small masters themselves. In addition, a mass of inherited guild notions still clung to the German artisan at that time. The greatest honour is due to them, in that they, who were themselves not yet full proletarians but only an appendage of the petty bourgeoisie, an appendage which was passing into the modern proletariat and which did not yet stand in direct opposition to the bourgeoisie, that is, to big capital—in that these artisans were capable of instinctively anticipating their future development and of constituting themselves, even if not yet with full consciousness, the party of the proletariat. But it was also inevitable that their old handicraft prejudices should be a stumbling block to them at every moment, whenever it was a question of criticising existing society in detail, that is, of investigating economic facts. And I do not believe there was a single man in the whole League at that time who had ever read a book on political economy. But that mattered little; for the time being "equality", "brotherhood" and "justice" helped them to surmount every theoretical obstacle.

Meanwhile a second, essentially different Communism was developing alongside that of the League and of Weitling. While I was in Manchester, it was tangibly brought home to me that the economic facts, which have so far played no role or only a contemptible one in the writing of history, are, at least in the modern world, a decisive historical force; that they form the basis of the origination of the present-day class antagonisms; that these class antagonisms, in the countries where they have become fully developed, thanks to large-scale industry, hence especially in England, are in their turn the basis of the formation of political parties and of party struggles, and thus of all political history. Marx had not only arrived at the same view, but had already, in the *German–French Annals* (1844), generalised it to the effect that, speaking generally, it is not the state which conditions and regulates civil society, but civil society which conditions and regulates the state, and, consequently, that policy and its history are to be explained from the economic relations and their development, and not *vice versa*. When I visited Marx in Paris in the summer of 1844, our complete agreement in all theoretical fields became evident and our joint work dates from that time. When, in the spring of 1845, we met again in Brussels, Marx had already fully developed his materialist theory of history in its main features from the above-mentioned basis and we now applied ourselves to the detailed elaboration of the newly-won mode of outlook in the most varied directions.

This discovery, which revolutionised the science of history and, as we have seen, is essentially the work of Marx—a discovery in which I can claim for myself only a very insignificant share—was, however, of immediate importance for the contemporary workers' movement. Communism among the French and Germans, Chartism among the English, now no longer appeared as something accidental which could just as well not have occurred. These movements now presented themselves as a movement of the modern oppressed class, the proletariat, as the more or less developed forms of its historically necessary struggle against the ruling class, the bourgeoisie; as forms of the class struggle, but distinguished from all earlier class struggles by this one thing, that the present-day oppressed class the proletariat, cannot achieve its emancipation without at the same time emancipating society as a whole from division into classes and, therefore, from class struggles. And Communism now no longer meant the concoction, by means of the imagination, of an ideal society as perfect as possible, but insight into the nature, the conditions and the consequent general aims of the struggle waged by the proletariat.

Now, we were by no means of the opinion that the new scientific results should be confided in large tomes exclusively to the "learned" world. Quite the contrary. We were both of us already deeply involved in the political movement, and possessed a certain following in the educated world, especially of Western Germany, and abundant contact with the organised proletariat. It was our duty to provide a scientific foundation for our view, but it was equally important for us to win over the European and in the first place the German proletariat to our conviction. As soon as we had become clear in our own minds, we set about the task. We founded a German workers' society in Brussels and took over the *Deutsche Brüsseler Zeitung*, which served us as an organ up to the February Revolution. We kept in touch with the revolutionary section of the English Chartists through Julian Harney, the editor of the central organ of the movement, *The Northern Star*, to which I was a contributor. We entered likewise into a sort of cartel with the Brussels democrats (Marx was vice-president of the Democratic Society) and with the French social-democrats of the *Réforme*, which I furnished with news of the English and German movements. In short, our connections with the radical and proletarian organisations and press organs were quite what one could wish.

Our relations with the League of the Just were as follows: The existence of the League was, of course, known to us; in 1843 Schapper had suggested that I join it, which I at that time naturally refused to do. But we not only kept up our continuous correspondence with the Londoners but remained on still closer terms with Dr. Ewerbeck, then the leader of the Paris communities. Without going into the League's internal affairs, we learnt of every important happening. On the other hand, we influenced the theoretical views of the most important members of the League by word of mouth, by letter and through the press. For this purpose we also made use of various lithographed circulars, which we dispatched to our friends and correspondents throughout the world on particular occasions, when it was a question of the internal affairs of the Communist Party in process of formation. In these, the League itself sometimes came to be dealt with. Thus, a young Westphalian student, Hermann Kriege, who went to America, came forward there as an emissary of the League and associated himself with the crazy Harro Harring for the purpose of using the League to turn South America upside down. He founded a paper in which, in the name of the League, he preached an extravagant Communism of love dreaming, based on "love" and overflowing with love. Against this we let fly with a circular that did not fail of its effect. Kriege vanished from the League scene.

Later, Weitling came to Brussels. But he was no longer the naïve young journeyman-tailor who, astonished at his own talents, was trying to clarify in his own mind just what a communist society would look like. He was now the great man, persecuted by the envious on account of his superiority, who scented rivals, secret enemies and traps everywhere—the prophet, driven from country to country, who carried a recipe for the realisation of heaven on earth ready-made in his pocket, and who was possessed with the idea that everybody intended to steal it from him. He had already fallen out with the members of the League in London; and in Brussels, where Marx and his wife welcomed him with almost superhuman forbearance, he also could not get along with anyone. So he soon afterwards went to America to try out his role of prophet there.

All these circumstances contributed to the quiet revolution that was taking place in the League, and especially among the leaders in London. The inadequacy of the previous conception of Communism, both the simple French equalitarian Communism and that of Weitling, became more and more clear to them. The tracing of Communism back to primitive Christianity introduced by Weitling—no matter how brilliant certain passages to be found in his *Gospel of Poor Sinners*—had resulted in delivering the movement in Switzerland to a large extent into the hands, first of fools like Albrecht, and then of exploiting fake prophets like Kuhlmann. The "true Socialism" dealt in by a few literary writers—a translation of French socialist phraseology into corrupt Hegelian German, and sentimental love dreaming (see the section on German or "True" Socialism in the *Communist Manifesto*)— that Kriege and the study of the corresponding literature introduced in the

League was found soon to disgust the old revolutionists of the League, if only because of its slobbering feebleness. As against the untenability of the previous theoretical views, and as against the practical aberrations resulting therefrom, it was realised more and more in London that Marx and I were right in our new theory. This understanding was undoubtedly promoted by the fact that among the London leaders there were now two men who were considerably superior to those previously mentioned in capacity for theoretical knowledge: the miniature painter Karl Pfänder from Heilbronn and the tailor Georg Eccarius from Thuringia.*

It suffices to say that in the spring of 1847 Moll visited Marx in Brussels and immediately afterwards me in Paris, and invited us repeatedly, in the name of his comrades, to enter the League. He reported that they were as much convinced of the general correctness of our mode of outlook as of the necessity of freeing the League from the old conspiratorial traditions and forms. Should we enter, we would be given an opportunity of expounding our critical Communism before a congress of the League in a manifesto, which would then be published as the manifesto of the League; we would likewise be able to contribute our quota towards the replacement of the obsolete League organisation by one in keeping with the new times and aims.

We entertained no doubt that an organisation within the German working class was necessary, if only for propaganda purposes, and that this organisation, in so far as it would not be merely local in character, could only be a secret one, even outside Germany. Now, there already existed exactly such an organisation in the shape of the League. What we previously objected to in this League was now relinquished as erroneous by the representatives of the League themselves; we were even invited to co-operate in the work of reorganisation. Could we say no? Certainly not. Therefore, we entered the League; Marx founded a League community in Brussels from among our close friends, while I attended the three Paris communities.

In the summer of 1847, the first League Congress took place in London, at which W. Wolff represented the Brussels and I the Paris communities. At this congress the reorganisation of the League was

---

* Pfänder died about eight years ago in London. He was a man of peculiarly fine intelligence, witty, ironical and dialectical. Eccarius, as we know, was later for many years Secretary of the General Council of the International Working Men's Association, in the General Council of which the following old League members were to be found, among others: Eccarius, Pfänder, Lessner, Lochner, Marx and myself. Eccarius subsequently devoted himself exclusively to the English trade union movement.

carried through first of all. Whatever remained of the old mystical names dating back to the conspiratorial period was now abolished; the League now consisted of communities, circles, leading circles, a Central Committee and a Congress, and henceforth called itself the "Communist League". "The aim of the League is the overthrow of the bourgeoisie, the rule of the proletariat, the abolition of the old, bourgeois society based on class antagonisms and the foundation of a new society without classes and without private property"—thus ran the first article. The organisation itself was thoroughly democratic, with elective and always removable boards. This alone barred all hankering after conspiracy, which requires dictatorship, and the League was converted—for ordinary peace times at least—into a pure propaganda society. These new Rules were submitted to the communities for discussion—so democratic was the procedure now followed— then once again debated at the Second Congress and finally adopted by the latter on December 8, 1847. They are to be found reprinted in Wermuth and Stieber, vol. I, p. 239, Appendix X.

The Second Congress took place during the end of November and beginning of December of the same year. Marx also attended this time and expounded the new theory in a fairly long debate—the congress lasted at least ten days. All contradiction and doubt were finally set at rest, the new basic principles were unanimously adopted, and Marx and I were commissioned to draw up the Manifesto. This was done immediately afterwards. A few weeks before the February Revolution it was sent to London to be printed. Since then it has travelled round the world, has been translated into almost all languages and today still serves in numerous countries as a guide for the proletarian movement. In place of the old League motto, "All Men Are Brothers", appeared the new battle cry, "Working Men of All Countries, Unite!" which openly proclaimed the international character of the struggle. Seventeen years later this battle cry resounded throughout the world as the watchword of the International Working Men's Association, and today the militant proletariat of all countries has inscribed it on its banner.

The February Revolution broke out. The London Central Committee functioning hitherto immediately transferred its powers to the Brussels leading circle. But this decision came at a time when an actual state of siege already existed in Brussels, and the Germans in particular could no longer assemble anywhere. We were all of us just on the point of going to Paris, and so the new Central Committee decided likewise to dissolve, to hand over all its powers to Marx and to empower him immediately to constitute a new Central Committee in Paris. Hardly had the five persons who adopted this decision (March 3, 1848) separated, before the police forced their way into Marx's house, arrested him and compelled him to leave for France on the following day, which was just where he was wanting to go.

In Paris we all soon came together again. There the following document was drawn up and signed by all the members of the new Central Committee. It was distributed throughout Germany and many a one can still learn something from it even today:

DEMANDS OF THE COMMUNIST PARTY
IN GERMANY

1. The whole of Germany shall be declared a single indivisible republic.

3. Representatives of the people shall be paid so that workers also can sit in the parliament of the German people.

4. Universal arming of the people.

7. The estates of the princes and other feudal estates, all mines, pits, etc., shall be transformed into state property. On these estates, agriculture is to be conducted on a large scale and with the most modern scientific means for the benefit of all society.

8. Mortgages on peasant holdings shall be declared state property; interest on such mortgages shall be paid by the peasants to the state.

9. In the districts where tenant farming is developed, land rent or farming dues shall be paid to the state as a tax.

11. All means of transport: railways, canals, steamships, roads, post, etc., shall be taken over by the state. They are to be converted into state property and put at the disposal of the non-possessing class free of charge.

14. Limitation of the right of inheritance.

15. Introduction of a steeply graded progressive taxation and abolition of taxes on consumer goods.

16. Establishment of national workshops. The state shall guarantee a living to all workers and provide for those unable to work.

17. Universal free elementary education.

It is in the interest of the German proletariat, of the petite bourgeoisie and peasantry, to work with all possible energy to put the above measures through. For only by their realisation can the millions in

Germany, who up to now have been exploited by a small number of people and whom it will be attempted to keep in further subjection, get their rights and the power that are their due as the producers of all wealth.

The Committee: *Karl Marx, Karl Schapper,*
H. Bauer, F. Engels, J. Moll, W. Wolff

At that time the craze for revolutionary legions prevailed in Paris. Spaniards, Italians, Belgians, Dutch, Poles and Germans flocked together in crowds to liberate their respective fatherlands. The German legion was led by Herwegh, Bornsted, Börnstein. Since immediately after the revolution all foreign workers not only lost their jobs but in addition were harassed by the public, the influx into these legions was very great. The new government saw in them a means of getting rid of foreign workers and granted them *l'étape du soldat*, that is, quarters along their line of march and a marching allowance of fifty centimes per day up to the frontier, whereafter the eloquent Lamartine, the Foreign Minister who was so readily moved to tears, quickly found an opportunity of betraying them to their respective governments.

We opposed this playing with revolution in the most decisive fashion. To carry an invasion, which was to import the revolution forcibly from outside, into the midst of the ferment then going on in Germany, meant to undermine the revolution in Germany itself, to strengthen the governments and to deliver the legionnaires—Lamartine guaranteed for that—defenceless into the hands of the German troops. When subsequently the revolution was victorious in Vienna and Berlin, the legion became all the more purposeless; but once begun, the game was continued.

We founded a German communist club, in which we advised the workers to keep away from the legion and to return instead to their homes singly and work there for the movement. Our old friend Flocon, who had a seat in the Provisional Government, obtained for the workers sent by us the same travel facilities as had been granted to the legionnaires. In this way we returned three or four hundred workers to Germany, including the great majority of the League members.

As could easily be foreseen, the League proved to be much too weak a lever as against the popular mass movement that had now broken out. Three-quarters of the League members who had previously lived abroad had changed their domicile by returning to their homeland; their previous communities were thus to a great extent dissolved and they lost all contact with the League. One part, the more ambitious among them, did not even try to resume this contact, but each one began a small separate movement on his own account in his own locality. Finally, the conditions in each separate petty state, each province and each town were so different that the League would have been incapable of giving more than the most general directives; such directives were, however, much better disseminated through the press. In short, from the moment when the causes which had made the secret League necessary ceased to exist, the secret League as such ceased to mean anything. But this could least of all surprise the persons who had just stripped this same secret League of the last vestige of its conspiratorial character.

That, however, the League had been an excellent school for revolutionary activity was now demonstrated. On the Rhine, where the *Neue Rheinische Zeitung* provided a firm centre, in Nassau, in Rhenish Hesse, etc., everywhere members of the League stood at the head of the extreme democratic movement. The same was the case in Hamburg. In South Germany the predominance of petty-bourgeois democracy stood in the way. In Breslau, Wilhelm Wolff was active with great success until the summer of 1848; in addition he received a Silesian mandate as an alternate representative in the Frankfort parliament. Finally, the compositor Stephan Born, who had worked in Brussels and Paris as an active member of the League, founded a Workers' Brotherhood in Berlin which became fairly widespread and existed until 1850. Born, a very talented young man, who, however, was a bit too much in a hurry to become a political figure, "fraternised" with the most miscellaneous ragtag and bobtail in order to get a crowd together, and was not at all the man who could bring unity into the conflicting tendencies, light into the chaos. Consequently, in the official publications of the association the views represented in the *Communist Manifesto* were mingled hodge-podge with guild recollections and guild aspirations, fragments of Louis Blanc and Proudhon, protectionism, etc.; in short, they wanted to please everybody [*allen alles sein*]. In particular, strikes, trade unions and producers' co-operatives were set going and it was forgotten that above all it was a question of first conquering, by means of political victories, the field in which alone such things could be realised on a lasting basis. When, afterwards, the victories of the reaction made the leaders of the Brotherhood realise the necessity of taking a direct part in the revolutionary struggle, they were naturally left in the lurch by the confused mass which they had grouped around themselves. Born took part in the

Dresden uprising in May, 1849 and had a lucky escape. But, in contrast to the great political movement of the proletariat, the Workers' Brotherhood proved to be a pure *Sonderbund* [separate league], which to a large extent existed only on paper and played such a subordinate role that the reaction did not find it necessary to suppress it until 1850, and its surviving branches until several years later. Born, whose real name was Buttermilch, has not become a big political figure but a petty Swiss professor, who no longer translates Marx into guild language but the meek Renan into his own fulsome German.

With June 13, 1849, in Paris, the defeat of the May insurrections in Germany and the suppression of the Hungarian revolution by the Russians, a great period of the 1848 Revolution came to a close. But the victory of the reaction was as yet by no means final. A reorganisation of the scattered revolutionary forces was required, and hence also of the League. The situation again forbade, as in 1848, any open organisation of the proletariat; hence one had to organise again in secret.

In the autumn of 1849 most of the members of the previous central committees and congresses gathered again in London. The only ones still missing were Schapper, who was jailed in Wiesbaden but came after his acquittal, in the spring of 1850, and Moll, who, after he had accomplished a series of most dangerous missions and agitational journeys—in the end he recruited mounted gunners for the Palatinate artillery right in the midst of the Prussian army in the Rhine Province —joined the Besançon workers' company of Willich's corps and was killed by a shot in the head during the encounter at the Murg in front of the Rotenfels Bridge. On the other hand Willich now entered upon the scene. Willich was one of those sentimental Communists so common in Western Germany since 1845, who on that account alone was instinctively, furtively antagonistic to our critical tendency. More than that, he was entirely the prophet, convinced of his personal mission as the predestined liberator of the German proletariat and as such a direct claimant as much to political as to military dictatorship. Thus, to the primitive Christian Communism previously preached by Weitling was added a kind of communist Islam. However, the propaganda of this new religion was for the time being restricted to the refugee barracks under Willich's command.

Hence, the League was organised afresh; the Address of March 1850 was issued and Heinrich Bauer sent as an emissary to Germany. The Address, composed by Marx and myself, is still of interest today, because petite-bourgeois democracy is even now the party which must certainly be the first to come to power in Germany as the saviour of society from the communist workers on the occasion of the next European upheaval now soon due (the European revolutions, 1815, 1830, 1848–52, 1870, have occurred at intervals of fifteen to eighteen years in our century). Much of what is said there is, therefore, still applicable today. Heinrich Bauer's mission was crowned with complete success. The trusty little shoemaker was a born diplomat. He brought the former members of the League, who had partly become laggards and partly were acting on their own account, back into the active organisation, and particularly also the then leaders of the Workers' Brotherhood. The League began to play the dominant role in the workers', peasants' and athletic associations to a far greater extent than before 1848, so that the next quarterly address to the communities, in June 1850, could already report that the student Schurz from Bonn (later on American ex-minister), who was touring Germany in the interest of petty-bourgeois democracy, "had found all fit forces already in the hands of the League". The League was undoubtedly the only revolutionary organisation that had any significance in Germany.

But what purpose this organisation should serve depended very substantially on whether the prospects of a renewed upsurge of the revolution were realised. And in the course of the year 1850 this became more and more improbable, indeed impossible. The industrial crisis of 1847, which had paved the way for the Revolution of 1848, had been overcome: a new, unprecedented period of industrial prosperity had set in; whoever had eyes to see and used them must have clearly realised that the revolutionary storm of 1848 was gradually spending itself.

"With this general prosperity, in which the productive forces of bourgeois society develop as luxuriantly as is at all possible within bourgeois relationships, *there can be no talk of a real revolution*. Such a revolution is only possible in the periods when both these factors, the modern productive forces and the bourgeois productive forms, come in collision with each other. The various quarrels in which the representatives of the individual factions of the continental party of order now indulge and mutually compromise themselves, far from providing the occasion for new revolutions are, on the contrary, possible only because the basis of the relationships is momentarily so secure and, what the reaction does not know, so *bourgeois*. From it all attempts of the reaction to hold up bourgeois development *willl rebound just as certainly as all moral indignation and all enthusiastic proclamations of the democrats*."

Thus Marx and I wrote in the "Revue of May to October 1850" in the *Neue Rheinische Zeitung, Politisch-ökonomische Revue*, Nos. V and VI, Hamburg, 1850, p. 153.

This cool estimation of the situation, however, was regarded as heresy by many persons, at a time when Ledru-Rollin, Louis Blanc, Mazzini, Kossuth and, among the lesser German lights, Ruge, Kinkel, Gögg and the rest of them crowded in London to form provisional governments of the future not only for their respective fatherlands but for the whole of Europe, and when the only thing still necessary was to obtain the requisite money from America as a loan for the revolution to realise at a moment's notice the European revolution and the various republics which went with it as a matter of course. Can anyone be surprised that a man like Willich was taken in by this, that Schapper, acting on his old revolutionary impulse, also allowed himself to be fooled, and that the majority of the London workers, to a large extent refugees themselves, followed them into the camp of the bourgeois-democratic artificers of revolution? Suffice it to say that the reserve maintained by us was not to the mind of these people; one was to enter into the game of making revolutions. We most decidedly refused to do so. A split ensued; more about this is to be read in the *Revelations*. Then came the arrest of Nothjung, followed by that of Haupt, in Hamburg. The latter turned traitor by divulging the names of the Cologne Central Committee and being slated as the chief witness in the trial; but his relatives had no desire to be thus disgraced and bundled him off to Rio de Janeiro, where he later established himself as a business-man and in recognition of his services was appointed first Prussian and then German Consul General. He is now again in Europe*.

For a better understanding of the *Revelations*, I give the list of the Cologne accused: (1) P. G. Röser, cigarmaker; (2) Heinrich Bürgers, who later died a progressive deputy to the Landtag; (3) Peter Nothjung, tailor, who died a few years ago a photographer in Breslau; (4) W. J. Reiff; (5) Dr. Hermann Becker, now chief burgomaster of Cologne and member of the Upper House; (6) Dr. Roland Daniels, physician, who died a few years after the trial as a result of tuberculosis contracted in prison; (7) Karl Otto, chemist; (8) Dr. Abraham Jacoby, now physician in New York; (9) Dr. I. J. Klein, now physician and town

---

* Schapper died in London at the end of the sixties. Willich took part in the American Civil War with distinction; he became Brigadier-General and was shot in the chest during the battle of Murfreesboro (Tennessee) but recovered and died about ten years ago in America. Of the other persons mentioned above, I will only remark that Heinrich Bauer was lost track of in Australia, and that Weitling and Ewerbeck died in America.

councillor in Cologne; (10) Ferdinand Freiligrath, who, however, was at that time already in London; (11) I. L. Ehrhard, clerk; (12) Friedrich Lessner, tailor, now in London. After a public trial before a jury lasting from October 4 to November 12, 1852, the following were sentenced for attempted high treason: Röser, Bürgers and Nothjung to six, Reiff, Otto and Becker to five and Lessner to three years' confinement in a fortress; Daniels, Klein, Jacoby and Ehrhard were acquitted.

With the Cologne trial the first period of the German communist workers' movement comes to an end. Immediately after the sentence we dissolved our League; a few months later the Willich-Schapper separate league was also laid to eternal rest.

A whole generation lies between then and now. At that time Germany was a country of handicraft and of domestic industry based on hand labour; now it is a big industrial country still undergoing continual industrial transformation. At that time one had to seek out one by one the workers who had an understanding of their position as workers and of their historico-economic antagonism to capital, because this antagonism itself was only just beginning to develop. Today the entire German proletariat has to be placed under exceptional laws, merely in order to slow down a little the process of its development to full consciousness of its position as an oppressed class. At that time the few persons whose minds had penetrated to the realisation of the historical role of the proletariat had to forgather in secret, to assemble clandestinely in small communities of 3 to 20 persons. Today the German proletariat no longer needs any official organisation, either public or secret. The simple self-evident interconnection of like-minded class comrades suffices, without any rules, boards, resolutions or other tangible forms, to shake the whole German Empire to its foundations. Bismarck is the arbiter of Europe beyond the frontiers of Germany, but within them there grows daily more threateningly the athletic figure of the German proletariat that Marx foresaw already in 1844, the giant for whom the cramped imperial edifice designed to fit the philistine is even now becoming inadequate and whose mighty stature and broad shoulders are growing until the moment comes when by merely rising from his seat he will shatter the whole structure of the imperial constitution into fragments. And still more. The international movement of the European and American proletariat has become so much strengthened that not merely its first narrow form—the secret League— but even its second, infinitely wider form—the open International

Working Men's Association—has become a fetter for it, and that the simple feeling of solidarity based on the understanding of the identity of class position suffices to create and to hold together one and the same great party of the proletariat among the workers of all countries and tongues. The doctrines which the League represented from 1847 to 1852, and which at that time could be treated by the wise philistines with a shrug of the shoulders as the hallucinations of utter madcaps, as the secret doctrine of a few scattered sectarians, has now innumerable adherents in all civilised countries of the world, among those condemned to the Siberian mines as much as among the gold diggers of California; and the founder of this doctrine, the most hated, most slandered man of his time, Karl Marx, was, when he died, the ever-sought-for and ever-willing counsellor of the proletariat of both the old and the new world.

London, October 8, 1885.

REVELATIONS CONCERNING THE COMMUNIST TRIAL IN COLOGNE

KARL MARX

REVELATIONS CONCERNING THE COMMUNIST TRIAL IN COLOGNE[1]

I

Introductory Remarks

Nothjung was arrested on May 10, 1851, in Leipzig and Bürgers, Röser, Daniels, Becker and the others were arrested shortly after. On October 4, 1852, the accused appeared before the Court of Assizes in Cologne on a charge of "plotting high treason" against the Prussian State. Thus the preliminary detention (in solitary confinement) had lasted a year and a half.

When Nothjung and Bürgers were arrested the police discovered copies of the "Manifesto of the Communist Party", the "Statutes of the Communist League" (a communist propaganda society), two Addresses[2] of the central committee of this league as well as a number of addresses and circulars. Eight days after Nothjung's arrest had become public knowledge there were further arrests and house-searches in Cologne. So if there had still been something to discover it would certainly have disappeared by then. And in fact the haul yielded only a few irrelevant letters. A year and a half later when the accused finally appeared before the jury, the bona fide evidence for the prosecution had not been augmented by a single document. Nevertheless we are assured by the public ministry (represented by von Seckendorf and Saedt) that the whole administrative machine of the Prussian State had undertaken the most strenuous and far-reaching researches. What then had they been doing? *Nous verrons!*

The unusually long period of detention was explained in the most ingenious way. At first it was claimed that the Saxon government refused to allow the extradition of Bürgers and Nothjung to Prussia. The court in Cologne appealed in vain to the ministry in Berlin, which appealed in vain to the authorities in Saxony. Then the Saxon authorities relented. Bürgers and Nothjung were handed over. Finally, enough progress had been made by October 1851 for the files to be presented to the Prosecution Council of the Cologne Court of Appeal. The Council ruled that "there was no evidence of an indictable offence and so . . . the investigation must start again from the beginning". Meanwhile the zeal of the courts had been kindled by a recently approved disciplinary law which enabled the Prussian government to dismiss any official of the judiciary who earned its displeasure. The case was dismissed on this occasion because there was insufficient evidence of an indictable offence. At the following quarter sessions it had to be further postponed, this time because there was too much evidence. The mass of documents was said to be so huge that the prosecution was unable to digest it. Gradually it did digest it, the bill of indictment was presented to the accused and the action was due to be heard on July 28th. But in the meantime the great driving wheel of the government's case, Police Commissioner Schulz, fell ill. The accused had to sit in gaol for another three months awaiting an improvement in Schulz's health. Fortunately Schulz died, the public became impatient and so the government had to ring up the curtain.

Throughout the whole period the police in Cologne, the police presidium in Berlin and the Ministries of Justice and of the Interior had continually intervened in the investigations, just as Stieber, their worthy representative, was to intervene later on as witness in the actual proceedings in Cologne. The government succeeded in assembling a jury that must be unique in the annals of the Province of the Rhineland. Together with members of the upper middle classes (Herstadt, Leiden, Joest) there were city patricians (von Bianca, von Rath), Squire Bumkins (Häbling von Lanzenauer, Freiherr von Fürstenberg, etc.), two advisers to the Prussian government, one of them a royal chamberlain (von Münch-Bellinghausen) and finally a Prussian professor (Kräusler). Thus in this jury every one of the ruling classes in Germany was represented and they were the only classes represented.

This jury enabled the Prussian government, so it seems, to stop beating about the bush and to make the case into a political trial pure and simple. The documents seized from Nothjung, Bürgers and the others and admitted by them to be genuine did not indeed prove the existence of a plot; in fact they did not prove the existence of any action provided for in the Penal Code. What they did show conclusively was the hostility of the accused to the existing government and the existing social order. But what the intelligence of the legislators had failed to achieve might well be made good (so it was hoped) by the conscience of the jury. What better proof of the craftiness of the accused than that they should have conducted their subversive activities so as not to violate any section of the Code? Does a disease cease to be infectious because it is not listed in the Police Medical Register? If the Prussian government had restricted itself to using the material actually available to prove the harmfulness of the accused and if the jury had confined itself to rendering them harmless by their verdict of guilty, who could censure either government or jury? Who indeed but the single-minded crank, who imagines in his folly that a Prussian government and the ruling classes in Prussia are strong enough to give their opponents a free rein as long as they confine themselves to discussion and propaganda.

Meanwhile the Prussian government had departed even from this— the broad highway of political trials. The delay in bringing the case before the court, the Ministry's direct intervention in the proceedings, the mysterious hints about unheard-of horrors, the rodomontade about a conspiracy in which the whole of Europe would be enmeshed and, finally, the signally brutal treatment meted out to the prisoners, all these things had swelled the trial into a *procès monstre*, the eyes of the European press were upon it and the curiosity and suspicions of the public were fully aroused. The Prussian government had put itself in a position in which for decency's sake the prosecution was simply obliged to produce evidence and the jury to demand it. The jury itself had to face another jury, the jury of public opinion.

To rectify its first blunder, the government was forced into a second one. The police, who had acted as examining magistrates during the preliminary investigation, had to appear as witnesses during the actual proceedings. By the side of the ordinary prosecutor the government had to put an extraordinary one, beside the judges the police, beside Saedt and von Seckendorf a Stieber together with his Wermuth, his Greif and Goldheim. Now that the legal prosecution had failed to uncover the facts whose shadows it had pursued in vain, it was inevitable that yet another agent of the state should intervene in court and, by virtue of his miraculous powers, should constantly make good this deficiency. The court was so thoroughly aware of the position that the President, the judge and the prosecutor abandoned their functions, now to Stieber the witness, now to Stieber the Police Superintendent and they continually disappeared behind with him with the most admirable submissiveness. But before we proceed to clarify these revelations made by the police, revelations which form the basis of the "indictable offence" that the Prosecution Council was unable to discover, one more preliminary observation remains to be made.

It became evident from the papers seized from the accused, as well as from their own statements, that a German Communist society had existed with a central committee originally based in London. On

September 15, 1850, the central committee split. The majority (referred to in the indictment as the *Marx Party*) moved its headquarters to Cologne. The minority, which was later expelled from the League by the Group in Cologne, established its own headquarters in London and founded branches in diverse places on the continent. The bill of indictment refers to this minority and its supporters as the *Willich–Schapper Party*.

Saedt–Seckendorf claim that the split in the London central committee had its origin solely in personal disagreements. Long before Saedt–Seckendorf the "chivalrous Willich" had spread the most scandalous and infamous rumours among the London *émigrés* about the causes of the split and had found in Mr. Arnold Ruge, that notorious fifth wheel on the state coach of European central democracy,[3] and in others of the same sort, people who were willing to act as sewage pipes conveying refuse to the German and American press. The democrats soon grasped the fact that they could gain an easy victory over the communists by hastily casting the "chivalrous Willich" for the role of the true representative of the League. The "chivalrous Willich" for his part soon realized that the Marx Party could not reveal the causes of the split without betraying the existence of a secret society in Germany and thereby confiding the central committee in Cologne to the paternal care of the Prussian police. This situation no longer obtains and so we may cite a few passages from the minutes of the last session of the London central committee, dated September 15, 1850.[4]

Here, verbatim, is the essence of Marx's defence of his motion calling for the breach:

> "The point of view of the minority is dogmatic rather than critical, idealistic rather than materialistic. For them revolutions are not the product of the realities of the situation but the result of a *mere effort of will*. What we say to the workers is: 'You will have 15, 20, 50 years of civil war and national struggle and this not merely to bring about a change in society but also to change yourselves and prepare yourselves for the exercise of political power.' Whereas you say on the contrary: 'Either we seize power at once, or else we might as well just take to our beds.' While we are at pains to show the German worker how rudimentary the development of the German proletariat is, you appeal to the patriotic feelings and the class prejudice of the German artisan, flattering him in the grossest way possible, and this is a more popular method, of course. Just as the word 'people' has been given an aura of sanctity by the

democrats, so you have made an idol of the word 'proletariat'. Like the democrats you ignore the idea of revolutionary development and substitute for it the slogan of revolution." etc., etc.

Mr. Schapper's verbatim reply is as follows:

"I have defended the opinions attacked here because in general I am an enthusiast about the whole business. The question at issue is: either we chop a few heads off right at the start or else ours will be chopped off."

(Schapper even promised to lose his own head in a year, i.e. on September 15, 1851.)

"In France it will be the workers' turn and when this happens it will be our turn here in Germany. Were this not the case I should certainly take to my bed and I should certainly be able to enjoy quite a different material position. When it is our turn we can take all the measures necessary to ensure the rule of the proletariat. I am fanatically in favour of this point of view but the central committee wants the very opposite." etc., etc.

It is apparent then that it was not for personal reasons that the central committee was divided. But it would be just as wrong to speak of a difference of principle. The Willich–Schapper Party have never laid claim to the dignity of having developed their own ideas. What is typical of them is the peculiar misunderstanding of other people's ideas which they transform into dogmas and, reducing these to a phrase, they fondly imagine they possess them. It would be no less misguided to agree with the prosecution in describing the Willich–Schapper Party as the *Party of Action*, unless by action one understands inaction concealed behind beerhouse bluster, simulated conspiracies and meaningless pseudo-alliances.

II

The Dietz Archive

The document found in the possession of the accused, the Manifesto of the Communist Party, had been printed before the February revolution and had been available from booksellers for some years so that neither in its form nor in its aims could it be the programme of a "plot". The confiscated "Addresses of the Central Committee" were concerned exclusively with the relations between the Communists and the future democratic government and not at all with the government of Frederick William IV. Lastly, the "Statutes" were indeed the statutes of a secret propaganda society, but the criminal code prescribes no penalties for secret societies. The ultimate aim of the propaganda is said to be the destruction of the social order; but the Prussian State has already perished once and could perish ten times more and indeed for good and all without the social order being even the slightest bit harmed. The Communists can help accelerate the dissolution of bourgeois society and yet leave the dissolution of the Prussian State in the hands of bourgeois society itself. If a man whose immediate aim was the overthrow of the Prussian State were to preach the destruction of the social order as a preliminary measure he would be like that deranged engineer who wished to blow up the whole world in order to remove a rubbish-heap.

But if the final goal of the League was the *overturning of the social order*, the method by which this was to be achieved was necessarily that of *political revolution* and this entailed the overthrow of the Prussian State, just as surely as an earthquake entails the overthrow of a henroost. And the accused did in fact proceed from the blasphemous assumption that the present Prussian government would collapse without their having to lift a finger. So they did not found a League to overturn the present government of Prussia, nor were they guilty of any "treasonable plot".

Has anyone ever accused the early Christians of desiring the overthrow of an obscure Roman prefect? The Prussian political philosophers from Leibniz to Hegel have laboured to dethrone God and if I dethrone God I must also dethrone the king who reigns by divine right. But has anyone ever prosecuted them for *lèse-majesté* against the house of Hohenzollern?

From whatever angle one looked at it, when the *corpus delicti* was subjected to public scrutiny it vanished like a ghost. The complaint of the Prosecution Council that there was no "indictable offence" remained valid and the "Marx Party" was spiteful enough to refrain from providing *one single iota for the indictment* during the whole year and a half of the preliminary investigation.

Such an embarrassing situation had to be remedied. So, in conjunction with the police, the Willich–Schapper Party remedied it. Let us see how Mr. Stieber, the midwife of this faction, introduces it into the trial in Cologne. (See Stieber's testimony in the session of October 18, 1852.)[5]

While Stieber was in London in the Spring of 1851, allegedly to protect the visitors to the Exhibition from thieves, the Berlin police sent him a copy of the papers found on *Nothjung*.

"Above all" Stieber swore, *"my attention was directed to the conspirators' archive which according to Nothjung's papers could be found in the possession of a certain Oswald Dietz and which would undoubtedly contain the whole correspondence of the League's members."*

The conspirators' archive? The whole correspondence of the League's members? But wasn't Dietz the secretary of the Willich–Schapper central committee? If the archive of a conspiracy could be found in his possession it had to be the archive of the Willich–Schapper conspiracy. If there was correspondence belonging to the League it could only be the correspondence of the separatist League that was hostile to the accused in Cologne. But even more became clear from the scrutiny of the documents found on Nothjung, namely that nothing in them points to the fact of Oswald Dietz being the keeper of an archive. And in any event how should Nothjung who was in Leipzig know what was hidden even from the "Marx Party" in London?

Stieber could not say outright: Now note this, Gentlemen of the Jury! I have made an amazing discovery in London. Unfortunately it refers to a conspiracy with which the accused in Cologne have nothing to do and which it is not the task of the Cologne jury to judge, but which provided a pretext for keeping the accused in solitary confinement for 1½ years. Stieber could not say this. The intermezzo with Nothjung was indispensable, for otherwise it would not have been possible to forge even the semblance of a link between the documents and revelations from London and the trial in Cologne.

Stieber then swore on oath that a man offered to buy the archive for cash from Oswald Dietz. The plain fact is that a certain Reuter, a spy of the Prussian police who has never belonged to a communist society, lived in the same house as Dietz and, during the latter's absence, broke into his desk and stole his papers. That Mr. Stieber paid him for the theft is only too credible, although it would hardly have protected him from a journey to Van Diemens' Land if the manoeuvre had become public knowledge while he was still in London.

C

On August 5, 1851, Stieber, who was in Berlin, received from London the Dietz Archive, "in a bulky parcel wrapped in oil-cloth" which turned out to be a heap of documents consisting of "60 separate items". To this Stieber could swear, and at the same time he swore that the parcel that he received on August 5, 1851, contained letters from the chief group in Berlin dated August 20, 1851.

Should any bold person say that Stieber was perjuring himself when he claimed that he received on August 5, 1851, letters dated August 20, 1851, Stieber would justly retort that a Royal Prussian Counsellor, like the Evangelist Matthew, has the right to perform chronological miracles.

En passant. From the list of documents stolen from the Willich–Schapper Party and from the dates of these documents it follows that although the party had been warned by Reuter's burglary, it still found ways and means of having further documents stolen and contriving that they fall into the hands of the Prussian police.

When Stieber found himself in possession of the treasure wrapped in stout oil-cloth he was beside himself with joy. "The whole network," he swore, "lay revealed before my eyes." And what did the treasure-trove reveal about the "Marx Party" and the accused in Cologne? According to Stieber's own testimony, nothing at all except for

"the original of a declaration by several members of the central committee, obviously the nucleus of the 'Marx Party'; it was dated from London, September 17, 1850 and concerned their resignation from the Communist League consequent on the well-known breach of September 15, 1850."

Stieber admits this himself but even in this simple statement he is unable to confine himself to the unvarnished truth. He is compelled to raise it on to a higher plane in order to make it truly worthy of the police. For the original declaration contained nothing more than a statement of three lines to the effect that the majority-members of the former central committee and their friends were resigning from the public Workers' Society of Great Windmill Street[6]; but they did not resign from a "communist league".

Stieber could have spared his correspondents the oil-cloth and our authorities the postal dues. He had only to rummage through the various German papers of September 1850 and he would have found in black and white the declaration of the "nucleus of the Marx Party" announcing its resignation from the Refugee Committee[7] and also from the Workers' Society of Great Windmill Street.

The immediate product of Stieber's researches was then the amazing discovery that the "nucleus of the Marx Party" had resigned from the Great Windmill Street Society on September 17, 1850. "The whole network of the Cologne plot lay revealed before his eyes." The public, however, couldn't trust his eyes, nor could they believe their own.

III

The Cherval Plot

Meanwhile Stieber did not let his treasure-trove lie idle. The papers that had come into his possession on August 5, 1851, led to the discovery of the so-called "Franco–German plot in Paris". They contained six reports sent from Paris by Adolph Majer an emissary of Willich–Schapper, as well as five reports from leaders of the Paris branch to the Willich–Schapper central committee. (Stieber's testimony of October 18th.) Stieber then went on a diplomatic pleasure trip to Paris and there he made the personal acquaintance of the great Carlier who in the recent notorious affair of the Goldbar Lottery[8] had just delivered proof that though a great enemy of the communists, he was an even greater friend of other people's private property.

"Accordingly I myself went to Paris in September 1851. Carlier, the Prefect of Police there at the time, was most eager and ready to lend me his support. . . . With the aid of the French police agents the threads laid bare in the London letters were speedily and surely taken up again; we were able to track down the addresses of the various leaders of the conspiracy and to keep all their movements, and especially all their meetings and correspondence, under observation. Some very sinister things came to light . . . . I was compelled to yield to Carlier's urgent request for action and so the police intervened during the night of September 4th." (Stieber's testimony of October 18th).

Stieber left Berlin in September. Let us assume it was September 1st. At best he could not have arrived in Paris before the evening of the 2nd. On the night of the 4th the police intervened. Thirty-six hours remain then for the conference with Carlier and for the necessary measures to be taken. In these thirty-six hours not only were the addresses of the various leaders "tracked down"; but *all* their movements, *all* their meetings and *all* their correspondence were "kept under observation", that is after their "addresses had been tracked down", of course. Stieber's arrival not only inspires the French police agents with a "speed and sureness" that works wonders, it also makes the conspiratorial leaders "eager and ready" to perpetrate so many movements, meetings and so much correspondence within twenty-four hours that the police can already intervene the following evening.

But it is not enough that by September 3 all the addresses of the individual leaders should have been traced and all their movements, meetings and correspondence put under observation:

> "French police agents", Stieber swears, "found an opportunity to be present at the meetings of the conspirators and to hear their decisions about the plan of campaign for the next revolution."

No sooner have the police observed the meetings, then, than the observation gives them an opportunity to be present, and no sooner have they been present at one meeting than it becomes several meetings, and no sooner has it become several meetings than resolutions are adopted about the plan of campaign during the next revolution — and all this on the same day. On that very same day when Stieber first meets Carlier, Carlier's agents first discover the addresses of the various leaders, the various leaders first meet Carlier's agents, invite them to their meetings, hold a whole series of meetings on the same day for their benefit and cannot bring themselves to part from them without hastily adopting resolutions for the plan of campaign for the next revolution.

However eager and ready Carlier might be—and no one will doubt his readiness to uncover a Communist plot three months before the *coup d'état*—Stieber expects more of him than he could achieve. Stieber asks miracles of the police; he does not merely ask for them, he believes them; he does not merely believe them, he swears to them on oath.

> "At the beginning of this venture, i.e. of this police intervention, a French Commissioner and I personally arrested the dangerous Cherval, the ring-leader of the French communists. He resisted vigorously and we had a violent tussle with him."

Thus Stieber's statement of October 18.

"Cherval made an attempt on my life in Paris, and in my own home where he had broken in during the night. In the course of the struggle consequent on this intrusion my wife, who came to my aid, was wounded."

Thus Stieber's testimony of October 27.

On the night of the 4th, Stieber intervenes at Cherval's dwelling and there is a tussle in which Cherval resists. On the night of the 3rd Cherval intervenes at Stieber's dwelling and there is a tussle in which Stieber resists. But during the day of the 3rd there reigned a veritable *entente cordiale* between conspirators and police agents without which so many great deeds could not have been performed in one day. For now not only have the conspirators been found out by Stieber on the 3rd, but Stieber has been found out on the 3rd by the conspirators. While Carlier's agents were tracking down the homes of the conspirators, the conspirators were tracking down Stieber's home. While he played the role of an "observer" towards them, they pursued an active rôle towards him. While he was dreaming about their plot against the government, they were engaged in an assault on his person.

Stieber's testimony of October 18 continues:

"In the course of the struggle" (this is Stieber on the attack) "I observed that Cherval was endeavouring to put a piece of paper into his mouth and swallow it. It was only with great difficulty that I managed to retrieve one half of the paper, the other half being already devoured."

So the paper was situated in Cherval's mouth, between his teeth in fact for only one half was saved, the other half having already been devoured. Stieber and his henchman, the Police Commissioner or whoever, could only rescue the other half by placing their hands in the jaws of the "dangerous Cherval". Cherval adopted the most obvious method of defence against such an onslaught: he *bit*, and the Paris papers actually announced that Cherval had bitten Mrs. Stieber, though in that account of the scene Stieber was supposed to be not with his wife but with the Police Commissioner. On the other hand, Stieber declares that when Cherval assaulted him in his own home, it was Mrs. Stieber who had been wounded while coming to his aid. If we try to reconcile Stieber's statements and the reports of the Paris papers it would appear that on the night of the 3rd Cherval bit Mrs. Stieber in an attempt to rescue the papers that Mr. Stieber tore from between his teeth on the night of the 4th. Stieber will retort that Paris is a city of miracles and that long before him La Rochefoucauld had said that in France all is possible.

Putting the belief in miracles to one side for a moment it becomes clear that the first miracles arose because Stieber compressed into one day, September 3, a whole series of events that were in reality spread over a long period of time, while the latter miracles arose when he claimed of different events that happened in one place and on one evening that they occurred in two places on two evenings. Let us confront his tale from a "Thousand and One Nights" with the actual facts. But first one very strange fact, though certainly no miracle. Stieber tore from Cherval one half of the paper that had been swallowed. What was in the rescued half? The whole that Stieber wanted.

> "This paper", he swears, "contains a vital instruction for Gipperich, the emissary in Strasbourg, together with his *complete postal address.*"

Now for the facts of the matter.

We know from Stieber that he received the Dietz archive in a stout oil-cloth wrapping on August 5, 1851. On August 8 or 9 a certain Schmidt arrived in Paris. Schmidt, it seems, is the name inevitably assumed by Prussian police agents travelling incognito. In 1845–46 Stieber journeyed to the Silesian Mountains under the name of Schmidt. Fleury, his London agent, went as Schmidt to Paris in 1851. Here he searched for the various leaders of the Willich–Schapper conspiracy and lit upon Cherval. He pretended that he had fled from Cologne rescuing the League's cash-box with 500 thalers. He produced credentials in the form of instructions from Dresden and various other places and spoke about reorganising the League, uniting the different parties, as the existing schisms were caused solely by personal disagreements (the police were in favour of unity and union even then), and promised to use the 500 thalers to inject fresh life into the League. Schmidt gradually made the acquaintance of all the leaders of the Willich–Schapper communes in Paris. He not only learned their addresses, but visited them, watched their post, observed their movements, found his way into their meetings and, as an *agent provocateur*, egged them on. Cherval in particular became more boastful than ever as Schmidt lavished more and more admiration on him, hailing him as the League's great Unknown, as the "Great Chief" who was only unaware of his own great merits, a fate that had befallen many a great man. One evening when Schmidt went with Cherval to a meeting of the League, the latter read out his famous letter to Gipperich before sending it off. In this way Schmidt learned of Gipperich's existence.

"As soon as Gipperich has returned to Stasbourg", Schmidt observed, "we can give him an order for the 500 thalers lying in Strasbourg. Here is the address of the man who is holding the money. Give me in exchange Gipperich's address to send to the man in advance as a credential for the moment when Gipperich presents himself."

In this way Schmidt obtained Gipperich's address. On the same evening a quarter of an hour after Cherval posted the letter a message was sent by electric telegraph and Gipperich was arrested, his house was searched and the famous letter was intercepted. Gipperich *was arrested before Cherval.*

Some little while after this Schmidt informed Cherval that a man called Stieber who was a tool of the Prussian police had arrived in Paris. He had not only learned his address but had also heard from a waiter in a café opposite that Stieber was plotting to have him (Schmidt) arrested. Would not Cherval be the man to give this wretched Prussian policeman a lesson he would not easily forget? "We'll throw him in the Seine" was Cherval's answer. They then agreed to gain entry into Stieber's house the next day under some pretext or other in order to confirm that he was there and to make a mental note of his personal appearance. The next evening our heroes really set out on their expedition. As they approached their goal Schmidt expressed the opinion that it would be better if Cherval were to enter the house while he patrolled in front of it.

"Just ask the porter for Stieber", he went on, "and when Stieber lets you in tell him that you want to speak to Herr Sperling and ask him whether he has brought the bill of exchange from Cologne. Oh, and one thing more. Your white hat is too conspicuous, it is too democratic. There, take my black one."

They exchanged hats, Schmidt prepared to stand guard, Cherval pulled the bell-rope and found himself in Stieber's house. The porter doubted whether Stieber was at home and Cherval was about to withdraw when a woman's voice called from upstairs: "Yes, Stieber is at home." Cherval followed the voice and the trail led to an individual wearing green spectacles who identified himself as Stieber. Cherval then produced the formula agreed on about Sperling and the bill of exchange.

"That won't do", Stieber interrupted, "You come into my house, ask for me, are shown up, try to withdraw, etc. That is extremely suspicious."

Cherval answered brusquely. Stieber pulled the bell, at once several men appeared, they surrounded Cherval, Stieber lunged at his coat pocket from where a letter was visible. It did not in fact contain Cherval's instructions to Gipperich, but it was a letter from Gipperich to Cherval. Cherval tried to eat the letter, Stieber attempted to take it from his mouth, Cherval hit out and bit and lashed out. Husband Stieber tried to save one half, wife Stieber the other half and an injury was all the reward she had for her zeal. The noise of the scene brought all the other tenants from their apartments. Meanwhile one of Stieber's thugs had thrown a gold watch down the stairs and while Cherval was shouting: "Spy!" Stieber and Co. screamed: "Stop thief!" The porter recovered the gold watch and the cry of "Stop thief!" became general. Cherval was arrested and on his way out he was welcomed at the door not by his friend Schmidt but by four or five soldiers.

When confronted with the facts, all the miracles conjured up by Stieber disappear. His agent Fleury was at work for a period of three weeks, he not only laid bare the threads of the plot, he also helped to weave them. Stieber had only to come to Paris and he could exclaim: *Veni, vidi, vici!* He could present Carlier with a ready-made plot and Carlier needed only to be "eager and ready" to intervene. There is no need for Mrs. Stieber to have been bitten by Cherval on the 3rd because Mr. Stieber put his hand into Cherval's mouth on the 4th. There is no need for Gipperich's address and the correct instructions to be salvaged whole from the jaws of the "dangerous Cherval", like Jonah from the whale's belly, after they have been half eaten. The only miracle that remains is the miraculous faith of the jurymen to whom Stieber is not afraid to serve up such fairy tales. Ever-loyal subjects! Fullblooded embodiments of narrow-minded servility!

"After I had confronted Cherval to his great astonishment" Stieber swears (in the sitting of October 18), "with all his original reports which he had himself sent to London, he realised that I knew all and so made a full confession."

The papers that Stieber showed Cherval at first were by no means the original reports to London. Stieber sent to Berlin for those later on, together with other documents from the Dietz Archive. He first showed him a circular signed by Oswald Dietz that Cherval had just received and, in addition, a few of the most recent letters from Willich. How did Stieber get possession of these? While Cherval was occupied biting and fighting Mr. and Mr. Stieber our valiant Schmidt-Fleury hurried to Mme. Cherval, an Englishwoman (Fleury being a German businessman in London naturally speaks English) and told her that her husband had been arrested, that the danger was great, that she should hand over all his papers so that he might be compromised no further, and that Cherval had instructed him to give them to a third person. As proof that he came as a genuine ambassador he showed her the white hat he had taken from Cherval because it looked too democratic. Thus Fleury obtained the letters from Mme. Cherval and Stieber obtained them from Fleury.

At any rate he now had a much more favourable base from which to operate than previously in London. Then he could only steal the Dietz Archive, but now he could give Cherval's evidence for him. Accordingly (in the session on October 18) he gave Cherval's views on "contacts in Germany";

"He had lived in the Rhineland for a considerable time and more particularly he had been in Cologne in 1848. There he made the acquaintance of Marx and the latter admitted him to the League which he then zealously laboured to propagate in Paris on the basis of already existing groups there."

In 1846 Cherval was nominated and admitted to the League in London by Schapper at a time when Marx was in Brussels and was himself not yet a member. So Cherval could not be admitted to the same league by Marx in Cologne in 1848.

On the outbreak of the March Revolution Cherval returned to the Prussian Rhineland for a few weeks and from there returned to London where he remained without interruption from the end of spring 1848 until the summer of 1850. He cannot therefore "have zealously laboured to propagate the League in Paris" unless Stieber, who can perform chronological miracles, also finds spatial miracles within his

c*

powers and can even confer the quality of ubiquity on third persons.

Marx came to know Cherval superficially along with a hundred other workers when he joined the Workers' Club in Great Windmill Street in 1849 after his expulsion from Paris. So he cannot possibly have met him in Cologne in 1848.

At first Cherval told Stieber the truth on all these points. Stieber tried to induce him to make false statements. Did he succeed? We have only Stieber's word that he did, that is to say, less than nothing. Stieber's prime concern was, of course, to establish a connection, however specious, between Cherval and Marx so as to be able to create a link artificially between the accused in Cologne and the Paris plot.

No sooner is Stieber required to go into details about the connections of Cherval and his colleagues in Germany, and their correspondence there, than he takes good care not even to mention Cologne and instead speaks complacently and at length of Heck in Brunswick, Laube in Berlin, Reininger in Mainz, Tietz in Hamburg, etc., etc., in short of the Willich–Schapper Party. This Party, says Stieber, had "the League's archives in its hands". Through a misunderstanding it changes from their hands to his. In the archive he found *not one single line* written by Cherval to anyone in London, let alone to Marx in person, *before the split* of the London central committee, that is to say before September 15, 1850.

With the help of Schmidt-Fleury he swindled Frau Cherval out of her husband's papers. But again, he could not find among them a single line written by Marx to Cherval. To deal with this embarrassing situation he attributed to Cherval the admission that:

> "he had fallen out with Marx because the latter had demanded that he should still maintain the correspondence even though the central committee was now situated in Cologne."

If Stieber found no Marx–Cherval correspondence *before* September 15, 1850, this must be due to the fact that Cherval ceased all correspondence with Marx *after* September 15, 1850. *Pends-toi, Figaro, tu n'aurais pas inventé cela!*

The documents that the Prussian government and, in part, Stieber himself had laboriously brought together during the year and a half that the investigation lasted refuted every suggestion of a connection between the accused and the Paris association no less than with the Franco–German plot.

The Address from the London central committee of June 1850[9] proved that the Paris association was in a state of dissolution even before the schism in the central committee. Six letters from the Dietz Archive showed that after the central committee was transferred to Cologne the Paris groups were refounded by A. Majer, an emissary of the Willich–Schapper party. The letters of the leading branches in Paris that were found in the Archive proved that the Paris association was decidedly hostile towards the Cologne central committee. Finally, the French bill of indictment against Cherval and his associates showed that all the evidence incriminating them did not occur until the year 1851 at the earliest. In the sitting of November 18 Saedt, despite Stieberian revelations, found himself reduced to the barest supposition that it was surely not impossible that the Marx Party had at some time somehow been involved in some plot or other in Paris but that nothing was known of this plot or the time when it took place other than the fact that Saedt, acting in his official capacity, deemed it possible. How dull-witted the German press must be to go on repeating the old myth of Saedt's incisive intelligence!

For a long time the Prussian police had sought to persuade the public that Marx and, through Marx, the defendants accused in Cologne were involved in the Franco–German plot. During the Cherval trial Beckmann, the police spy, sent the following notice from Paris to the *Kölnische Zeitung* on February 25, 1852:

"Several of the accused have fled, among them a certain A. Majer, who is said to be an agent of Marx and Co."

Whereupon the *Kölnische Zeitung* printed a declaration by Marx that

"A. Majer is one of the closest friends of Herr Schapper and the former Prussian lieutenant Willich, and that relations with him (Marx) could not be more distant."

Then, in his testimony of October 18, 1852, Stieber himself admitted:

"The members of the central committee expelled by the Marx Party on September 15, 1850, sent A. Majer to Frankfurt, etc."

and he even divulged the contents of the correspondence between A. Majer and Willich–Schapper.

In September 1851 during the police-campaign against aliens, a member of the Marx Party, Konrad Schramm, was arrested, together with 50 or 60 other people sitting in a café, and was detained for almost two months on the suspicion of being implicated in the plot instigated by the Irishman Cherval. On October 16 while still in the depot of the Prefecture of Police he received a visit from a German who addressed him as follows:

> "I am a Prussian official. You are aware that all over Germany and especially in Cologne there have been a large number of arrests following the discovery of a communist club. The mere mention of a person's name in a letter is enough to bring about his arrest. The government is slightly embarrassed by the hordes of prisoners of whom it is uncertain whether or not they are really implicated. *We know that you had no part in the complot franco-allemand but on the other hand you are very closely acquainted with Marx and Engels and are doubtless very well informed about all the details of the communist network in Germany.* We would be very much in your debt if you could help us and give us more detailed information as to who is guilty and who innocent. In this way you could bring about the liberation of a large number of people. If you wish we can draw up an official statement. You will have nothing to fear from such a declaration." etc., etc.

Schramm naturally showed this gentle Prussian official the door, protested to the French Ministry about such visits and was expelled from France at the end of October.

That Schramm was a member of the "Marx Party" was known to the Prussian police from the official resignation found in the Dietz Archive. That the "Marx Party" had no connection with the Cherval plot, they admitted personally to Schramm. If a connection between the "Marx Party" and the Cherval plot were to be established this could not happen in Cologne but only in Paris where a member of that party sat in gaol together with Cherval. But the Prussian government feared nothing more than the confrontation of Cherval and Schramm, for this would nullify in advance the advantage they hoped for from the Paris trial in their own case against the accused in Cologne. By his acquittal of Schramm the French examining magistrate ruled implicitly that the trial in Cologne was in no way connected with the Paris plot.

Stieber then made a last attempt:

> "With reference to the above-mentioned leader of the French communists, Cherval, we laboured, for a long time in vain, to

discover Cherval's true identity. It finally came clear from a remark made in confidence to a police agent by Marx that he had escaped from gaol in Aachen in 1845 where he was serving a sentence for forgery, that he was then granted admittance to the League by Marx during the troubles of 1848 and that he went as an emissary from there to Paris."

Just as Marx was unable to inform Stieber's *spiritus familiaris*, the police agent that he had admitted Cherval in London as early as 1846, or that he had induced him to live in London while at the same time hawking propaganda around in Paris, so too, he was unable to inform Stieber's *alter ego*, the police agent as such, that Cherval had served a sentence in Aachen and that he had forged banknotes, facts that he learnt from Stieber himself in his testimony. Such a *hysteron-proteron* is possible only for a Stieber. Antiquity has bequeathed to us its "*dying gladiator*";[10] the Prussian state will leave us its "*swearing Stieber*".

Thus for a long, long time they had vainly endeavoured to discover Cherval's true identity. On the evening of September 2 Stieber arrived in Paris. On the evening of the 4th Cherval was arrested, on the evening of the 5th he was taken from his cell to a dimly lit room. Stieber was there but not alone; there was also a French police official present, an Alsatian who spoke broken German but who understood perfectly, had a policeman's memory and who was not favourably impressed by the arrogantly servile Prussian police superintendent. In the presence of this French official the following conversation took place:

> *Stieber* in German: "Now look here, Herr Cherval, we know what's at the bottom of this business with the French name and the Irish passport. We know who you are, you are a Rhineland Prussian. Your name is K. and if you want your freedom it is really in your own hands. All we ask of you is a full confession." etc., etc.
>
> Cherval denied this.
>
> Whereupon *Stieber:* "People who have forged banknotes and have escaped from Prussian gaols have in the past been extradited to Prussia by the French authorities. So I would urge you to think carefully; the penalty is twelve years solitary confinement."
>
> *The French official:* "We must give the man time to think it over in his cell."

And so Cherval was led back to his cell.

Naturally enough Stieber could not afford to blurt out the truth, he could not admit openly that he was trying to force false admissions from Cherval by conjuring up the ghost of extradition and twelve years in gaol.

And even now Stieber had still not been able to discover Cherval's true identity. He still referred to him in front of the jury as Cherval and not as K. And that was not all. He did not know where Cherval really lived. In the sitting of October 23 he had him living in Paris. When in the sitting on October 27 Schneider II, Counsel for the Defence, pressed him to say whether "the aforementioned Cherval was at present in London?" Stieber answered that

"He could not give the court any precise information on this point; he knew only of a rumour that Cherval had escaped in Paris."

The Prussian government suffered its customary fate of being the dupe. The French government had allowed it to pull the chestnuts of the Franco–German plot out of the fire but not to eat them. Cherval had found a means of gaining the sympathy of the French government and so a few days after the Assizes they let him and Gipperich flee to London. The Prussian government had hoped that in Cherval it would have a valuable tool for the trial in Cologne, whereas in fact it only provided the French government with yet another agent.

One day before Cherval's pretended flight he received a visit from a Prussian ruffian dressed in a black dress-coat and cuffs, with a bristling black moustache, and sparse grey hair cut short, in a word, a very pretty fellow who, he was told later, went by the name of Police Inspector Greif and who later introduced himself as Greif. Greif had obtained access to him by means of an entrance ticket which he had obtained (having bypassed the prefect of police) directly from the Minister of Police. The Minister of Police thought it great fun to deceive the dear Prussians.

> Greif: "I am a Prussian official. I have been sent here to negotiate with you. You will never get out of here without our aid. I have a proposal to make to you. We need you as a witness in Cologne. If you submit a request to the French government to hand you over to Prussia they have agreed to grant permission. After you have fulfilled your obligations in court and the case is over we promise on our word of honour to release you."
> Cherval: "I'll get out without your help."
> Greif: (emphatically) "That is impossible!"

Greif also had Gipperich brought to him and proposed that he should spend five days in Hannover as a communist emissary. Likewise without success. The next day Cherval and Gipperich escaped. The French authorities smirked, the telegraph brought the bad news to Berlin and as late as October 23 Stieber swore in court that Cherval was in Paris, and as late as October 27 he could not give any information and could only pass on the rumour that Cherval had escaped "in Paris". Meanwhile, Inspector Greif had visited Cherval three times during the Cologne proceedings in order to discover, among other things, Nette's address in Paris in the hope that he could be bribed to testify against the defendants in Cologne. This plan misfired.

Stieber had his reasons for casting a veil of obscurity over his relations with Cherval. So K. remained Cherval, the Prussian remained Irish and Stieber does not know to this day where Cherval is and what is "his true identity".*

In Cherval's correspondence with Gipperich the trifolium Seckendorf–Saedt–Stieber had at last found what it was looking for:

> *Schinderhannes, Karlo Moor,*
> *Nahm ich mit als Muster vor.*[12]

> [Schinderhannes, Karlo Moor
> Heroes whom I held in awe.]

In order that Cherval's letter to Gipperich might be deeply engraved upon the lethargic cerebral matter of the 300 top tax-payers whom the jury represented, it received the honour of being read aloud three times in court. Behind this harmless gipsy pathos no experienced person could fail to see the figure of the buffoon who tries to impress both himself and others with his terrifying ferocity.

Cherval & Co., moreover, shared the general expectation of the

---

* Even in the "Black Book"[11] Stieber still does not know who Cherval really is. It is written there (Part II, p. 38, under Nr. III) Cherval: see Crämer, and under Nr. 116 Crämer: "has been very active in the Communist League under the name of Cherval (see Nr. III). In the League he is also known as Frank. Under the name of Cherval he was sentenced to 8 years imprisonment by the Paris Assizes in February 1853" (this should read 1852) "but he soon escaped and fled to London." So ignorant is Stieber in Part II where he provides an alphabetical, numbered list of suspects with their particulars. He has already forgotten that in Part I, p.81 he has let slip the admission: "Cherval is the son of a Rhineland official called Joseph Krämer and he" (who? the father or the son?), "abused his craft of lithography to forge banknotes, and was arrested for this but escaped from prison in Cologne" (false, it was Aachen!) "and in 1848 fled to England and later to Paris." Compare this with Stieber's evidence before the jury quoted above. The plain fact is that the police are absolutely incapable of telling the truth. (Note by Engels in the edition of 1885.)

democrats that the second Sunday in May[13] would inaugurate an age of miracles and so they decided to join the revolution on that day. Schmidt-Fleury had helped to bestow upon this *idée fixe* the form and dignity of a plan and so the activities of Cherval and Co. now came within the legal definition of a plot. Through them proof was obtained that the plot that the accused in Cologne had omitted to put into action against the Prussian government had at least been perpetrated by the Cherval Party against France.

With the help of Schmidt-Fleury the Prussian government had sought to fabricate the semblance of a connection between the accused in Cologne and the plot in Paris, a connection to the reality of which Stieber then swore on oath. This trinity of Stieber, Greif, Fleury played the chief role in the Cherval plot. We shall see them at work again.

Let us then sum up:

A is a republican, B also calls himself a republican. A and B are enemies. B is commissioned by the police to construct a bomb. Whereupon A is dragged before the courts. If B rather than A has built the bomb this is due to the enmity between A and B. In order to find proof of A's guilt B is called as a witness against him. This was the comedy of the Cherval plot.

It will be readily understood that as far as the general public was concerned the logic of this was a flop. Stieber's "factual" revelations dissolved amidst malodorous vapours; the complaint of the Prosecutions Council that "there was no evidence of an indictable offence" was as valid as ever. New police miracles had become necessary.

IV

The Original Minute-Book

During the sitting on October 23, the President of the Court announced: "Police Superintendent Stieber has indicated to me that important new evidence has come to light" and he called the witness back into the box so that the court might hear it. Up jumped Stieber and the performance began.

Hitherto Stieber had described the activities of the Willich–Schapper Party, or more briefly, the Cherval Party, activities that took place both *before* and after the arrest of the accused in Cologne. The activities of the accused themselves he had not described either *before* or *after* their arrest. The Cherval Plot took place *after* their arrest and Stieber himself now declared:

> "In my earlier testimony I described the development of the Communist League and the activities of its members only *up to the time* when the men now accused *were arrested.*"

Thus he admitted that the Cherval Plot had nothing to do with "the development of the Communist League and the activities of its members". He confessed to the *nullity* of his previous testimony. Indeed, he was so complacent about his statements on October 18 that he regarded it as quite superfluous to continue to identify Cherval with the "Marx Party".

> "Firstly", he said, "the Willich Party still exists and of its members hitherto only Cherval in Paris has been seized, etc."

Aha! so the ringleader Cherval is a leader of the Willich Party.

But now Stieber wished to reveal his *most important* discoveries, not merely his *very latest* discoveries that is, but his *most important* ones. The very latest and most important! This most important information would have lost some of its significance if the insignificance of his earlier information were not emphasised. Up to now, Stieber announced, I have not really said anything, but just wait. Pay attention! Hitherto I have merely talked about the Cherval Party which is in fact hostile to the accused, and strictly speaking, none of that has been in place here. But now I shall discuss the "Marx Party", for that alone is truly relevant to this case. Naturally Stieber could not put the matter as plainly as this. So he says:

> "Up to now I have described the Communist League *before* the arrest of the accused; I shall now describe the League *after* their arrest."

With characteristic virtuosity he manages to convert even empty rhetorical phrases into perjury.

After the arrest of the accused in Cologne Marx formed a new central committee.

> "This emerges from the statement of a police agent whom the late Police Commissioner Schulz had contrived to smuggle unnoticed into the London League and into the immediate vicinity of Marx himself."

The new central committee kept a minute-book and this, the *Original Minute-Book*, was now in Stieber's possession. Horrifying machinations in the Rhineland provinces, in Cologne and even in the courtroom itself, all this is proved by the Original Minute-Book. It even contains evidence to show that the accused had maintained an uninterrupted correspondence with Marx through the very walls of the prison. In a word, if the Dietz Archive had been the Old Testament, the New Testament was the Original Minute-Book. The Old Testament had been bound in stout oil-cloth, but the New Testament is bound in a sinister red morocco leather. Now the red morocco is indeed a *demonstratio ad oculos*, but we live in a sceptical age and doubt even more readily than Thomas; for we do not even believe what we see with our own eyes. Who still believes in Testaments, let them be Old or New, now that the religion of the Mormons has been invented? But Stieber, who is not wholly unsympathetic to Mormonism, has foreseen even this.

> "It might be objected", Stieber the Mormon observed, "that these are nothing but the tales of contemptible police agents but", Stieber swore, "I have irrefutable proofs of the truthfulness and reliability of their contents."

Just listen to that! Proofs of their truthfulness and proofs of their reliability! and irrefutable proofs at that. *Irrefutable* proofs! And what are these proofs?

> Stieber had long known "that a secret correspondence existed between Marx and the accused men in the gaol, but had been unable to obtain definite proofs. Then on the previous Sunday a special courier from London arrived bringing me the news that we had finally managed to discover the secret address from which the correspondence had been conducted. It was the address of D. Kothes a businessman in the Old Market here. The same courier brought me the Original Minute-Book used by the London central committee which had been procured from a member of the League for money."

Stieber then consulted with Police Commissioner Geiger and the postal authorities.

> "The necessary precautionary measures were taken and *after no more than two days* the evening post from London brought with it a letter addressed to Kothes. On the instructions of the Postmaster-

General the letter was detained and opened and in it was found a seven-page-long briefing for Schneider II, the Counsel for the Defence, in Marx's own handwriting. It indicated the method of defence that Counsel should adopt . . . . On the reverse side of the letter there was a large Latin B. The letter was copied and an easily detachable piece of the original was retained together with the original envelope. The letter was then put into a new envelope, sealed and given to a policeman from another town with the orders that he should go to Kothes, and introduce himself as an emissary from Marx." etc.

Stieber then narrated at length the rest of the disgusting hole-and-corner farce, about how the policeman from another town had pretended to be an emissary from Marx, etc. Kothes was arrested on October 18 and after 24 hours he explained that the B on the inside of the letter stood for Bermbach. On October 19 Bermbach was arrested and his house searched. On October 21 Kothes and Bermbach were released.

Stieber gave this evidence on Saturday, October 23. "The previous Sunday", that is Sunday, October 17, was the day the special courier arrived with Kothes' address and the Original Minute-Book! Two days after the courier, Kothes received the letter, that is on October 19th. But Kothes had already been arrested on October 18 because of the letter the policeman from another town had delivered on October 17. The letter to Kothes, then, arrived two days before the courier with Kothes' address, or else Kothes was arrested on October 18 for a letter that he did not receive until October 19. A chronological miracle?

Later, when Counsel had sounded the alarm, Stieber declared that the courier with Kothes' address and the Original Minute-Book arrived on October 10. Why on October 10? Because October 10 was likewise a Sunday and on October 23 it too would be a "previous" Sunday" and in this way the original statement about "the previous" Sunday could be sustained and to this extent the perjury could be kept secret. In that event, however, the letter did not arrive two days but a whole week after the courier. The perjury now fell on the letter rather than on the courier. Stieber's oath is like Luther's peasant. If you help it to mount the horse from one side it falls down on the other.[14]

And finally during the sitting of November 3 Police Inspector Goldheim of Berlin declared that Police Inspector Greif of London had delivered the Minute-Book to Stieber on October 11, that is to say on a Monday, in his presence and that of Police Commissioner Wermuth. So Goldheim's statement makes Stieber guilty of perjury twice over.

As the original envelope with the London postmark shows, Marx posted the letter to Kothes on Thursday, October 14. So the letter should have arrived on Friday evening, October 15. For a courier to deliver Kothes' address and the Minute-Book two days before the letter arrived, he must have come on Wednesday, October 13. He could not arrive on October 17th, nor on the 10th nor on the 11th.

Greif, in his role of courier, did indeed bring Stieber the Original Minute-Book from London. Stieber was as well aware as his crony Greif of the real value of this book. He hesitated therefore to produce it in court for this time it would not be as easy as in the case of statements taken behind prison bars in Mazas.[15] Then came the letter from Marx and Stieber was saved. Kothes is a mere address, for the contents of the letter were not intended for Kothes but for the Latin B on the back of the sealed letter inside the envelope. Kothes is then nothing but an address. Let us suppose he is a *secret* address, Stieber reasoned. Let us suppose further he is the secret address through which Marx communicates with the accused in Cologne. Let us then suppose lastly that our London agents had sent by the same courier at the same time both the secret addresses and the Original Minute-Book but that the letter arrived two days after the courier, the address and the Minute-Book. In this way we kill two birds with one stone. Firstly we have proof of the secret correspondence with Marx and secondly we prove that the Original Minute-Book is authentic. The authenticity of the Minute-Book is shown by the correctness of the address, the correctness of the address is shown by the letter. The truthfulness and reliability of our agents is shown by the address and the letter, the authenticity of the Minute-Book is shown by the truthfulness and reliability of our agents. *Quod erat demonstrandum.* Then comes the merry comedy with the police official from another town and then come the mysterious arrests. Public, jurymen and accused, all stand thunderstruck.

But why did not Stieber let his special courier arrive on October 13? Because in that case he would not have been special, because, as we have seen, chronology was not his strong point and the common calendar is beneath the dignity of a Prussian Police Superintendent. Moreover, he kept the original envelope; so who would be able to question his evidence?

However, Stieber's evidence is compromised by the omission of one fact. If his agents knew of Kothes' address they would also know to whom the mysterious B referred on the reverse of the inside letter. Stieber was so little initiated into the mysteries of the Latin B that on October 17 he had Becker searched in gaol in the hope of finding the letter from Marx on him. He only learnt from Kothes that the B stood for Bermbach.

But how did Marx's letter fall into the hands of the Prussian government in the first place? Very simply. The Prussian government regularly opens the letters entrusted to its postal service and during the trial in Cologne it did this with particular assiduity. In Aachen and Frankfurt-am-Main they could tell some pretty stories about it. It was a pure chance whether a letter would slip through or not.

When the story about the Original Courier collapsed, the one about the Original Minute-Book had to share its fate. Naturally, Stieber did not yet suspect this in the sitting on October 23 when he triumphantly proclaimed the Gospel according to the New Testament, that is the red book. The immediate effect of his announcement was the re-arrest of Bermbach who was present at the trial as a witness.

Why was Bermbach re-arrested?

Because of the papers found on him? No, because after his house had been searched he was released again. He was arrested 24 hours after Kothes. If he had possessed incriminating documents they would certainly have disappeared by then. Why then was this one witness Bermbach arrested, when the witnesses Hentze, Hätzel, Steingens, who had been shown to be accomplices or members of the League, still sat unmolested on the witness bench.

Bermbach had received a letter from Marx which contained a mere criticism of the indictment and nothing else besides. This Stieber admitted—for the letter was there for the jury to see. But he couched the admission in his hyperbolic policeman's manner thus: "Marx continues to exercise an uninterrupted influence on the present case from London." And the jury might well ask themselves, as Guizot asked his voters: *"Est-ce que vous vous sentez corrompus?"* What then was the reason for Bermbach's arrest? From the beginning of the inquiry the Prussian government strove *systematically and on principle*, to prevent the accused from making use of all proper means of defence. In direct contradiction to the law, defence counsel, as they made plain in open court, were refused access to the accused even after receipt of the bill of indictment. On his own testimony Stieber had been in possession of the Dietz Archive ever since August 5, 1851. But the Dietz Archive was not appended to the indictment. Not until October 18,

1852, was it produced in the middle of the proceedings — and only so much of it was produced as Stieber thought politic. The jury, the accused and the public were all to be caught off their guard and over-whelmed; defence counsel were to stand by defencelessly in the face of this unforeseen revelation.

But their amazement was increased a thousandfold when Stieber produced the Original Minute-Book! The Prussian government simply quivered with revelations. Bermbach however had received material for the defence from Marx; it would no doubt include information about the Minute-Book. His arrest implicitly proved that a new crime had been added to the Statutes: to correspond with Marx was now a felony punishable by gaol. That would deter every Prussian citizen from permitting his address to be used. *À bon entendeur demi mot.* Bermbach was *locked up* so that evidence for the defence might be *locked out.* And Bermbach remained in gaol for five weeks. For the Prussian courts to have released him immediately after the case was concluded would have been to proclaim publicly their docile sub-servience to the Prussian police. So Bermbach remained in gaol, *ad majorem gloriam* of the Prussian judicature.

Stieber swore on oath

"that after the arrest of the accused in Cologne, Marx rebuilt his party in London from the ruins and formed a new central committee with about eighteen people", etc.

The ruins required no reconstruction for they were so joined to-gether that they had formed a private society ever since September 1850. But at a word from Stieber they promptly vanished only to be revived by another command from Stieber after the arrest of the accused in Cologne and this time they appear in a new form, recon-stituted as a new central committee.

On Monday, October 25 the *Kölnische Zeitung* arrived in London with Stieber's testimony of October 23.

The "Marx Party" had neither formed a new central committee nor had they kept minutes of its meetings. They guessed at once who had been the chief author of the New Testament—*Wilhelm Hirsch from Hamburg.*

Early in December 1851 Hirsch appeared at the "Marx Society" and announced that he was a communist refugee. Simultaneously, letters arrived from Hamburg denouncing him as a spy. It was decided to allow him to remain in the society for the time being and to keep a watch on his activities with a view to procuring convincing evidence of his innocence or guilt.

At the meeting on January 15, 1852, a letter from Cologne was read aloud in which a friend of Marx referred to another postponement of the trial and to the difficulty experienced even by relatives in gaining access to the accused. On this occasion mention was made of Frau Dr. Daniels. People were struck by the fact that Hirsch was not seen again after this meeting either in anyone's immediate vicinity or at a distance. On February 2, 1852, Marx was notified from Cologne that Frau Dr. Daniels' house had been searched as the result of a police denunciation which claimed that a letter from Frau Daniels to Marx had been read out in the communist society in London and that Marx had been instructed to write back to her telling her that he was busy reorganising the League in Germany, etc. This denunciation literally fills the first page of the Original Minute-Book. Marx replied by return of post that as Frau Daniels had never written to him he could not possibly have read out a letter from her; the whole denunciation had been invented by a certain Hirsch, a dissolute young man who had no objection to fobbing the Prussian police off with as many lies as they had a mind to pay for in cash.

From January 15 Hirsch disappeared from the meetings; he was now formally expelled from the society. At the same time it was resolved to change the time and place of the meetings. Hitherto, meetings had taken place on *Thursdays* on premises belonging to J. W. Masters, Markethouse, in Farringdon Street, City. From now on it was agreed that the society would meet on *Wednesdays* in the Rose and Crown Tavern, Crown Street, Soho. Hirsch, whom "Police Commissioner Schulz had managed to smuggle unrecognised into the immediate vicinity of Marx", was unaware despite his being in the vicinity even eight months later of the time and venue of the meetings. He persisted even after February in manufacturing his Original Minute-Book on a Thursday and dating the meetings on Thursdays. if the *Kölnische Zeitung* is consulted the following excerpt from Hirsch's report can be found: Minutes of January 15 (Thursday), item January 29 (Thursday), and March 4 (Thursday), and May 13 (Thursday) and July 22 (Thursday) and July 29 (Thursday) and September 23 (Thursday) and September 30 (Thursday).

The landlord of the Rose and Crown Tavern made a declaration before the magistrate in Marlborough Street to the effect that "Dr. Marx's society" had met in his tavern every Wednesday since February

1852. Liebknecht and Rings whom Hirsch had nominated as the secretaries for his Original Minute-Book, had their signatures witnessed by the same magistrate. And finally, the minutes Hirsch had kept in Stechan's Workers' Club were obtained so that his handwriting might be compared with that in the Original Minute-Book.

In this way the inauthentic nature of the Original Minute-Book was demonstrated without its being necessary to embark upon a criticism of the contents which were in any event nullified by their own internal contradictions.

The real difficulty was how to send these documents to Counsel. The Prussian Post was merely an outpost, situated between the Prussian frontier and Cologne, and designed to frustrate the passage of munitions to the Defence.

It was necessary to have recourse to subterfuge and so the first documents, dispatched on October 25, did not arrive in Cologne before October 30.

Counsel were at first forced to make do with the very meagre resources that lay at hand in Cologne. The first blow against Stieber came from a completely unforeseen direction. Frau Dr. Daniels' father Müller, a Q.C. and a man in high repute as a legal expert and well known for his conservative views, declared in the *Kölnische Zeitung* on October 26, that his daughter had never corresponded with Marx and that Stieber's Original Book was simply a piece of "mystification". The letter Marx had sent to Cologne on February 3, 1852, in which Hirsch was alluded to as a *mouchard* and a forger of inauthentic police notices, was found by chance and put at the disposal of the Defence. In the "Marx Party's" notice of resignation from the Great Windmill Street Club which was included in the Dietz Archive, a genuine specimen of W. Liebknecht's handwriting was discovered. Lastly, Schneider II, Counsel for the Defence, received from Birnbaum, the secretary of the Council for Poor-Relief in Cologne, some genuine letters from Liebknecht while genuine letters by Rings were forthcoming from a private correspondent called Schmitz. At the offices of the court Counsel compared the Minute-Book with Liebknecht's handwriting in the notice of resignation and also with letters by Rings and Liebknecht.

Stieber was already alarmed by Counsellor Müller's declaration, and now when these calligraphic researches came to his notice he sensed a disaster. To forestall the imminent blow he again leaped up in court during the sitting on October 27, and declared that "he had become very suspicious of the fact that Liebknecht's signature in the Minute-Book differed greatly from a signature that already appeared on other documents. He had therefore made further enquiries and had learnt that the signatory in the Minute-Book in question was H. Liebknecht while the initial W. occurred in the other documents."

When Schneider II asked him: "Who informed you that an H. Liebknecht actually exists?", Stieber refused to answer. Schneider II then asked for further information about Rings and Ulmer who appear together with Liebknecht as secretaries in the Minute-Book. Stieber smelt a new trap. He misheard the question three times, tried to conceal his embarrassment and strove to regain his composure by recounting three times and for no reason how the Minute-Book had come into his possession. At last he stammered: The names Rings and Ulmer are probably not real names at all but only "League names". Stieber explained the frequent mention in the Minute-Book of Frau Dr. Daniels as a correspondent of Marx by surmising that perhaps Bermbach was really *meant*, when the Book said Frau Dr. Daniels. Herr von Hontheim cross-examined him about Hirsch for the defence.

"He did not know this man Hirsch either", Stieber swore, "Contrary to rumour however it is obvious that he is not a Prussian agent if only because the Prussian police are on the lookout for him."

At a signal from Stieber Goldheim buzzed into sight and said that "In October 1851 he was sent to Hamburg in order to apprehend Hirsch."

We shall see how the very same Goldheim was sent to London on the following day to apprehend the very same Hirsch. So the very same Stieber who claimed that he had bought the Dietz Archive and the Original Minute-Book from refugees for cash, that same Stieber now asserts that Hirsch cannot be a Prussian agent simply because he is a refugee! You have only to be a refugee and Stieber will guarantee your absolute venality or absolute incorruptibility, just as it suits his book. And is not Fleury likewise a political refugee, the same Fleury whom Stieber denounced as a police agent in the sitting on November 3rd?

When the defences of his Original Minute-Book had been breached on every side Stieber summed up the situation on October 27 with a classical display of impudence, stating that "his belief in the authenticity of the Minute-Book is firmer than ever".

At the sitting of October 29 an expert compared the letters of Liebknecht and Rings, that had been submitted by Birnbaum and

Schmitz, with the Minute-Book and declared the signatures in the latter to be *false*.

In his summing-up the Chief Prosecutor, Seckendorf, said:

> "The information contained in the Minute-Book coincides with facts derived from other sources. The only thing that the prosecution is unable to prove is the Book's authenticity."

The book is authentic, but its authenticity cannot be proved. The New Testament! Seckendorf continued:

> "But the Defence has itself shown that at the very least the book contains much that is true, for example it gives us much information about the activities of Rings about whom no-one knew anything before."

If no-one knew anything about Rings' activities before, that knowledge was not increased by the Minute-Book. The statements about Rings' activities could not confirm the truth of the Minute-Book's *contents* and in their form they demonstrated that the signature of a member of the "Marx Party" was *in truth false*, and had been forged. They proved then, according to Seckendorf, that "the book contains much that is true"—it was indeed *a true forgery*. The chief Prosecutors (Saedt–Seckendorf) together with the postal authorities and Stieber had opened the letter to Kothes. Therefore they knew the date of its arrival. Therefore they knew that Stieber committed perjury when he caused the courier to arrive at first on October 17 and, later, on the 10th, whereas the letter came according to Stieber's first account as late as October 19th and on the 12th according to the second one. They were his accomplices.

At the sitting on October 27 Stieber tried in vain to preserve a calm appearance. Any day the incriminating documents might arrive from London. Stieber felt ill at ease and the Prussian State, incarnate in him, felt ill at ease too. The public scandal was becoming dangerous. So Police Inspector Goldheim was sent to London on October 26 to save the fatherland. What did Goldheim do in London? Aided by Greif and Fleury he attempted to persuade Hirsch to go to Cologne and, under the name of H. Liebknecht, to swear to the authenticity of the Minute-Book. Hirsch was offered a State pension outright, but Hirsch's policeman's instincts were as good as Goldheim's. Hirsch knew that he was neither Prosecutor nor Police Inspector, nor a Police

Superintendent, and therefore could not commit perjury with impunity. His instincts told him that he would be dropped as soon as things began to go wrong. Hirsch was no lamb, and least of all did he want to be the sacrificial lamb. Hirsch flatly refused. But the Christian Germanic government of Prussia deserves undying fame for having attempted to bribe a witness to commit perjury in the course of criminal proceedings in which the heads of its own citizens were at stake.

Nothing achieved, Goldheim returned to Cologne.

In the sitting on November 3, when the prosecution had concluded its final address and before Counsel for the defence could commence his, Stieber, caught between the two, leaped once again into the breach swearing that "he had now ordered further research into the Minute-Book. He sent Police Inspector Goldheim to London to pursue the inquiry there. Goldheim left on October 28 and returned on November 2. Here is Goldheim."

At a signal from his master Goldheim buzzed into view and swore that

"on arriving in London he went first to Police Inspector Greif and he took him to Police agent Fleury in the borough of Kensington for it was Fleury from whom Greif had originally obtained the book. Fleury admitted as much to him and maintained that he had acquired the book from a member of Marx's party with the name H. Liebknecht. Fleury definitely recognised the receipt H. Liebknecht had given him for the money he had received for the book. Goldheim himself was unable to arrange a personal meeting with Liebknecht in London because he is, according to Fleury, reluctant to make public appearances. During his stay in London he became quite convinced that a few errors apart, the content of the book was *absolutely genuine*. Reliable agents who had been present at Marx's meetings had persuaded him of this. The book itself however was not the Original Minute-Book but only a *notebook* on the proceedings at Marx's meetings. There are two possible explanations for the admittedly somewhat obscure origin of the book. Either as Fleury insists it really comes from Liebknecht who has refused to give a specimen signature in order that there should be no proof of his treachery; or else the agent Fleury obtained the notes from Dronke and Imandt, two *émigré* friends of Marx, and put them in the form of an Original Minute-Book in order to increase their market value. Police Inspector Greif has officially stated that Dronke and Imandt frequently consorted with Fleury. Goldheim was wholly convinced in London that everything that has been said about Marx's secret meetings, about

the contacts between London and Cologne and the secret correspondence was true in every particular. As evidence of how well
informed Prussian agents are in London even today, he would
inform the Court that a meeting shrouded in secrecy took place in
Marx's house on October 27 to discuss what steps should be taken
to counteract the Minute-Book and above all the activities of Police
Superintendent Stieber who was a thorn in the side of the London
Party. The relevant decisions and documents have been sent in
complete secrecy to the lawyer, Schneider II. In particular, among
the papers sent to Schneider II was a private letter that Stieber
himself wrote to Marx in Cologne in 1848 and that Marx had hitherto
kept very secret in the hope that it might be used to compromise the
witness Stieber."

Witness Stieber leaped up and declared that he had written to Marx
about an infamous slander, that he had threatened to sue him, etc.

"No one but Marx and he could know this and this was indeed
the very best proof of the accuracy of the information from London"

So according to Goldheim the Original Minute-Book is "absolutely
genuine", apart from the false parts. What convinced him of its
authenticity is above all the circumstance that the Original Minute-
Book is no Original Minute-Book but only a "Notebook". And
Stieber? Stieber was by no means taken aback; on the contrary a great
weight had been lifted from his mind. Just on closing time, the prosecutor's last words still echoing in his ears, Stieber swiftly and with
the aid of his Goldheim transformed the Original Minute-Book into
a notebook. When two policemen accuse each other of lying, does that
not prove that they are both disciples of the truth? Through Goldheim
Stieber was able to cover his retreat.

Goldheim testified that "on arriving in London he went first to
Police Inspector Greif who took him to Police agent Fleury in the
borough of Kensington".

Now who would not swear an oath that poor Goldheim and Police
Inspector Greif must have worn themselves out walking on that long
journey to Fleury's house in the remote suburb of Kensington? But
Police Inspector Greif lives in the same house as Police agent Fleury, in
fact he lives on the second floor, above the Fleury household, so that in
reality it was not Greif who took Goldheim to Fleury but Fleury who
took Goldheim to Greif.

"Police agent Fleury in the borough of Kensington!" What precision! Can you still doubt the truthfulness of a Prussian government that denounces its own spies, gives their name and address and every detail, body and soul? If the Minute-Book is inauthentic you can still rely on "Police agent Fleury in Kensington". Yes, indeed. On Private Secretary Pierre in the 13th arrondissement. If you wish to specify a person you must give his Christian name as well as his surname. Not *Fleury* but *Charles* Fleury. And you must also name the profession that he practises in public, and not his clandestine activities. So it is Charles Fleury, a businessman, not Fleury, police agent. And when you state his address you do not merely name a London borough, a town in itself, but you give the borough, the street and the number of the house. So it is not Police agent Fleury in Kensington but *Charles Fleury, a businessman, 17 Victoria Road, Kensington.*

But Police Inspector Greif, that at any rate is frankly spoken! But when Police Inspector Greif attaches himself to the embassy in London and the Inspector turns into an attaché that of course is an attachment of no concern to the courts. For *"Der Zug des Herzens ist des Schicksals Stimme"*. ["The heart's desire is the voice of fate."]

So Police Inspector Goldheim asserts that Police agent Fleury asserts that he has the book from a man who really asserts that he is H. Liebknecht and who has given Fleury a receipt. The only drawback is that Goldheim was unable "to apprehend" the said H. Liebknecht in London. So Goldheim could have stayed quietly at home in Cologne for Police Superintendent Stieber's assertion does not look any healthier for the fact that it appears as an assertion of Police Inspector Goldheim's, which had been asserted by Police Inspector Greif who in his turn had been so favoured by Police agent Fleury that this latter had agreed to assert his assertion.

Goldheim's London experiences were hardly encouraging but, undeterred and with the aid of a faculty unique in him for convincing himself (which in his case must do duty for the faculty of judgement), he convinced himself "completely" that "everything" that Stieber had affirmed concerning the "Marx Party", about its contacts in Cologne, etc. was all "true *in every particular*". And now that Goldheim, his junior official has issued him with a *testimonium paupertatis*, surely Police Superintendent Stieber is fully covered now? Stieber's method of swearing has at least one achievement to its credit: he has turned the whole Prussian hierarchy upside down. You don't believe the Police Superintendent? Very well. He has compromised himself. But surely you will not doubt the Police Inspector? You doubt him too? Better still. Then you have no other choice than to believe at least the Police agent alias *mouchardus vulgaris*. Such is the heretical conceptual confusion that our *swearing* Stieber has created.

When Goldheim had delivered the proof that the only thing he had established in London about the non-existence of the Original Minute-Book and about the existence of H. Liebknecht was that he was unable "to apprehend" them in London, and when he had thereby convinced himself that "all" Stieber's statements about the "Marx Party" "were true in every particular", he had of necessity to augment his negative arguments (which in Seckendorf's view contained "much that was true") by the positive demonstration of "how well informed the Prussian agents in London were to this very day". As evidence of this he mentions that on October 27 there had been an "absolutely secret meeting in Marx's house". In this absolutely secret meeting steps were discussed to combat the Minute-Book and Police Superintendent Stieber, that "thorn in their side". The relevant decisions and documents were sent with the utmost secrecy to the lawyer Schneider II.

Although the Prussian agents were present at these meetings the route taken by these letters remained so very "secret" that all the efforts of the postal authorities to intercept them were in vain. Listen to our Goldheim chirping sadly from among the ageing and venerable ruins:

"The relevant letters and documents were sent with the most absolute secrecy to the lawyer Schneider II."

Absolutely secret from Goldheim's secret agents.

The imaginary decisions about the Minute-Book cannot have been made in the absolutely secret session in Marx's house on October 27 because already on October 25 Marx had sent the chief reports about the inauthenticity of the Minute-Book not indeed to Schneider II, but to Herr von Hontheim.

It was not merely the police's bad conscience that first gave them the idea that documents were being sent to Cologne. On October 29th Goldheim arrived in London. On October 30 Goldheim found a declaration[17] signed by Engels, Freiligrath, Marx and Wolff in the *Morning Advertiser*, the *Spectator*, the *Examiner*, *Leader* and the *People's Paper* in which the attention of the English public was drawn to the revelations that the defence would make of forgery, perjury, the falsification of documents, in short of all the infamies perpetrated by the Prussian Police. The sending of the documents was veiled in such "absolute secrecy" that the "Marx Party" openly informed the English public about them, though of course not until October 30 by which time Goldheim had arrived in London and the documents in Cologne.

Meanwhile, however, yet other documents were sent to Cologne on October 27. How did the omniscient Prussian police learn of this?

The Prussian police did not pursue their activities with quite such "absolute secrecy" as the "Marx Party". Quite the reverse in fact: they had openly posted two of their informers for some weeks in front of Marx's house and from the street they watched him *du soir jusqu'au matin* and *du matin jusqu'au soir* and dogged his every step. Now on October 27th Marx had received the absolutely secret documents containing the genuine specimens of Rings' and Liebknecht's handwriting together with the statement of the landlord of the Crown Tavern concerning the days of the society's meetings. He then took these absolutely secret documents and had them witnessed in the absolutely public police court in Marlborough Street in the presence of reporters from the English daily press. His Prussian guardian angels followed him from his house to Marlborough Street and from Marlborough Street back to his house and from his house to the post office. They did not in fact disappear until Marx had gone in absolute secrecy to the local magistrate in order to obtain a warrant for the arrest of his two "followers".

Moreover, yet another way lay open to the Prussian police. For Marx sent the documents that were dated October 27 and had been witnessed on October 27 directly to Cologne through the post in order to ensure that the talons of the Prussian eagle would have no chance to grasp hold of the *duplicates* that had been sent in *absolute secrecy*. Both postal authorities and the police in Cologne knew then that documents dated October 27 had been forwarded by Marx and there was no need for Goldheim to make the journey to London in order to unravel the mystery.

Goldheim felt finally that he ought *"in particular"* to reveal something "particular" that "the absolutely secret meeting on 27th October" had resolved to send to Schneider II, and so the particular fact that he lit upon was the letter written by Stieber to Marx. Unfortunately Marx had sent this letter not on October 27 but as early as October 25 and it was sent not to Schneider II but to Herr von Hontheim. But how did the police know that Marx still had Stieber's letter in his possession and that he intended to send it to the defence? But let us permit Stieber to leap up once more.

Stieber hoped to forestall Schneider II and thus prevent him from reading aloud in court what was for him a very "unpleasant letter". Stieber calculated: If Goldheim says that Schneider II has my letter and that he has it thanks to his "criminal contact" with Marx, then Schneider II will suppress the letter so as to prove that Goldheim's agents were misinformed and that he himself does not maintain any criminal contact with Marx. So Stieber leaped up, gave a false account of the content of the letter and concluded with an astonishing declaration that "no one but himself and Marx can be aware of that and this is in fact the very *strongest proof of the credence* that can be given to the information from London".

Stieber has a strange method of keeping secret facts that he finds unpalatable. If he remains silent, the whole world must hold its tongue. Hence "no one can know" apart from him and a certain elderly lady that he once lived near Weimar as an *homme entretenu*. But if Stieber has every reason to make sure that no one but Marx should know of the letter, Marx had every reason to let everyone apart from Stieber know about it. We now know the "strongest proof" of the information from London. What would Stieber's weakest proof look like?

But once again Stieber knowingly commits perjury when he says "no one other than Marx and himself can be aware of that". He knew that it was not Marx but another editor of the *Rheinische Zeitung* who had answered his letter. So there had been at least "one man besides Marx and himself".

In order that even more people may learn of it we print it here:

"Nr. 177 of the *Neue Rheinische Zeitung* contains a news item from your correspondent in Frankfurt-on-Main in which a base lie is reported to the effect that I under the pretence of being a democrat went to Frankfurt as a police spy to search for the murderers of Prince Lichnowsky and General Auerswald. I was in fact in Frankfurt on the 21st but as you can see from the accompanying testimonial I was engaged in purely private business on behalf of a lady from here, Frau von Schwezler. I have long since returned to Berlin and resumed my work as defence counsel. I would refer you to the official apologies in this matter that have already appeared in Nr. 338 of the *Frankfurter-Oberamts-Postzeitung* of December 21st and in Nr. 248 of the local *National-Zeitung*. I believe that I may expect from your respect for the truth that you will print the relevant correction in your paper without delay and that you will also give me the name of your slanderous informant in accordance with your legal obligations for I cannot possibly permit such a libel to go unpunished. In the event of my not obtaining this satisfaction I shall be compelled to proceed against your worthy editorial board.

I believe that in recent times democracy is indebted to no one more than *myself*. It was I who rescued hundreds of democrats from the nets of the criminal courts. It was I who during the recent period of martial law persistently and fearlessly challenged the authorities (and do so to this very day), while all the cowardly and contemptible fellows (the so-called democrats) had long since fled the field. When democratic organs treat me in this fashion it is scarcely an encouragement to me to make further efforts.

The real joke, however, in the present case lies in the clumsiness of the organs of democracy. The rumour that I went to Frankfurt as a police spy was spread first by that notorious organ of reaction, the *Neue Preussische Zeitung* in order to undermine my activities as defence counsel that gave that paper such offence. The other Berlin papers have long since corrected this report. But the democratic papers have been so misguided as to parrot this stupid lie. If I had wished to go to Frankfurt as a spy it would certainly not be announced beforehand in the press. And how could Prussia send a police official to Frankfurt which has enough competent officials of its own? Stupidity has always been the failing of the democrats and their opponents' cunning has always brought them to victory.

It is no less a monstrous lie to say that years ago I was a police spy in Silesia. At that time I was openly employed as a police officer and as such I did my duty. Monstrous lies have been circulated about me. If anyone can prove that I insinuated my way into his favour let him come forth and do so. Anyone can make assertions and tell lies. I think of you as an honest decent man and so I expect from you a satisfactory answer by return of post. The democratic papers are generally in disrepute here because of the many lies they publish. I hope that you are a man of a different stamp.

Berlin, 26th December, 1848   Respectfully yours,
                              Stieber, Doctor at Law, etc., Berlin
                              Ritterstrasse 65."

How then did Stieber know that on October 27 Marx had sent his letter to Schneider II? But it was not sent on October 27 but on October 25, and it was not sent to Schneider II but to von Hontheim. So Stieber knew only that the letter still existed and he suspected that Marx would put it in the hands of some defence counsel or other.

Whence this suspicion? When the *Kölnische Zeitung* brought Stieber's testimony on October 18 about Cherval, etc., to London, Marx sent a declaration dated October 21 to the *Kölnische Zeitung*, the *Berliner Nationalzeitung* and the *Frankfurter Journal* and at the end of this declaration Stieber was threatened with this very letter. In order to keep this letter "absolutely secret" Marx himself announced it to the press. He failed, but only because of the cowardice of the daily press in Germany. Be that as it may, the Prussian post was now informed and with the Prussian post, its—Stieber.

What then was the message our Goldheim chirruped back from London?

That Hirsch did not commit perjury, that H. Liebknecht has no tangible existence, that the Original Minute-Book is no Original Minute-Book and that the all-knowing London agents know all that the "Marx Party" has published in the London Press. To save the honour of the Prussian agents Goldheim placed in their mouths the few titbits of information that Stieber gleaned from letters he had opened or purloined.

In the sitting on November 4 after Schneider II had annihilated Stieber and his Minute-Book and shown him to be guilty of forgery and perjury, Stieber leaped into the breach for the last time and gave vent to his moral indignation. "They even dare", he cried out, his soul mortally wounded, "they even dare to accuse Herr Wermuth, Police Commissioner Wermuth, of perjury!" Stieber thereby returned to the orthodox hierarchy, to the rising scale. Earlier he had moved on the heterodox, descending scale. If he, a police superintendent could not be trusted, well then surely his police inspector could be; and if not the police inspector, then surely his police agent; and if not agent Fleury, then surely sub-agent Hirsch. But now it is in reverse. He, the *police superintendent*, can perhaps commit perjury, but Wermuth, a *Commissioner of Police?* Unbelievable! In his rage he praised Wermuth with mounting bitterness, he served Wermuth up to the public neat, Wermuth as a human being, Wermuth as a lawyer, Wermuth as paterfamilias, Wermuth as police commissioner, Wermuth for ever.

Even now, Stieber did not stop trying to isolate the accused in open court and to erect a barrier between the defence and the defence materials. He accused Schneider II of "criminal contact" with Marx. In attacking him Schneider was impugning the highest authorities of Prussia. Even Göbel, the President of the court, even a Göbel felt intimidated by Stieber's forcefulness. He could not overlook it and even though timorous and servile he did lash Stieber with a few stern rebukes. But Stieber was in the right for all that. It was not merely he as a person that stood exposed to public view: it was the prosecution, the courts, the postal authorities, the government, the police headquarters in Berlin, it was the ministries and the embassy in London, in short it was the whole Prussian state that stood in the pillory with him, Original Minute-Book in hand.

Mr. Stieber is herewith granted permission to print the answer the *Neue Rheinische Zeitung* returned to his letter.

Let us now return once more to London with Goldheim.

Just as Stieber is still ignorant of Cherval's true identity and address so too, for Goldheim (in the sitting on November 3), the origin of the Minute-Book is an enigma that is still not fully resolved. To resolve it Goldheim put forward two hypotheses.

> "There are only two possible explanations", he said, "for the as yet somewhat obscure origin of the book. *Either*, as Fleury insists, it really comes from Liebknecht who has refused to give a specimen signature in order that there should be no proof of his treachery."

W. Liebknecht is well known as a member of the "Marx Party". But it is no less well known that the signature in the Minute-Book does not belong to *W.* Liebknecht. In the sitting on October 27 Stieber swore that the signature was not that belonging to W. Liebknecht but to another Liebknecht, an *H.* Liebknecht. He had apparently learnt of the existence of this double without being able however to disclose the source of his discovery. Goldheim swore:

> "Fleury claimed he had really obtained the book from a member of the 'Marx Party' by the name of *H.* Liebknecht." Goldheim swore further: "I was not able to apprehend the said H. Liebknecht in London."

What *signs of life* has the H. Liebknecht that Stieber has uncovered actually given to the world in general and to Police Inspector Goldheim in particular? No sign of life other than his *signature* in the Original Minute-Book; but now Goldheim declares: "Liebknecht has refused to give a specimen signature."

Up to the present H. Liebknecht existed only as a signature. Now nothing remains of H. Liebknecht at all, not even a signature, not even the dot on the i. How Goldheim could possibly know that H.

Liebknecht's real signature differs from the signature in the Minute-Book, when the signature in the Minute-Book is his only proof of H. Liebknecht's existence, that is Goldheim's secret. If Stieber has his miracles, why should not Goldheim have his miracles too?

Goldheim forgot that his superior, Stieber, had just sworn to H. Liebknecht's existence before him, and that he too had just sworn to it. In the same breath in which he swears to H. Liebknecht he recollects that H. Liebknecht is nothing but a makeshift, a necessary expedient invented by Stieber, and necessity knows no law. He remembers that there is but one genuine Liebknecht, W. Liebknecht, but that if W. Liebknecht is genuine then the signature in the Minute-Book is a forgery. He cannot confess that Fleury's underling Hirsch had manufactured the false signature along with the false Minute-Book. Accordingly he invents the hypothesis: "Liebknecht was unwilling to give a specimen signature." Let us likewise construct a hypothesis. Goldheim once forged banknotes. He is brought before the courts; it is proved that the signature on the banknote is not that of the bank director. Don't take offence, gentlemen, Goldheim will say, don't take offence. The banknote is genuine. It comes from the bank director himself. If his name appears signed by someone other than him what does that matter? "He merely refused to give a specimen signature."

Or else, Goldheim continues, if the hypothesis with Liebknecht turns out to be false:

> "*Or* the agent Fleury obtained the notes for the book from Dronke and Imandt, two *emigré* friends of Marx and then put them in the form of an Original Minute-Book to increase their market value. Police Lieutenant Greif has officially stated that Dronke and Imandt frequently consorted with Fleury."

Or? How so, or? If a book like the Original Minute-Book is signed by three people, Liebknecht, Rings and Ulmer, no one will deduce that "it was written either by Liebknecht"—or by Dronke and Imandt, but: It was written either by Liebknecht or by Rings and Ulmer. Should our unfortunate Goldheim, now that he has climbed to the dizzy heights of a disjunction—either-or—should he now repeat: "Rings and Ulmer have refused to give specimen signatures"? Even Goldheim realises the need for new tactics.

If the Original Minute-Book is not by Liebknecht as the agent Fleury claimed then it must have been written by Fleury himself, but the notes for it were provided by Dronke and Imandt of whom Police Inspector

Greif has officially stated that they frequently consorted with Fleury.

"To increase their market value" says Goldheim, Fleury put the notes in the form of an Original Minute-Book. He not only commits a fraud, he also forges signatures and all this to "increase their market value". A man so conscientious as this Prussian agent who for profit manufactures forged minutes and forged signatures is obviously incapable of manufacturing *false notes* for profit. Such is Goldheim's inference.

Dronke and Imandt did not come to London until April 1852, after they had been expelled by the Swiss authorities. However, one-third of the Original Minute-Book consists of entries for the months of January, February and March 1852. Fleury manufactured one-third of the Original Minute-Book *without* Dronke and Imandt although Goldheim had affirmed that either Liebknecht wrote the Minute-Book —or else Fleury wrote it, following, however, the notes of Dronke and Imandt. Goldheim swore to it, and although Goldheim is no Brutus he is still Goldheim.

But the possibility still remains that Dronke and Imandt furnished Fleury with notes after April for, Goldheim swore:

"Police Inspector Greif has officially stated that Dronke and Imandt frequently consorted with Fleury."

Let us examine this association.

As we have noted above Fleury was known in London not as a Prussian police agent but as a businessman in the City, as a democratic businessman in fact. Born in Altenburg he had come to London as a political refugee, had later married an Englishwoman from a wealthy and respected family and apparently enjoyed a quiet life with his wife and his father-in-law, an old *Quaker* industrialist. On October 8th or 9th Imandt began to "consort frequently "with Fleury, in the capacity, that is, of tutor. But according to the improved version of Stieber's evidence the Original Minute-Book arrived in Cologne on October 10th—according to Goldheim's final version on the 11th. By the time that Imandt, whom he had never set eyes on till then, had given him his first French lesson, Fleury had not only had the Original Minute-Book bound in red Morocco leather, he had also dispatched it with the special courier who brought it to Cologne. So heavily did Fleury rely on Imandt's notes when writing the Original Minute-Book. As for Dronke, Fleury only saw him *once* and by chance with Imandt, and this was on October 30 by which time the Original Minute-Book had long since dissolved into its original nothingness.

Thus the Christian Germanic government is not content with breaking into desks, stealing papers, obtaining false testimony, creating false plots, forging false documents, swearing false oaths, and attempting to suborn witnesses—all this to bring about the condemnation of the Cologne defendants. The government attempts also to cast suspicion on the London friends of the accused so that Hirsch might be held blameless now that Stieber has sworn that he does not know him and Goldheim has sworn that he is no spy.

On Friday, November 5, the *Kölnische Zeitung* arrived in London with the report of the court session on November 3 with Goldheim's evidence. Inquiries about Greif were instituted at once and the very same day it was learnt that he lived in Fleury's house. At the same time Dronke and Imandt paid Fleury a visit taking with them a copy of the *Kölnische Zeitung*. They gave him Goldheim's testimony to read. He went pale, tried to regain his composure, pretended to be utterly astonished and declared himself perfectly willing to make a statement against Goldheim before an English magistrate. But he said he must consult his solicitor first. They agreed to meet the following afternoon, Saturday, November 6. Fleury promised to have his statement officially witnessed and said he would bring it to the meeting. Of course, he did not appear. Dronke and Imandt then went to his house on Saturday evening and found there the following note addressed to Imandt:

> "With the solicitor's help everything has been arranged; further steps can be taken as soon as the guilty party has been discovered. The solicitor sent the relevant documents off today. Business commitments have made it imperative for me to be in the City today. If you would like to visit me tomorrow I shall be at home the whole afternoon until 5 o'clock. Fl."

On the other side of the note there was the following postcript.

> "I have just arrived home but had to go out again with Herr Werner and my wife—I *can prove this to you* tomorrow. Leave me a note saying when you would like to come."

Imandt left the following reply:

> "I am extremely surprised not to find you at home especially as you did not appear at the appointed time and place this afternoon.

I must confess that in the circumstances my opinion of you is already fixed. If you wish me to revise it you will visit me by tomorrow morning at the latest for I cannot guarantee that your activities as a Prussian police spy might not find their way into the English newspapers. Imandt."

Fleury did not appear on Sunday morning either, so in the evening Dronke and Imandt went to his house once again to obtain his declaration, putting on an appearance of great astonishment as if their confidence in him had only just then been shaken. Finally, after all sorts of procrastinations and doubts the declaration was formulated. Fleury hestitated most when it was pointed out to him that he must sign with his Christian name as well as his surname. The declaration went literally as follows:

"To the editors of the *Kölnische Zeitung*
The undersigned declares that he has known Herr Imandt for about a month during which time the latter gave him tuition in the French language and at that he met Herr Dronke for the first time on October 30 of this year.
He declares further that neither of them gave him any information in connection with the Original Minute-Book mentioned in the Cologne Trial.
Lastly he is not acquainted with any person by the name of Liebknecht nor has he ever known anyone of that name.
Kensington, London, November 8, 1852.

Charles Fleury."

Dronke and Imandt, were, of course, quite sure that Fleury would instruct the *Kölnische Zeitung* not to print any statement signed by him. Accordingly they sent his declaration not to the *Kölnische Zeitung* but to Schneider II. Unfortunately the case was too far advanced for him to make any use of it.

So Fleury is not indeed the Fleur de Marie of the police prostitutes, but he is a flower and he will bear blossom, albeit only the *fleur de lys*.*

But the story of the Minute-Book is not yet finished. On Saturday, November 6, W. Hirsch of Hamburg made a statutory declaration before the magistrate at Bow Street, London, to the effect that he

---

* Fleur-de-lys (lilies) is the word used in the French colloquial language to betoken the letters T. F. (*travaux forcés*, forced labour) which are branded on criminals. The accuracy of Marx's judgment is demonstrated in the Appendix to *Herr Vogt*, see pp. 7-8. (Note by Engels to the edition of 1885.)

himself had fabricated the Original Minute-Book that figured so prominently in the Cologne trial and that he had done this at the instigation of Greif and Fleury.

Thus, it had at first been the Original Minute-Book of the "Marx Party"—after that it was the notebook of the police spy Fleury— and lastly it became the fabrication of the Prussian police, a simple police fabrication, a police fabrication *sans phrase*.

On the same day that Hirsch revealed the secret of the Original Minute-Book to the English magistrate at Bow Street another representative of the Prussian State was busy packing at Fleury's house in Kensington, and the things he was packing in stout oil-cloth were neither stolen nor forged nor even documents at all, but his own personal belongings. It was none other than our friend Greif of sweet memory in Paris, the special courier to Cologne, the chief of the Prussian police agents in London, the official director of mystifications, the Police Inspector attached to the Prussian Embassy. Greif had received instructions from the Prussian government to leave London at once. There was no time to be wasted.

Just as at the end of spectacular operas the rising amphitheatrical set that had been obscured by curtains now suddenly flares up in a blaze of fireworks so that all eyes are dazzled, so too at the end of this Prussian police tragicomedy the hidden amphitheatrical workshop is revealed in which the Original Minute-Book was forged. On the lowest level we see the wretched informer Hirsch working at piece rates; a little higher up is the respectably situated spy and agent provocateur, the City businessman Fleury; higher still is the diplomatic Police Inspector Greif and highest of all the Prussian Embassy itself to which he was attached. For 6–8 months Hirsch had laboured week by week to forge the Original Minute-Book in his study, under the watchful eyes of Fleury. But one floor above Fleury dwelt the Prussian Police Inspector Greif who supervised and inspired him. However, Greif himself regularly spent a part of his day in the Prussian Embassy where he in his turn was supervised and inspired. Thus the Prussian Embassy was the real hothouse where the Original Minute-Book grew and flowered.* So Greif had to disappear. He disappeared on November 6, 1852.

The authenticity of the Original Minute-Book could not be sustained any longer, not even as a notebook. The Prosecutor, Saedt, buried it in

* The Basel edition of 1853 included this sentence: The scandal that awaited him in London now fell back onto the shoulders of the Prussian Embassy.

the address he gave in reply to the concluding speeches by Counsel for the Defence.

The trial had now reached the point at which the Prosecution Council of the Court had begun when it ordered a new investigation because "*there was no evidence of an indictable offence*".

V

The Document accompanying the "Red Catechism"

In his evidence during the sitting on October 27 Police Inspector *Junkermann* of Crefeld said that

"he took possession of a parcel addressed to the waiter in an inn in Crefeld which bore a Düsseldorf post mark and in it were some copies of the 'Red Catechism'. It contained also an unsigned document. It had not been possible to identify the sender." "As the Prosecution has pointed out, the accompanying document appeared to *be written in Marx's hand*."

In the sitting on October 28 the expert (???) Renard disovered that the document was in fact in Marx's handwriting. The accompanying document said:

"Citizens! As we have complete confidence in you, we herewith present you with 50 copies of the 'Red'. Your task is to push them under the doors of citizens, preferably of workers who are known to sympathize with the Revolution on Satuday, June 5th at eleven o'clock at night. We are definitely counting on your civic courage and accordingly expect you to carry out this instruction. The revolution is closer than many people think. Long live the Revolution! Berlin, May 1852 with Fraternal Greetings. The Revolutionary Committee."

Witness Junkermann declared further that "the parcels in question had been sent to the witness *Chianella*".

Chief Commissioner *Hinckeldey* of Berlin was the Supreme Commander in charge of operations against the defendants during the preliminary investigations. The laurels won by Maupas prevented him from sleeping.

The actors in the proceedings include two commissioners of police,
D*

one alive and one dead, one superintendent (only one, but that one a Stieber), two police inspectors one of whom was constantly en route from London to Cologne, the other constantly journeying from Cologne to London, myriads of police agents and sub-agents, named, anonymous, heteronymous, pseudonymous, with tails and without. Lastly a Chief Inspector.

No sooner had the *Kölnische Zeitung* arrived in London with the evidence heard on October 27–28, than Marx went to the Magistrate in Marlborough Street, where he copied out from the paper the text of the "accompanying document" given there, had the copy witnessed and at the same time the following statutory declaration:

1. that he had not written the document in question;
2. that he learnt of its existence from the *Kölnische Zeitung*;
3. that he had *never seen* the "Red Catechism";
4. that he had never helped in any way at all to distribute it.

It may be pointed out in passing that if such a declaration made before an English magistrate is found to be false, then it counts as perjury with all the consequences attendant thereupon.

The above document was sent to Schneider II but it appeared simultaneously in the London *Morning Advertiser*[18] as the conviction had gained ground during the trial that the Prussian post seems to have put upon the requirement of the privacy of the post the strange interpretation that letters entrusted to its care should be kept so very private that even the addressees should not be allowed to see them. The prosecution resisted the attempt to produce the document, even for purposes of *comparison*. For the prosecution was aware that a single glance from the original accompanying document to the officially attested copy by Marx would reveal the deception, the deliberate imitation of his handwriting could not remain hidden even from such a sharpsighted jury as this. Therefore, in order to defend the morality of the Prussian State, the prosecution denounced any attempt at comparison.

Schneider II observed "that Chianella, the addressee who had freely given information to the police about the supposed identity of the sender and who had *offered to act as a spy*, had not even dreamt of mentioning Marx in this connection".

No one who has ever read a single line by Marx could possibly attribute to him the authorship of this melodramatic accompanying document. The midsummer night's dream hour on June 5, and the whole tiresomely naïve idea of pushing the "Red" under the doors of the revolutionary philistines—all that could point to the hand of Kinkel, just as the references to "civic courage" and the way in which they are "definitely counting on" this military "instruction being carried out" all seems to reflect the imagination of a Willich. But how could such typically Kinkel–Willich precepts for revolution come to be written in Marx's hand?

If it is permissible to form a hypothesis about the "as yet somewhat obscure origins" of this accompanying document written in an imitated hand: the police found the 50 Reds in Crefeld as well as the convenient high sounding accompanying document. In Cologne or in Berlin *qu'importe?* they copied the text in Marx's handwriting. For what purpose? "So as to give it a correspondingly higher market value."

However, even the Chief Prosecutor did not dare to revert to the accompanying document in his catalinarian speech. He let it drop. It was not able to do duty for the still wanting "*indictable offence*".

VI

The Willich–Schapper Party

With the suppression of the revolution of 1848–49 the party of the proletariat on the continent lost every right it had enjoyed for once in a way during that short interval: a press, freedom of speech and the right to associate, i.e. the legal instruments of party organisation. The social status of the classes they represented enabled both the bourgeois liberal and the petit-bourgeois democratic parties to remain united in one form or another and to function more or less effectively despite the reaction. After 1849 just as before 1848, only one path was open to the proletarian party—that of *secret association*. And so after 1849 a whole series of clandestine proletarian societies sprang up on the continent, were discovered by the police, condemned by the courts, broken up by the gaols and invariably resuscitated by the force of circumstances.

Some of these secret societies had as their goal the direct overthrow of the existing power of the state. This was fully justified in France where the proletariat had been crushed by the bourgeoisie and hence to attack the existing government and the bourgeoisie were one and the same thing. Others aimed at organising the proletariat into a party, without concerning themselves with the existing governments. This was necessary in countries like Germany where both proletariat and bourgeoisie had succumbed to their semi-feudal governments and where in consequence a victorious assault on the existing governments instead of breaking the power of the bourgeoisie or the so-called middle classes, would at first help them to gain power. There is no doubt that here too the members of the proletarian party would take part once again in a revolution against the *status quo*, but it was no part of their task to prepare for this revolution, to agitate, conspire or to plot for it. They could leave this preparation to circumstances in general and to the classes directly involved. They could not help leaving it to them if they were not to abandon the position of their own party and the historic tasks that follow of themselves from the conditions governing the existence of the proletariat. For them the contemporary governments were but ephemeral phenomena, the *status quo* a brief stopping place and the task of toiling away at it could be left to the petty narrow-minded democrats.

The "Communist League", therefore, was no conspiratorial society, but a society which secretly strove to create an organised proletarian party because the German proletariat is publicly debarred, *igni et aqua*, from writing, meeting and speaking. Such a society can only be said to conspire against the *status quo* in the sense that steam and electricity conspire against it.

It is self-evident that a secret society which strives to form not the *government of the future* but the *opposition party* could have but few attractions for individuals who on the one hand concealed their personal insignificance by strutting around in the theatrical cloak of the conspirator, and on the other wished to satisfy their stupid ambition on the day of the next revolution, and who wished above all to seem important at the moment, to snatch their share of the fruits of demagogy and to find a welcome among the quacks and charlatans of democracy.

Thus a splinter broke off from the Communist League, or rather it was broken off, a group that demanded, if not real conspiracies, at any rate the *appearance* of conspiracies, and accordingly favoured an alliance with the democratic heroes of the hour; this was the Willich–Schapper party. It is typical of them that Willich was, together with Kinkel, one of the entrepreneurs in the German–American revolutionary loan.[19]

Such then is the relation of this party to the majority of the Communist League to which the Cologne defendants belonged. Bürgers and Röser defined it succinctly and exhaustively in the sessions of the Cologne Assizes.

Let us pause before finally bringing our narrative to a close in order to take a glance at the behaviour of the Willich–Schapper Party during the Cologne Trial.

As was pointed out above, the data contained in the documents purloined from the party by Stieber make it plain that their documents contrived to find their way to the police even after Reuter's theft. To this day the party has been at a loss for an explanation of this phenomenon.

Schapper knew the facts about Cherval's past better than anyone. He knew that Cherval had entered the League on his nomination in 1846 and not on that of Marx in 1848, etc. But his silence seems to verify Stieber's lies.

The Party knew that it was Hake, who was their member, that had written the threatening letter to the witness, Haupt; but it let the suspicion fall on the heads of the party of the accused.

Moses Hess, a member of the party and the author of the "Red Catechism"—that unfortunate parody of the "Manifesto of the Communist Party"—Moses Hess who not only writes but also retails his own works, knew exactly to whom he had distributed parcels of his "Red". He knew that Marx would have declined to diminish his wealth of "Reds" by taking even a single copy. But Moses calmly let suspicion fall on the accused, as if it were their party that had hawked his "Red", together with its melodramatic accompanying document from door to door in the Rhineland Provinces.

That the Party has made common cause with the Prussian police is apparent not only in their silence but also in their utterances: whenever they enter the trial it is not in the dock with the accused, but as *witnesses for the Crown*.

Hentze, Willich's friend and benefactor, and, on his own admission, an accomplice of the League, spent a few weeks in London with Willich and then journeyed to Cologne where he falsely testified that Becker (against whom there was far less evidence than against himself) had been a member of the League in 1848.

Hätzel who, as the Dietz Archive reveals, was a member of the Party, from which he received financial support. He had already been put on trial in Berlin for his association with the League and now he appeared as a witness for the prosecution. His testimony was false for he invented a wholly fictitious connection between the statutes of the

League and the exceptional arming of the Berlin proletariat during the revolution.

Steingens, whose own letters proved him to be the Party's chief agent in Brussels (in the session on October 18), appeared in Cologne not as a defendant, but as a witness.

Not long before the court action in Cologne Willich and Kinkel sent a journeyman tailor as emissary to Germany. Kinkel is not indeed a member of the Party but Willich was co-director of the German–American revolutionary loan.

Kinkel was at that time already threatened by the danger that was later to become a reality, of seeing himself and Willich removed by the London guarantors from control of the Loan moneys and seeing the money itself drift back to America despite the energetic protests of Willich and himself. He was just then in need of the pseudo-mission *to* Germany and a pseudo-correspondence *with* Germany, partly in order to demonstrate that an area still existed for his revolutionary activities and the American dollars, and partly to provide a pretext for the enormous costs of the correspondence, stamps, etc., that he and Willich managed to charge to the account. (See Graf O. Reichenbach's lithographed circular.) Kinkel knew he had no contacts either with the bourgeois liberals or with the petit bourgeois democrats in Germany. As he could not afford to be particular he used an emissary of the Party as the emissary of the German–American Revolutionary League. This emissary's sole function was to promote antagonism among the workers towards the accused in Cologne. It must be admitted that the moment was well chosen and it offered a new pretext in the nick of time to reopen the investigation. The Prussian police had been fully apprised of the emissary's identity, of the day of his departure and of his route. Who thus apprised them? We shall see. Their spies were present at the secret meetings he held in Magdeburg and they reported on the debates. The friends of the accused in Germany and London trembled.

We have already narrated how on November 6th Hirsch went before the Magistrate at Bow Street and admitted to having forged the Original Minute-Book under the guidance of Greif and Fleury. It was Willich who induced him to take this step, and it was Willich and Schärttner the innkeeper who accompanied him to the magistrate. Three copies were made of Hirsch's confession and these were sent through the post to three different addresses in Cologne.

It was of supreme importance to arrest Hirsch as soon as he left the court. With the aid of the officially witnessed statement in his possession it would have been possible for the case lost in Cologne to be won in London. If not *for* the accused at any rate *against* the government. However, Willich did everything in his power to see to it that this step was not taken. He observed the strictest silence both towards the "Marx Party" and even towards his own people not excluding Schapper. Schärttner alone was taken into his confidence. Schärttner declares that he and Willich had accompanied Hirsch to the ship. For Willich's plan was for Hirsch to give evidence against himself.

Willich informed Hirsch of the route by which the documents had been sent, Hirsch for his part informed the Prussian Embassy, and the Prussian Embassy informed the post. The documents did not arrive at their destination; they disappeared. Some time after this, Hirsch, who had also vanished, re-appeared in London and declared at a public meeting of democrats that Willich was his accomplice.

Although it had been on a motion from him that Hirsch had been expelled as a spy from the Great Windmill Street Club in 1851, Willich admitted, when questioned, that he had resumed relations with Hirsch early in August 1852. This was because Hirsch had revealed to him that Fleury was a Prussian spy and had intercepted all of Fleury's incoming and outgoing correspondence. He, Willich, made use of this to keep himself informed of the activities of the Prussian police.

It was notorious that Willich had been on terms of intimate friendship with Fleury for about a year and that he received monetary assistance from him. But if Willich had known ever since August 1852 that he was a Prussian spy and if he was familiar with his activities how was it possible that he should have remained ignorant of the Original Minute-Book?

That he did not intervene until the Prussian government itself had *admitted* that Fleury was a spy?

That the manner of his intervention was such as to remove his ally Hirsch from English soil and the officially witnessed proofs of Fleury's guilt from the hands of the "Marx Party"?

That he continued to receive contributions from Fleury who boasts that he has in his possession Willich's receipt for £15 sterling?

That Fleury continued to be actively engaged in the German–American loan?

That he informed Fleury of the meeting place of his own secret society so that Prussian agents in the next room could make records of the debates?

That he revealed to Fleury the route of the above-mentioned journeyman tailor and that he even received money from him to cover the costs of this mission?

That, lastly, he told Fleury that he had instructed Hentze who lived with him, how he should testify *against* Becker at the trial in Cologne? It must be admitted—*que tout cela n'est pas bien clair.**

VII

Judgement and Sentence

As the police mysteries were gradually explained, public opinion declared itself increasingly in favour of the defendants. When at last the Original Minute-Book was shown to be a forgery an acquittal was generally expected. The *Kölnische Zeitung* felt bound to defer to public opinion and to dissociate itself from the government. Little notices favourable to the defendants and casting suspicion on Stieber found their way into columns that had earlier contained nothing but police insinuations. Even the Prussian government admitted defeat. Its correspondent in *The Times* and the *Morning Chronicle* suddenly began to prepare public opinion abroad for an unfavourable decision. Monstrous and destructive as the teachings of the defendants were, horrifying as were the documents found in their possession, conclusive evidence of a conspiracy was nevertheless wanting and a conviction was therefore unlikely. Downcast and resigned, the Berlin correspondent of *The Times* obsequiously echoed the fears that were circulating among the most highly-placed authorities in the city on the Spree. All the more extravagant then was the rejoicing of the eunuchs at the Byzantine court when the electric telegraph flashed its message of the jury's verdict of "guilty!" from Cologne to Berlin.

With the unmasking of the Minute-Book the case had advanced to a new stage. The jury was no longer free merely to find the defendants guilty or not guilty; they must either find the defendants guilty—or

---

* As to relations between Willich and Becker:

"Willich writes me the funniest letters; I do not reply, but this does not prevent him from describing his latest plans for a revolution. He has appointed me to subvert the Cologne garrison! ! ! We laughed till the tears came. His idiocy will spell disaster for countless people yet; for a single letter would suffice to guarantee the salaries of a hundred 'Demagogue judges' for three years at least. As soon as I have completed the revolution in Cologne he would *have no objection* to assuming the leadership for all subsequent operations. Very kind of him!"

(From a letter by Becker to Marx, January 27, 1851) (Note by Marx).

else the government. To acquit the accused would mean condemning the government.

Replying to the summing-up for the defence, Saedt, speaking for the prosecution, let the Minute-Book be set aside. He was unwilling to make use of such an unreliable document, he was convinced that it was "inauthentic", it was an "unfortunate" book, it had resulted in much time being wasted, it added nothing to what was already known, Stieber's praiseworthy zeal had led in this instance to his being deceived, etc.

But the prosecution itself had maintained that there was "much that was true" in the book. Far from declaring it to be a forgery the prosecution had regretted only that it could not prove it to be authentic. But if the Original Minute-book was a forgery despite Stieber's having pronounced it genuine, Cherval's statement in Paris was also forgery, though no less genuine according to Stieber's sworn statement, and though Saedt was to return to it in his summing up; indeed all the facts established by all the authorities of the Prussian state for $1\frac{1}{2}$ years were now discredited at one stroke. The court session set down for July 28 was postponed for three months. Why? Because Police Commissioner Schulz had been taken ill. And who was Schulz? The original discoverer of the Original Minute-Book. Let us go back even further. In January and February 1852, Frau Dr. Daniels's house had been searched. On what grounds? On the grounds discovered in the *first few* pages of the Original Minute-Book that Fleury had sent to Schulz, that Schulz had sent to the police authorities in Cologne, that the police authorities in Cologne had sent to the examining magistrate, that led the examining magistrate to the house of Frau Dr. Daniels.

In October 1851, despite the Cherval conspiracy, the Prosecution Council was still unable to discover the missing indictable offence and on instructions from the Ministry it therefore ordered a new investigation. Who was in charge of this investigation? Police Commissioner Schulz. Schulz was to discover the offence. What did Schulz discover? The Original Minute-Book. The only new material he found were the loose leaves of the Minute-Book which Stieber later completed and bound. Twelve months solitary confinement for the accused simply to give the Original Minute-Book the time necessary to be born and to grow. "Bagatelles!" Saedt exlaims and finds evidence of the guilt of the accused in the mere fact that it took them and their counsel eight days to clean out an Augean stable that all the authorities of the Prussian State had needed $1\frac{1}{2}$ years to fill while the accused had to remain $1\frac{1}{2}$ years in gaol. The Original Minute-Book was no mere single item of evidence; it was the junction where all the threads spun by the various Prussian authorities met—embassy and police, ministry and magistrates, prosecution and postal authorities, London, Berlin and Cologne. The Original Minute-Book meant so much to the case that it was invented so that a case might be made out. Couriers, telegrams, the intercepting of letters, arrests, perjuries to support the Original Minute-Book, forgeries to bring it into existence, attempted bribery to authenticate it. When the mystery of the Original Minute-Book was revealed the mystery of the whole monster trial was revealed with it.

The miracles performed by the police were originally necessary to make the public forget that it was really political opinions that were on trial. The revelations you are about to witness, Gentlemen of the Jury, said Saedt when opening for the prosecution, will prove to you that it is not political opinions that are to be put on trial. But now he emphasises the importance of these opinions so as to ensure that the police revelations are forgotten. After the 1½ year preliminary investigation the jury needed objective evidence in order to justify itself before public opinion. After the five-week long police comedy they needed "opinions *pure and simple*" to extricate themselves from the sheer mess. Saedt therefore did not only confine himself to the material that had led the Prosecution Council to the conclusion that "there was no evidence of an indictable offence". He went even further. He attempted to prove that the law against conspiracy does not in fact require any conspiracy to take place but only that it be advocated so that in effect the word "plot" is only a pretext which enables the law to burn political heretics. The success of his attempt promised to be all the greater because of the decision to apply the new Prussian Penal Code that had been promulgated after the accused had been arrested. On the pretext that this code contained milder provisions the servile court brought itself to permit its application to be retroactive.

But if people were on trial because of their political opinions, then why a preliminary investigation lasting 1½ years? Because of yet other opinions.

As it is however a matter of opinion are we to engage in a discussion of fundamental opinions with a Saedt–Stieber–Seckendorf, with a Göbel, with a Prussian government, with the 300 most highly taxed people in the district of Cologne, with the Royal Chamberlain von Münch-Bellinghausen and with the Freiherr von Fürstenberg? *Pas si bête.*

Saedt admits (in the sitting on November 8th) that

"when some few months ago, the Attorney General commissioned
him to join him in representing the Ministry in this affair, and when,
as a result, he began to read through the files he first hit upon the
idea of making a somewhat more thorough study of communism
and socialism. He felt that it would be not wholly superfluous to
impart the results of his studies to the jury, as he thought he might
proceed on the assumption that many of them like himself may have
not greatly concerned themselves with the subject hitherto."

So Saedt bought the well-known compendium by Stein.[20]

> "*Und was er heute gelernt
> das will er morgen schon lehren.*"
>
> ["And what he has learnt today,
> he'll teach to others tomorrow."][21]

But the Ministry was afflicted by a singular misfortune. It sought to
find the offence called Marx and found instead the offence called
Cherval. It went in search of the communism propagated by the
defendants and found the communism they combated. In Stein's compendium many sorts of communism are to be found, but not the sort
Saedt was seeking. Stein had not progressed as far as German, critical
communism. It is true that Saedt had in his possession a copy of the
"Manifesto of the Communist Party" that the defendants recognise as
the manifesto of their party. But in this manifesto there is a chapter
devoted to a criticism of the whole previous literature of socialism and
communism, i.e. of the whole of the wisdom recorded in Stein. From
this chapter the distinction between the brand of communism pro-
pounded by the defendants and all previous kinds must become apparent; that is to say the specific content and *the specific direction* of the
theory that Saedt requires. But no Stein will help him over this stumb-
ling-block. Understanding was unavoidable, if only in order to
prosecute. How did Saedt manage when Stein left him in the lurch?
He claimed:

"The 'Manifesto' consists of 3 *sections*. The first section contains a
historical account of the social status of the various citizens [Bürger](!)
from the communist point of view (very fine)....The second section
expounds the communist point of view *vis à vis* the proletariat. . . .

Lastly, the final section treats of the position of the communists in different countries. . . ."(!) (Sitting of November 6th).

Now in fact the "Manifesto" consists of 4 sections, not of 3, but what the eye does not see the heart does not grieve over. Saedt claims therefore that there are 3 sections and not 4. The fourth section which for him does not exist is that same accursed section with the critique of communism as recorded by Stein, that is to say the section that contains the *specific brand* of communism advocated by the defendants. Poor Saedt! First he cannot find the indictable *offence*, and then even the indictable *opinions* elude him.

But "grey, dear friends, is every theory".[22] The "so-called social question" and its solution, Saedt observed, "is one that in recent times has attracted the qualified and the unqualified". Saedt surely belongs to the qualified, for the Attorney General, Seckendorf officially "qualified" him three months ago to study communism and socialism. The Saedts of all times and all places have agreed from time immemorial that Galileo was "unqualified" to explore the movements of the heavenly bodies, whereas the inquisitor who declared him a heretic was of course "qualified" to do so. *E pur si muove.*★

Embodied in the defendants the revolutionary proletariat stood helplessly before the ruling classes who were embodied in the jury; so the defendants were condemned because they stood before *this* jury. What, for one moment, deeply affected the bourgeois conscience of the jury, just as it had deeply affected public opinion, was the unmasking of the intrigues of the government, the corruption of the Prussian government that had been laid bare before their eyes. But, the members of the jury reasoned, if the Prussian government could risk using such infamous and at the same time such foolhardy methods against the accused, if it could, as it were, stake its European reputation, then the accused must be damnably dangerous, however small their party, and their theories at least must be a real power. The government has offended against every law in the penal code in order to protect us from these monstrous criminals. Let us for our part not be backward in sacrificing our little *point d'honneur* to save the government's honour. Let us be thankful and let us condemn.

★ Saedt was not only "qualified". He became still further "qualified", for as a reward for his performance in this trial he was promoted to Attorney-General for the whole of the Rhine Province and remained in this post until he was pensioned, when, provided with the holy sacraments, he passed on. (Note by Engels in the edition of 1885.)

With their verdict of guilty the Rhenish nobility and the Rhenish bourgeoisie joined in the cry uttered by the French bourgeoisie after December 2:

"Property can be saved only by theft, religion only by perjury, the family only by bastardy, order only by disorder!"

In France the whole machinery of state prostituted itself. And yet no institution prostituted itself so deeply as French courts of law and French juries. Let us surpass the French judges and jurymen, the judge and jury exclaimed in Cologne. In the Cherval case immediately after the *coup d'état* the Paris jury acquitted Nette though there was more evidence against him than against *any one* of the accused in Cologne. Let us surpass the jury of the *coup d'état* of December 2. Let us, in condemning Bürgers, Röser, etc., also condemn Nette retrospectively.

Thus the superstititious faith in the jury, still rampant in the Prussian Rhineland, was broken. It became evident that the jury was the summary court of the privileged classes; it was created to bridge the gaps in the law with the fullness of the bourgeois conscience.

Jena![23] . . . that is our last word to a government that requires such methods in order to survive and to a society that needs such a government for its protection. The word that should stand at the end of the Communist trial in Cologne is . . . Jena!

NOTES ON REVELATIONS CONCERNING THE COMMUNIST TRIAL IN COLOGNE

1. Written October–December 1852. Published anonymously in Basle, January 1853 and Boston, April 1853. Published in instalments in the *Volksstaat*, October–December 1874 under Marx's name. It appeared in book-form in 1875.
2. See Appendix A, I, II, IV, V.
3. The Central Committee of European Democracy was founded in London in June 1850 on Mazzini's initiative. It consisted of bourgeois and petit-bourgeois immigrants of various nationalities, including e.g. Kossuth. Dissolved in effect in March 1852 because of the growing tensions between the Italian immigrants and those from France and Germany.
4. See Appendix A, III.
5. Here and throughout the pamphlet Marx quotes from the reports of the trial in the *Kölnische Zeitung*.
6. "The German Educational Society for Workers in London" was founded on February 7, 1840, by Karl Schapper, Joseph Moll, Heinrich Bauer and other members of the League of the Just. Marx and Engels were actively involved in the Society in 1847 and 1849–50. They resigned from it on September 17, 1850, together with a number of their associates following the split in the League. They were again active in the affairs of the Society in the late 1850s. The Society was finally dissolved by the English government in 1918.
7. Refugee Committee: a committee of the German Educational Society. Marx had been elected a member in September 1849.
8. A lottery organised by Bonaparte in 1850. The profits were to be used to ship Parisian vagabonds to California. Marx gives an account of it in *The Eighteenth Brumaire of Louis Bonaparte*.
9. See Appendix A, II.
10. The Dying Gladiator is a Greek statue of the second half of the third century B.C. It represents a warrior collapsing on his shield after killing himself in order to escape the enemy.
11. Wermuth and Stieber, *Die Communisten-Verschwörungen des neunzehnten Jahrhunderts*. Part Two of this work contains a "black list" of people connected with the democratic and workers' movements.
12. From Heinrich Heine's *Buch der Lieder*; Schinderhannes and Karl Moor (the hero of Schiller's *Die Räuber*) both symbolise great rogues in this context.
13. According to the Constitution of November 4, 1848, the election of a new president of the republic should have taken place on May 9, 1852. Petit-bourgeois democrats and above all emigrant groups hoped that this would mean the victory of the democratic parties.
14. In his "Table-Talk" Luther compared the world to a drunken peasant unable to keep his seat in the saddle.
15. Former prison in Paris in which Cherval and the other people involved in the so-called Franco–German Plot were detained.
16. Schiller.
17. See Appendix B, III.

18. See Appendix B, V.
19. See *Heroes of the Exile*, p. 334.
20. Lorenz Stein, *Der Socialismus und Communismus des heutigen Frankreichs. Ein Beitrag zur Zeitgeschichte.*
21. Schiller, *Die Sonntagskinder*, in an amended form.
22. Goethe, *Faust.*
23. Refers to the defeat of the Prussian army by Napoleon on October 14, 1806. The defeat revealed at a single stroke the complete inner decadence of the state created by Frederick the Great.

THE COMMUNIST TRIAL IN COLOGNE

APPENDIX 4 TO *Herr Vogt* BY KARL MARX

In this section (of *Herr Vogt*) I wish to make public information concerning the Prussian Embassy in London and its transactions with Prussian authorities on the Continent at a time when the Cologne Trial was still proceeding. This information is based on the confessions of Hirsch which were published by A. Willich in April 1853 in the *New-Yorker Criminal-Zeitung* under the title "The Victims of Police-denunciations; an Apologia by Wilhelm Hirsch". Hirsch who is at present in a Hamburg gaol was the principal tool of Chief Inspector Greif and his agent Fleury. It was on instructions from them and under their guidance that he forged the *false* Minute-Book submitted as evidence by Stieber in the course of the trial. I give here a number of excerpts from Hirsch's memoirs.

(During the Great Exhibition) "the German Clubs were kept under close surveillance by a Police Triumvirate: Police Superintendent Stieber for Prussia, a Mr. Kubesch for Austria and Police Commissioner Huntel of Bremen."

Having volunteered to act as an informer, Hirsch had an interview in London with Alberts who was Secretary at the Prussian Embassy. He gives this account of their first meeting:

"For its assignations with its secret agents the Prussian Embassy in London has discovered a public house entirely worthy of them. The Cock in Fleet St., Temple Bar is so very unobtrusive that but for a golden cock pointing to the entrance the casual passer-by would never even notice it. I went through a narrow passage leading to the interior of this old English tavern and asked for Mr. Charles whereupon a corpulent personage introduced himself to me with such an amiable smile that anyone seeing us would have taken us to be old friends. The Embassy agent (for this is what he was) seemed to be in very high spirits and his mood was still further improved by great amounts of brandy and water. He was enjoying himself so much that for a long time he seemed to have completely forgotten the purpose of our meeting. Mr. Charles at once revealed that his true name was Alberts and that he was the Embassy Secretary. He informed me that he did not in fact engage on any police business but that he would act as an intermediary in this case. . . . A second meeting took place at his home in 34 Brewer St., Golden Square and it was here that I met Police Inspector Greif. Greif looked the true policeman: medium height, dark hair and a beard of the same colour cut in the regulation style i.e. with the moustache meeting the side-whiskers and the chin left shaven. His eyes looked anything but intelligent and they protruded fiercely in a permanent glare, doubtless the result of his habitual association with thieves and rogues. . . . Like Mr. Alberts, Mr. Greif introduced himself to me by the pseudonym of Mr. Charles. The latest Mr. Charles was at least in a more serious mood and he even felt it was necessary to test me. . . . The meeting ended with his instructing me to give him a complete report on all the activities of the revolutionary *émigrés*. . . . On the next occasion Mr. Greif introduced me to what he called 'his right hand', namely 'one of his agents' he added. This turned out to be a tall elegantly dressed young man who also gave his name as Mr. Charles. The whole Prussian police seems to have adopted this name and I now had three on my hands. The latest specimen was easily the most remarkable. He said that he too had been a revolutionary but that all things were possible and I had only to go along with him."

Greif left London and parted from Hirsch "expressly commending me to the latest Mr. Charles who, he said, acted always on his instructions. I should not hesitate to confide in him. Moreover, even if certain things should appear strange to me I should not take offence. To make this clearer he added: 'The Ministry sometimes requires various articles, chiefly *documents*; *if these are unobtainable we should not let this deter us!*' "

Hirsch states further that the latest Charles was Fleury.

"He had earlier been employed in the office of the 'Dresdner Zeitung' which was edited by L. Wittig. When he was in Baden, as a result of recommendations he had brought from Dresden, he was sent by the provisional government to the Palatinate to take in hand the organisation of the local militia etc. When the Prussians occupied Karlsruhe he was taken prisoner etc. He reappeared in London towards the end of 1850 or early in 1851; here he went by the name of de Fleury and was known by this name in the *émigré* circles which he frequented. He seemed to be down at heel, stayed in the *émigré* barracks built by the Refugee Committee and drew subsidies. Early in the summer of 1851 his position suddenly improved; he rented a respectable apartment and at the end of the year he married the daughter of an English engineer. He turned up later in Paris as a police agent. . . . His real name is *Krause* and he is the son of Krause the cobbler who was executed some 15 or 18 years ago in Dresden together with Backhof and Beseler for the murder of Countess Schönberg and her maid. . . . Fleury–Krause told me many times that he had been working for different governments since he was 14."

It is this same Fleury–Krause whom Stieber admitted in open court in Cologne to be a secret Prussian police agent working directly under Greif. In my "Revelations concerning the Communist Trial in Cologne" I wrote of Fleury: "So Fleury is not indeed the Fleur de Marie of the police prostitutes, but he is a flower and he will bear blossom, albeit only the *fleur de lys*." This prophecy has since been fulfilled; some months after the Communist Trial Fleury was sentenced to several years in the hulks for forgery.

"As the right-hand man of Police Inspector Greif", Hirsch writes, "Fleury dealt directly with the Prussian Embassy during Greif's absence."

Fleury was in contact with Max Reuter who committed the theft from Oswald Dietz, at that time archivist of the Willich-Schapper League.

"Stieber", says Hirsch, "had learned from the agent of the Prussian ambassador Count Hatzfeldt, the notorious Cherval, of the letters written by the latter to London. He got Reuter to find out where they were whereupon Fleury stole them on Stieber's orders and with Reuter's aid. These are the stolen letters which Mr. Stieber was not ashamed to exhibit 'as such' to the jury in Cologne. . . . In Autumn 1851 Fleury had come to Paris with Greif and Stieber after the latter had already made contact with Cherval, or better, Joseph Crämer, through the mediation of Count Hatzfeldt with whose assistance he hoped to create a plot. With this end in view consultations were held in Paris between Messrs. Stieber, Greif, Fleury, two other police agents, Beckmann★ and Sommer, and the famous French spy Lucien de la *Hodde* (who went by the name of Duprez) and they gave Cherval directions according to which he was to tailor his correspondence. Fleury often laughed in my presence over the scuffle he had

★ The same man who figured in the Arnim Trial. (Note by Marx in the edition of 1875.) He was Paris correspondent for the *Kölnische Zeitung* already at this period and was to remain so for many years. (Engels' addition to the edition of 1885.)

provoked between Stieber and Cherval. And the man called Schmidt who in the guise of secretary of a revolutionary league in Strasbourg and Cologne, had gained admission to the society founded at the behest of the police by Cherval, was none other than M. de Fleury. . . . Fleury was undoubtedly the sole agent of the Prussian secret police in London and all proposals and offers that the embassy received went through his hands. . . . Messrs. Greif and Stieber were accustomed to relying on his judgment."

Fleury informed Hirsch:

"Mr. Greif has told you what has to be done. . . . At Police Head-quarters in Frankfurt they are themselves of the opinion that our primary aim must be to make *the position of the political police secure*; the means we use to achieve this are immaterial; the September plot in Paris is already *one step in this direction.*"

Greif returned to London and expressed satisfaction with Hirsch's work but demanded more. In particular he wanted to receive reports on the *"secret meetings of the Marx Party"*.

"At all costs," the Police Inspector concluded, we must make reports on the League meetings. Do it any way you wish as long as you don't overstep the limits of probability. I am too occupied to attend to it myself. M. de Fleury will work with you as my representative."

Greif's occupation at that time consisted, as Hirsch states, in a correspondence via de la Hodde-Duprez with Maupas concerning the mock escape of Cherval and Gipperich from the St. Pélague gaol.

On being assured by Hirsch that "Marx had not founded any new League Headquarters in London. . . . Greif agreed with Fleury that in the circumstances we should prepare reports ourselves on meetings of the League. He, Greif, would vouch for their authenticity, and in any case his submissions were always approved."

So Hirsch and Fleury set to work.

"The content" of their reports on Marx's secret meetings of the League "was provided", Hirsch states, "by reports of discussions that took place from time to time; the admission of new members, the founding of new communes in obscure corners of Germany, or a new organisation; the fact that in Cologne Marx's friends did or did not have any prospects of being acquitted; letters that had come from this person or that, and so on. On this last point Fleury took care to mention people in Germany who had become suspect as a result of political investigations or who had been involved in some political activity or other. Very often, however, we had to have recourse to our imagination and then we would discuss the activities of a non-existent member of the League. But Mr. Greif said that the reports were excellent and that we had to have them at all costs. Some of the writing was done by Fleury alone but mostly I had to help him as he was unable to describe the smallest detail without errors of style. In this way the reports came into being and without a moment's hesitation Mr. Greif declared his willingness to vouch for their accuracy."

Hirsch then describes how Fleury and he visited Arnold Ruge in Brighton, and Edward Meyen and stole letters and lithographed notices from them. But as if that were not enough, Greif-Fleury rented a lithographic press from Stanbury Press, Fetter Lane and together with Hirsch he produced "radical broadsheets". That democrat, F. Zabel, could learn a lesson or two here. Let him take note of this:

"The first broadsheet I (Hirsch) made was entitled 'To the Rural Proletariat' at Fleury's suggestion; and we managed to make a few good copies of it. Mr. Greif sent these copies to Prussia as documents emanating from the Marx Party. To make it seem more plausible we included in the reports of the so-called League meetings which came into being in the manner described above, a few words about the distribution of such a broadsheet. One other product of this kind was fabricated; its title was 'To the Children of the People' and I do not know under whose auspices Mr. Greif sent this one in. We later abandoned this method chiefly because it was so costly."

At this point Cherval arrived in London after his pretended flight from Paris. He became attached to Greif at a weekly salary of £1–10–0, "in return for which he was required to make reports on the contacts between the French and German émigrés".

Publicly exposed and expelled from the Workers' Club as a spy, "Cherval very understandably described the German émigrés and their organs from then on as being as insignificant as he could make them out to be—since he found it quite impossible to get hold of any information which he could pass on. By way of compensation he compiled a report on the non-German revolutionary party which put Münchhausen's tall stories in the shade."

Hirsch now returns to the Cologne Trial.

"Mr. Greif had already been questioned a number of times about the contents of the reports prepared at his instance by Fleury in so far as they had any bearing on the Cologne Trial. . . . There were also particular commissions in connection with the Trial. On one occasion Marx was alleged to be corresponding with *Lassalle* via an *ale-house* and the Public Prosecutor required further information. . . . Rather more naïve was the Public Prosecutor's request asking for precise information about the financial assistance that Lassalle in Düsseldorf was allegedly having sent to the defendant Röser in Cologne . . . it was believed that the true source of the money was in London."

I have already recounted in Section III, 4 (of *Herr Vogt*) how Fleury, acting on instructions from Hinckeldey, was supposed to look for someone in London who would be willing to appear before the jury in Cologne in the guise of Haupt, the witness who had disappeared, etc. After a detailed account of this incident Hirsch goes on:

"Mr. Stieber had meanwhile urgently requested Greif to supply him, if at all possible, with the original minutes of the reports of the League meetings that he had sent in. Fleury was of the opinion that he could produce an original minute-book if only some more people could be placed at his disposal. Above all, however, he would need *specimens of the handwriting of some of Marx's friends*. I made use of this last remark in order to extricate myself from the whole undertaking; Fleury alluded to the topic only once again and after that he said nothing more. . . . Around this time Stieber suddenly appeared in the court in Cologne with a minute-book of the League Central Committee in London. . . . I was even more astonished when I found that the minutes as reported in extract in the papers were absolutely identical with the reports concocted by Fleury at Greif's behest. It was evident that Mr. Greif or Mr. Stieber had had a *copy* made somehow or other, *for the minutes in this allegedly original document bore signatures while those submitted by Fleury had none.* From Fleury himself I learned only that 'Stieber can put anything right, it will be a sensation!'

As soon as Fleury heard that 'Marx' had had the handwriting of the ostensible signatories of the minute-book (Liebknecht, Rings, Ulmer, etc.) "witnessed in a London Police Court he wrote the following letter:

'To the Royal Police Presidium in Berlin; dated from London.

It is the intention of Marx and his friends here to discredit the signatures on the League Minutes by having handwriting specimens witnessed. These specimens are to be produced in the Court of Assizes as the really authentic ones. Everyone familiar with the

English Laws knows that on this point they can be manipulated and
that a person who vouches for the authenticity of a thing is not
required to give any true guarantee. The person who gives you this
information does not recoil from giving you his name in a matter
like this where the truth is at stake.

    Becker, 4, Litchfield St.'

Fleury knew the address of Becker, a German *émigré* living in the
same house as Willich. It might very easily happen later on that
suspicion would fall on the latter who was an opponent of Marx. . . .
Fleury looked forward eagerly to the scandal that would result. The
letter would be read out in court, but too late, he thought, for any
doubts about its authenticity to arise before the trial was over. . . .
The letter, signed by Becker, was addressed to the *Police Presidium in
Berlin*, but it went not to Berlin but to 'Police Officer Goldheim',
Frankfurter Hof in Cologne', and an *envelope* for this letter arrived at
the Police Presidium in Berlin with a note stating that *Mr. Stieber in
Cologne would give a complete explanation as to its use. . . .*' Mr. Stieber
made no use of this letter; he was unable to do so because he was
forced to drop the whole Minute-Book."

    With regard to the Minute-Book Hirsch says that "Mr. Stieber
declared" (in court) "that he had had the Minute-Book in his hands
for two weeks but had scrupled to produce it; he declared further
that it had come to him by a courier called Greif. . . . Hence Greif had
personally delivered his own work. How can this be reconciled with
a letter of Mr. Goldheim's in which he informed the Embassy that
'the Minute-Book was produced so late only in order to avoid scrutiny as to its authenticity . . .' ."

On Friday, October 29th, Mr. Goldheim arrived in London.

    "As Mr. Stieber had to face the fact that it was not possible to
uphold the authenticity of the Minute-Book he sent a deputy to
negotiate with Fleury about it on the spot. At issue was the question
whether a proof could not be obtained after all. His discussions were
fruitless and he returned without any decision having been reached.
Fleury was left in a state of despair for Stieber was resolved to expose
him rather than compromise the police chiefs. But I did not realise
that this was the cause of Fleury's disquiet until Stieber made his
next declaration soon afterwards. In panic, Fleury now resorted to
his last piece of trickery. He brought me a specimen of handwriting
for me to use to copy out a dcelaration, sign it 'Liebknecht' and take
an oath before the Lord Mayor of London that I was Liebknecht. . . .
Fleury told me that the handwriting was identical with that in the

Minute-Book and that *Mr. Goldheim had brought it with him*" (from Cologne). "But how was it possible for Mr. Goldheim to bring a specimen of the handwriting of the alleged author of the Minute-Book from Cologne at the very moment when Greif the courier, having handed the Minute-Book over to Mr. Stieber, had just arrived back in London? . . . . What Fleury gave me consisted of a signature and a few phrases" . . . Hirsch "copied the writing as closely as he could and wrote that the undersigned, i.e. Liebknecht, solemnly declared that the signature legally witnessed by Marx and Co. was false and that this, his signature was the only genuine one. When I had finished and had the handwriting in my hands" (i.e. the specimen given him by Fleury to copy), "which fortunately I still possess, I told Fleury who was not a little taken aback, that I had had second thoughts and would not go through with it. Though inconsolable at first he then announced that he would swear to it himself. . . . For safety's sake *he would have the writing countersigned by the Prussian Consul*; and he did go to the Consulate. I waited for him in a tavern; when he got back he had the countersignature and he next went to the Lord Mayor for the oath. But the plan fell through as the Lord Mayor wanted further guarantees and Fleury could not give them— so the oath remained unsworn. . . . Late in the evening I saw Fleury again, and for the last time. He had that very day been surprised to read Mr. Stieber's declaration concerning him in the 'Kölnische Zeitung'. 'But I know that Stieber could not have done otherwise: he would have had to compromise himself', M. de Fleury said very truly by way of consoling himself . . ." *There will be a great explosion in Berlin if the Cologne prisoners are convicted*, Fleury said to me at one of our last meetings."

Fleury's last meeting with Hirsch took place at the *end* of October 1852. Hirsch's confessions are dated the *end of November 1852*; and at the *end of March 1853* came the "explosion in Berlin" (the Ladendorf conspiracy).

The reader will be interested to see the testimonials that Stieber gave his two accomplices Fleury-Krause and Hirsch. He writes of the first in the Black Book II, p. 69.

"No 345 *Krause* Karl Friedrich August, from Dresden. He is the son of Friedrich August Krause and his widow Johanna Rosine née Göllnitz. Krause was a farmer who was executed for his part in the murder of Countess Schönberg in Dresden, and who afterwards" (after his execution??) "became a corn-dealer. Carl Friedrich was born on January 9, 1824, in the vineyard houses at Coswig near Dresden.

From October 1, 1832, he went to the charity school in Dresden; in 1836 he was admitted to the orphanage in Antonstadt-Dresden and in 1840 he was confirmed. He was then apprenticed to Mr. Gruhle, a Dresden merchant, but in the following year he was arrested and detained by the City Court for *repeated theft*. However, the period of detention was counted towards his sentence and he was released. After this he lived with his mother without taking a job, but in March 1842 he was arrested again for breaking and entering and this time he was sentenced to four years' imprisonment. On October 23, 1846, he came out of gaol and returned to Dresden and began to *associate with the most notorious thieves*. Then, the Rehabilitation Society took him up and found him a job in a cigar factory and he remained in this job without interruption or any further misdemeanour until March 1848. But after that date he gave in to a tendency to be unemployed and began to frequent political societies," (as a government spy; see his admission to Hirsch above). "Early in 1849 he found employment as a salesman for E. L. Wittig who is now in America but who at that time was in Dresden where he edited the *Dresdner Zeitung*. In May 1849 he took part in the Dresden uprising and became commandant of the barricade in the Sophienstrasse. He fled to Baden after the revolt was quelled and there, he was empowered by the provisional government of Baden to apply the decrees of June 9 and 23, 1849, concerning the confiscation of supplies for the insurgents and the raising of the militia. He was taken prisoner by Prussian soldiers but on October 8, 1849, he escaped from Rastatt."

(Just as, later on, Cherval "escaped" from Paris. But now comes the part of the bouquet which has the authentic police aroma—it should be borne in mind that this was printed two years after the Cologne Trials.)

"In the *Berliner Publizist* No. 39 of May 15, 1853, there was a report which was taken from a book printed in New York with the title 'The Victims of Espionage' by Wilhelm Hirsch, a Hamburg shop-assistant" (Oh Stieber, you innocent angel!). "In consequence of this Krause turned up in London late in 1850 or early in 1851 disguised as a political *émigré* and bearing the name Charles de Fleury. At first he lived in somewhat straitened circumstances but later, in 1851 his manner of life improved. For after he was admitted to the Communist League," (another Stieber lie), "he worked as an agent for a number of governments in the course of which, however, he became involved in a number of swindles."

So much for Stieber's gratitude to his friend Fleury who, moreover, (as we noted above) was sentenced to a number of years' imprisonment in London for forgery just a few months after the Cologne Trials. Concerning the worthy Hirsch we can read (*op. cit.*, p. 58):

"No. 265. Hirsch, Wilhelm, shop-assistant from Hamburg. It appears that he went to London not as a refugee but of his own accord." (Why this wholly superfluous lie? After all, Goldheim tried to arrest him in Hamburg!) "But once there he associated with refugees and especially with the Communist Party. He then played a double game. On the one hand he was active on behalf of the revolutionary party, while, on the other, he offered to spy on political criminals and forgers for a number of continental governments. . . . But he himself became implicated in the *worst possible frauds and swindles.* In particular, he was guilty of forgery on several occasions so that everyone should be on their guard against *him.* Together with various other individuals he even manufactured *false paper money* merely in order to extract huge rewards from the police for uncovering forgeries. He was unmasked by both sides," (namely, both by police forgers and other forgers?) "and he has now returned to Hamburg where he lives in poor circumstances."

Thus far Stieber on his London accomplices to whose "reliability and truthfulness" he is never tired of testifying. It is interesting to see how utterly impossible it is for this model Prussian to speak the simple truth. He cannot even restrain himself from scattering quite new and purposeless lies into the—true and false—facts already recorded. On the testimony of such professional liars—and they are more numerous now than ever—hundreds of people are sent to prison and in this fact lies what is usually called nowadays the salvation of the state.

E

NOTES ON *THE COMMUNIST TRIAL IN COLOGNE*
(APPENDIX 4 TO HERR VOGT)

1. This appeared first in 1860 as an appendix to *Herr Vogt* but was republished in the 1875 edition of the *Revelations*.
2. A conspiracy led by Dr. August Ladendorf, the son of a senator from Prenzlau. He was a bourgeois democrat who had long been active as the president of a popular club in Berlin. Together with other democrats some of whom had contacts with the workers' movement he was arrested in March 1853 thanks to the efforts of Hentze who acted as a police agent. Ladendorf was finally sentenced to five years hard labour. The trial, like the Cologne case was another instance of the determination of the Prussian government to smash the left-wing opposition.

[POSTSCRIPT TO THE *REVELATIONS CONCERNING THE COMMUNIST TRIAL* 1875]

KARL MARX

The editors of the *Volksstaat* think that the time is propitious for a reprint of the *Communist Trial in Cologne* which originally appeared in Boston, Mass., and in Basle. Almost the whole of the latter edition was confiscated at the German frontier. This work saw the light of day only a few weeks after the end of the trial. At that time the most pressing need was to make the facts known quickly and so errors of detail were unavoidable. For example, in the names of the Cologne jurymen. Also, it appears that the "Red Catechism" was written not by Moses Hess but by a man called Levy.[1] Furthermore, Wilhelm Hirsch maintains in his "Apologia" that Cherval's flight from gaol in Paris was the result of an arrangement between Greif, the French police and Cherval himself with the aim of using the latter as an informer in London while the trial was still proceeding. This is very plausible as Crämer (this was Cherval's true name) was wanted for forgery in Prussia and the threat to have him extradited would have made him amenable to such plans. My account of the course of events was based on "confessions" that Cherval made to a friend of mine. Hirsch's story shows up Stieber's perjury even more clearly, as well as the intrigues of the Prussian Embassies in London and Paris, and the shameless machinations of Hinckeldey.

When the *Volksstaat* started to reprint the pamphlet in its columns I hesitated a moment whether or not to omit Section VI (The Willich-Schapper Party). But on further reflection I decided that any mutilation of the text would entail the distortion of the historical record.

The violent suppression of a revolution leaves a powerful imprint upon the minds of those involved, especially if they are torn away from their homes and cast into exile. So that even people with steady personalities may lose their heads for a longer or shorter period. They can no longer keep pace with the march of events. They refuse to admit that history has changed direction. Hence that playing around with conspiracies and revolutions which compromises the cause they are serving no less than themselves; hence, too, the errors of Willich and Schapper. Willich has shown in the American Civil War that he is something more than a visonary and Schapper who had been a lifelong champion of the workers' movement saw and admitted his momentary aberration soon after the Cologne trial. On his deathbed many years later he spoke to me with cutting irony of the folly of the *émigrés* (*Flüchtlingstölpelei*) at that time. As opposed to this, however, the circumstances in which the "Communist Trial" was written may explain the bitterness of the attack on those who involuntarily aided and abetted the common enemy. To lose your head at moments of crisis is a crime against the Party, one which requires public atonement.

"*The whole existence of the political police depends on the result of this trial!*" These words were written by Hinckeldey to the Embassy in London during the court proceedings (See *Herr Vogt*, 1860, p. 27) and they contain the key to the Communist trial. "The whole existence of the political police", means more than the existence and the activities of the people directly concerned with police work. It means that the whole machinery of government including the courts (see the Prussian Disciplinary Law concerning the Judiciary of May 7, 1851) and the press (see the so-called "reptile fund")[2] was subordinated to the political police just as the state of Venice was made entirely subject to the Inquisition. The political police had been paralysed during the revolutionary outbreaks in Prussia and was now in need of reorganisation on the model of its counterpart in the Second French Empire.

After the revolution of 1848 was defeated the German workers' movement existed only as a theoretical propaganda organ and this only within very narrow limits; its nullity as a practical threat was quite evident to the Prussian government at all times. For the government the communist witchhunt was merely the overture to the reactionary crusade against the liberal bourgeoisie and the bourgeoisie itself strengthened the arm of the reaction, i.e. the political police by condemning the workers' leaders and condoning Stieber-Hinckeldey. So Stieber won his spurs at the Cologne Assizes. At that time the name Stieber meant no more than an obscure police official on the look-out for promotion and higher salary. Now Stieber is the symbol of the unfettered rule of the political police in the new Holy Prussian–German Empire. In a sense he has been transformed into a moral being—but only in the figurative sense in which, e.g., the Reichstag is a moral being. And on this occasion the political police does not hit out at the workers in order to beat the bourgeoisie. But the other way round. It is just because of his position as dictator of the German liberal bourgeoisie that Bismarck thinks himself strong enough to "Stieber" the workers' party out of existence. The very increase in Stieber's importance can be used by the German proletariat as an index to the progress made by the movement since the communist trial in Cologne.

The infallibility of the Pope is child's-play compared to the infallibility of the political police. For decades they incarcerated youthful hotheads who enthused over German unity, the German Reich and the German Emperor, and now they will happily imprison even old men with bald pates who decline to enthuse about such gifts of God. And the attempt to root out the enemies of the Reich is just as futile as earlier attempts to eliminate its friends. What more crushing proof could be wanted of the fact that the police is not called upon to make history, even though it be no more than the history of the conflict over the Emperor's beard!

The Communist Trial in Cologne itself laid bare the impotence of the state in its battle to halt the development of social processes. His Prussian Majesty's State Prosecutor ultimately based his proof of the guilt of the accused on the fact that they had secretly circulated the subversive principles of the "Communist Manifesto". And despite this, is it not so that twenty years later these very same principles are proclaimed on the streets in Germany? Do they not resound in the speeches in the Reichstag itself? Have they not defied all governmental interdicts and travelled all over the world in the "Programme of the International Workingmen's Association"? The fact is that Society will not recover its equilibrium until it rotates around the sun of labour. The "Communist Trial" ends with the words: "Jena! . . . that is our last word to a government that requires such methods in order to survive and to a society that needs such a government for its protection. The word that should stand at the end of the Communist Trial is . . . Jena!" A Treitschke will sneer and say this was a fine prophecy and he will point proudly to the Mauser gun and Prussia's latest victorious passage of arms. It is enough for me to recall that just as there is an "inner" victory at Düppel[3] so too is there an *inner Jena!*

NOTES ON THE POSTSCRIPT (TO THE *REVELATIONS CONCERNING THE COMMUNIST TRIAL IN COLOGNE*) 1875

1. Marx was right the first time: the Red Catechism was in fact written by Moses Hess.
2. The "reptile funds" were funds derived from the confiscated property of the Hanoverian royal household. Bismarck used them for "special purposes", in particular to bribe the bourgeois press (the *Pressereptile*) and to make it dependent on him.
3. The Prussian war against Denmark of 1864 was decided by the storming of the fortifications of Düppel by the Prussian troops. It signalled also the further strengthening within Prussia of the supremacy of the Junkers over the middle classes.

HEROES OF THE EXILE

KARL MARX
AND FREDERICK ENGELS

HEROES OF THE EXILE[1]

"Singe, unsterbliche Seele,
der sündigen Menschen Erlösung"[2]—
[Sing, immortal soul
the redemption of fallen
mankind]—through Gottfried Kinkel.

Gottfried Kinkel was born some 40 years ago. The story of his life has been made available to us in an autobiography, *Gottfried Kinkel. Truth without Poetry. A biographical sketch-book.* Edited by Adolph Strodtmann. (Hamburg, Hoffmann & Campe, 1850, octavo.)

Gottfried is the hero of that democratic Siegwart[3] epoch that flooded Germany with endless torrents of tearful lament and patriotic melancholy. He made his debut as a simple lyrical Siegwart.

We are indebted to Strodtmann the Apostle, whose "narrative compilation" we follow here, both for the diary-like fragments in which his pilgrimage on this earth is paraded before the reader, and for the glaring lack of discretion of the revelations they contain.

"Bonn, February–September 1834
Like his friend, Paul Zeller, young Gottfried studied Protestant theology and his piety and industry earned him the admiration of his celebrated teachers" (Sack, Nitzsch and Bleck, p. 5).

From the very beginning he is "obviously immersed in weighty speculations" (p. 4), he is "tormented and gloomy" as befits a budding genius. "Gottfried's gloomily flashing brown eyes" "lit upon" some youths "in brown jackets and pale-blue overcoats"; he at once sensed that these youths wished "to make up for their inner emptiness by outer show" (p. 6). He explains his moral indignation by pointing out that he had "defended Hegel and Marheinicke" when these lads had called Marheinicke a "blockhead"; later, when he himself goes to study in Berlin and is himself in the position of having to learn from Marheinicke he characterises him in his diary with the following belletristic epigram (p. 61):

"Ein Kerl ,der spekuliert,
ist wie ein Tier auf dürrer Heide
von einem bösen Geist im Kreis herumgeführt,
und ringsumher ist schöne grüne Weide."

[I tell you a chap who's intellectual
Is like a beast on a blasted heath
Driven in circles by a demon
While a fine green meadow lies round beneath.][4]

Gottfried has clearly forgotten that other verse in which Mephisto-
pheles makes fun of the student thirsting for knowledge:

"Verachte nur Verstand und Wissenschaft!"
[Only look down on knowledge and reason!][5]

However, the whole moralising Student Scene serves merely as an
introduction enabling the future Liberator of the World to make the
following revelation (p. 6).
    Listen to Gottfried:

"This race will not perish, unless a great war comes. . . . Only
strong remedies will raise this age up from the mire!"
"A second Flood with you as a second and improved edition of
Noah!" his friend replied.

The light brown overcoats have helped Gottfried to the point where
he can proclaim himself the "Noah in a new Flood". His friend responds
with a comment that might well have served as the motto to the whole
biography.

"My father and I have often had occasion to smile at your *passion
for unclear ideas!*"

Throughout these Confessions of a Beautiful Soul[6] we find repeated
only one "clear idea", namely that Kinkel was a great man from the
moment of his conception. The most trivial things that occur to all
trivial people become momentous events; the petty joys and sorrows
that every student of theology experiences in a more interesting form,
the conflicts with bourgeois conditions to be found by the dozen in
every consistory and refectory in Germany become world-shaking
events from which Gottfried, overwhelmed by Weltschmerz, fashions
a perpetual comedy. [Thus we find that these confessions consistently
present a double aspect—there is firstly the *comedy*, the amusing way
in which Gottfried interprets the smallest trivia as signs of his future
greatness and casts himself in relief from the outset. And then there is
the *rodomontade*, his trick of complacently embellishing in retrospect

every little occurrence in his theologico-lyrical past. Having established these two basic features we can return to the further developments in Gottfried's story.]*

The family [of his "friend Paul" leaves Bonn and] returns to Württemberg. Gottfried stages this event in the following manner.

Gottfried loves Paul's sister and uses the occasion to explain that he has "already been in love twice before"! His present love, however, is no ordinary love but a "fervent and authentic act of divine worship" (p. 13). Gottfried climbs the Drachenfels together with friend Paul and against this romantic backcloth he breaks into dithyrambs:

> "Farewell to friendship!—I shall find a brother in our Saviour;— Farewell to love—Faith shall be my bride;—Farewell to sisterly loyalty—I am come to the commune of many thousands of just souls! Away then, O my youthful heart, learn to be alone with your God; struggle with him until you conquer him and force him to give you a new name, that of Holy Israel which no-one knows but he who receives it! I give you greetings, you glorious rising sun, image of my awakening soul!" (p. 17).

We see how the departure of his friend gives Gottfried the opportunity to sing an ecstatic hymn to his own soul. As if that were not enough, his friend too must join in the hymn. For while Gottfried exults ecstatically he speaks "with exalted voice and glowing countenance", he "forgets the presence of his friend", "his gaze is transfigured", "his voice inspired", etc. (p. 17)—in short we have the vision of the Prophet Elijah as it appears in the Bible complete in every detail.

> "Smiling sorrowfully Paul looked at him with his loyal gaze and said: 'You have a mightier heart in your bosom than I and *will surely outdistance me*—but let me be your friend—even when I am far away.' Joyfully Gottfried clasped the proferred hand and renewed the ancient covenant" (p. 18).

Gottfried has got what he wants from this Transfiguration on the Mount. Friend Paul who has just been laughing at "Gottfried's passion for unclear ideas" humbles himself before the name of "holy Israel" and acknowledges Gottfried's superiority and future greatness. Gottfried is as pleased as Punch and graciously condescends to renew the ancient covenant.

* Passages in square brackets were struck out by Marx in the MS.

The scene changes. It is the birthday of Kinkel's mother, the wife of Pastor Kinkel of Upper Cassel. The family festival is used to proclaim that "his mother, like the mother of our Lord, was called Mary" (p. 20)—certain proof that Gottfried, too, was destined to be a saviour and redeemer. Thus within the space of twenty pages our student of theology has been led by the most insignificant events to cast himself as *Noah*, as the holy *Israel*, as *Elijah*, and, lastly, as *Christ*.

Inevitably, Gottfried, who when it comes to the point has experienced nothing, constantly dwells on his inner feelings. The Pietism that has stuck to this parson's son and would-be scholar of divinity is well adapted both to his innate emotional instability and his coquettish preoccupation with his own person. We learn that his mother and sister were both strict Pietists and that Gottfried was powerfully conscious of his own sinfulness. The conflict of this pious sense of sin with the "carefree and sociable joie de vivre" of the ordinary student appears in Gottfried, as befits his world-historical mission, in terms of a struggle between religion and poetry. The pint of beer that the parson's son from Upper Cassel downs with the other students becomes the fateful chalice in which Faust's twin spirits are locked in battle. In the description of his pietistic family life we see his "Mother Mary" combat as sinful "Gottfried's penchant for the theatre" (p. 28), a momentous conflict designed to prefigure the poet of the future but which in fact merely highlights Gottfried's love of the theatrical. The harpy-like puritanism of his sister Johanna is revealed by an incident in which she boxed the ears of a five-year-old girl for inattention in church—sordid family gossip whose inclusion would be incomprehensible were it not for the revelation at the end of the book that this same sister Johanna put up the strongest opposition to Gottfried's marriage to Mme. Mockel.

One event held to be worthy of mention is that in Seelscheid Gottfried preached "a wonderful sermon about the wilting wheat".

The Zelter family and "beloved Elise" finally take their departure. We learn that Gottfried "squeezed the girl's hand passionately" and murmured the greeting, "Elise, farewell! I must say no more". This interesting story is followed by the first of Siegwart's laments.

"Destroyed!" "Without a sound." "Most agonising torment!" "Burning brow." "Deepest sighs," "His mind was lacerated by the wildest pains", etc. (p. 37).

It turns the whole Elijah-like scene into the purest comedy, performed for the benefit of his "friend Paul" and himself. Paul again makes his appearance in order to whisper into the ear of Siegwart who is sitting there alone and wretched: "This kiss is for my Gottfried" (p. 38).

And Gottfried at once cheers up.

"My plan to see my sweet love again, honourably and *not without a name*, is firmer than ever" (p. 38).

Even amid the pangs of love he does not fail to comment on the name he expects to make, or to brag of the laurels he claims in advance. Gottfried uses the intermezzo to commit his love to paper in extravagant and vainglorious terms, to make sure that the world is not deprived of even his diary-feelings. But the scene has not yet reached its climax. The faithful Paul has to point out to our barnstorming maestro that if Elise were to remain stationary while he continued to develop, she might not satisfy him later on.

"O no!" said Gottfried. "This heavenly budding flower whose first leaves have scarcely opened already smells so sweetly. How much greater will be her beauty when... [—] the burning summer *ray* of manly *vigour* unfolds *her innermost calix!*" (p. 40).

Paul finds himself reduced to answering this sordid image by remarking that rational arguments mean nothing to poets.

"'And all your wisdom will not protect you from the whims of life better than our *lovable* folly' Gottfried *replied with a smile*" (p. 40).

What a moving picture: Narcissus smiling to himself! The gauche student suddenly enters as the lovable fool, Paul becomes Wagner[7] and admires the great man; and the great man "smiles", "indeed, he smiles a kind, gentle smile". The climax is saved.

Gottfried finally manages to leave Bonn, He gives this summary of his educational attainments to date.

"Unfortunately I am increasingly unable to accept Hegelianism; my highest aspiration is to be a rationalist, at the same time I am a supernaturalist and a mystic, *if necessary* I am even a Pietist" (p. 45).

This self-analysis requires no commentary.

"Berlin, October 1834–August 1835."
Leaving his narrow family and student environment Gottfried arrives in Berlin. In comparison with Bonn Berlin is relatively metropolitan but of this we find no trace in Gottfried any more than we find evidence of his involvement in the scientific activity of the day. Gottfried's diary entries confine themselves to the emotions he experiences together with his new *compagnon d'aventure*, Hugo Dünweg from Barmen, and also to the minor hardships of an indigent theologian: his money difficulties, shabby coats, employment as a reviewer, etc. His life stands in no relation to that of the public life of the city, but only to the Schlössing family in which Dünweg passes for *Master Wolfram* [von Eschenbach] and Gottfried for Master *Gottfried von Strasbourg* (p. 67).[8] Elise fades gradually from his heart and he conceives a new itch for Miss Maria Schlössing. Unfortunately he learns of Elise's engagement to someone else and he sums up his Berlin feelings and aspirations as a "dark longing for a woman he could [call] *wholly* his own".

However, Berlin must not be abandoned without the inevitable climax:

"Before he left Berlin Weiss, the old theatre producer, took him *once again* into the theatre. A strange feeling came over the youth as the friendly old man led him into the great auditorium where the busts of German dramatists have been placed and with a gesture towards a few empty niches said meaningfully:
'There are still some vacant places!' "

Yes, indeed, there is still a place vacant awaiting our Platenite[9] Gottfried who solemnly allows an old clown to flatter him with the exquisite pleasure of "future immortality".

"Bonn, Autumn 1835—Autumn 1837"
"Constantly balancing between art, life and science, unable to reach a decision, active in all three without firm commitment, he resolved to learn, to gain and to be creative in all three as much as his indecision would permit" (p. 89).

Having thus discovered himself to be an irresolute dilettante Gottfried returns to Bonn. Of course, the feeling that he is a dilettante does not deter him from taking his Licentiate examination and from becoming a Privatdozent at the university of Bonn.

"Neither Chamisso nor Knapp[10] had published the poems he had sent them in their magazines and this upset him greatly" (p. 99).

This is the public debut of the great man who in private circles lives on intellectual tick on the promise of his future eminence. From this time on he definitely becomes a hero of dubious local significance in belletristic student circles until the moment when a glancing shot in Baden suddenly turns him into the hero of the German Philistines.

"But more and more there arose in Kinkel's breast the yearning for a firm, true love, a yearning that no devotion to work could dispel" (p. 103).

The first victim of this yearning is a certain Minna. Gottfried dallies with Minna and sometimes for the sake of variety he acts the compassionate Mahadeva[11] who allows the maiden to worship him while he meditates on the state of her health.

"Kinkel could have loved her had he been able to deceive himself about her condition; but his love would have *killed* the wilting rose even more quickly. Minna was the first girl that could understand him; but she was a second Hecuba and would have borne him torches and not children, and through them the passion of the parents would have burnt down their own house as Priam's passion burned Troy. Yet he could not abandon her, his heart bled for her, *he was indeed wretched not through love, but through pity.*"

The godlike hero whose love can kill, like the sight of Jupiter, is nothing but an ordinary self-regarding young puppy who in the course of his marriage studies tries out the role of the cad for the first time. His revolting meditations on her health and its possible effects on children become the occasion for the base decision to prolong the relationship for his own pleasure and to break it off only when it provides him with the excuse for yet another melodramatic scene.

Gottfried goes on a journey to visit an uncle whose son has just died; at the midnight hour in the room where the corpse is laid out he stages a scene from a Bellini opera with his cousin, Mlle. Elise II. He becomes engaged to her, "in the presence of the dead" and on the following morning his uncle gladly accepts him as his future son-in-law.

"Now that he was lost to her forever, he often thought of Minna and of the moment when he would see her again. But he was not afraid as she could have no claims on a heart that was already bound" (p. 117).

The new engagement means nothing but the opportunity to bring about a dramatic explosion in his relationship with Minna. In this crisis we find "duty and passion"[12] confronting each other. This explosion is produced in the most philistine and rascally way because our bonhomme denies Minna's legal claims upon his heart which is already committed elsewhere. Our virtuous hero is of course not at all disturbed by the need to compound this lie to himself by reversing the order of events in the matter of his "bound heart".

Gottfried has plunged into the interesting necessity of being forced to break "a poor, great heart".

"After a pause Gottfried went on: 'At the same time, Minna, I feel I owe you an apology—I have sinned against you—the hand which I let you have yesterday with such feelings of friendship, that hand is no longer free—I am engaged!' " (p. 123).

Our melodramatic student takes good care not to mention that this engagement took place a few hours after he had given her his hand "with such feelings of friendship".

"Oh God!—Minna—can you forgive me?" (*loc. cit.*)
"I am a man and must be faithful to my *duty*—I *may* not love you! But I have not deceived you" (p. 124).

After re-arranging his duty after the fact it only remains to produce the unbelievable. He dramatically reverses the whole relationship so that instead of Minna forgiving him, our moral priest forgives the deceived woman. With this in mind he conceives the possibility that Minna "might hate him from afar" and he follows this supposition up with this final moral:

" 'I would gladly forgive you for that and if that were the case you can be assured of my forgiveness in advance. And now farewell, my duty calls me, I must leave you!' He slowly left the arbour . . . from that hour on Gottfried was unhappy" (p. 124).

The actor and self-styled lover is transformed into the hypocrytical priest who extricates himself from the affair with an unctuous blessing; Siegwart's sham conflicts of love have led to the happy result that he is able in his imagination to think himself unhappy.

It finally becomes apparent that all of these arranged love stories were nothing but Gottfried's coquettish infatuation with himself. The whole affair amounts to no more than that our priest with his dreams of future immortality has produced Old Testament stories and modern lending-library phantasies after the manner of Spiess, Clauren and Cramer[13] so that he may indulge his vanity by posing as a romantic hero.

"Rummaging among his books he came across Novalis' *Ofter-dingen*[14] the book that had so often inspired him to write poetry a year before. While still at school he and some friends had founded a society by the name of *Teutonia* with the aim of increasing their understanding of German history and literature. In this society he had assumed the name of *Heinrich von Ofterdingen*. . . . Now the meaning of this name became clear to him. *He saw himself as that same Heinrich* in the charming little town at the foot of the Wartburg and a longing for the 'Blue Flower' took hold of him with overwhelming force. Minna could not be the glorious fairy-tale bloom, nor could she be his bride, however anxiously he probed his heart. Dreaming, he read on and on, the phantastic world of magic enveloped him and he ended by hurling himself weeping into a chair, thinking of the 'Blue Flower'."

Gottfried here unveils the whole romantic lie which he had woven around himself; the carnival gift of disguising oneself as other people is his authentic "inner being". Earlier on he had called himself Gottfried von Strasbourg; now he appears as *Heinrich von Ofterdingen*[14] and he is searching not for the "Blue Flower" but for a woman who will acknowledge his claims to be Heinrich von Ofterdingen. And in the end he really did find the "Blue Flower", a little faded and yellow, in a woman who played the much longed-for comedy in his interest and in her own.

The sham Romanticism, the travesty and the caricature of ancient stories and romances which Gottfried *re-lives* to make up for the lack of any inner substance of his own, the whole emotional swindle of his vacuous encounters with Mary, Minna and Elise I & II have brought him to the point where he thinks that his experiences are on a par with those of Goethe. Just as Goethe had suddenly rushed off to Italy, there

to write his *Roman Elegies* after undergoing the storms of love, so too
Gottfried thinks that his day-dreams of love qualify him for a trip to
Rome. Goethe must have had a premonition of Gottfried:

> *Hat doch der Walfisch seine Laus,*
> *Kann ich auch meine haben.*
>
> [And if the whale has his lice
> I can have them too][15]

"Italy, October 1837–March 1838"

The trip to Rome opens in Gottfried's diary with a lengthy account
of the journey from Bonn to Coblenz. This new epoch begins as the
previous one had concluded, namely with a narrative richly embellished
by allusions to the experiences of others. While on the steamer Gottfried
recalls the "splendid passage in Hoffmann" where he "made Master
Johannes Wacht produce a highly artistic work immediately after
enduring the most overwhelming grief". As a confirmation of the
"splendid passage" Gottfried follows up his "overwhelming grief"
about Minna by *"meditating"* about a "tragedy he had long since
intended to write" (p. 140).

During Kinkel's journey from Coblenz to Rome the following
events take place:

> "The friendly letters he frequently receives from his fiancée and
> which he answers for the most part on the spot, dispel his gloomy
> thoughts" (p. 144).
> "His love for the beautiful Elise II struck root deeply in the
> youth's yearning bosom" (p. 146).

In Rome we find:

> "On his arrival in Rome Kinkel had found a letter from his
> fiancée awaiting him which further intensified his love for her and
> caused the image of Minna to fade even more into the background.
> His heart assured him that Elise could make him happy and he gave
> himself up to this feeling with the purest passion. . . . Only now did
> he realize what love is" (p. 151).

We see that Minna whom he only loved out of pity has re-entered
the emotional scene. In his relationship with Elise his dream is that she

will make him happy, not he her. And yet in his "Blue Flower" fantasy he had already said that the fairy-tale blossom which had given him such a poetic itch could be neither Elise nor Minna. His newly aroused feelings for these two girls now serve as part of the mis-en-scène for a new conflict.

"Kinkel's poetry seemed to be slumbering in Italy" (p. 151). Why?

"Because he lacked *form*" (p. 152).

We learn later that a six-month stay in Italy enabled him to bring the "form" back to Germany well wrapped up. As Goethe had written his *Elegies* in Rome so Kinkel too meditated on an elegy called "*The Awakening of Rome*" (p. 153).

Kinkel's maid brings him a letter from his fiancée. He opens it joyfully—

"and sank back on his bed with a cry. Elise announced that a wealthy man, a Dr. D. with an extensive practice and even a riding horse had asked for her hand in marriage. As it would probably be a long time before he, Kinkel, an indigent theologian, would have a permanent position she asked him to release her from the bonds that tied her to him".

A scene taken over lock, stock and barrel from [Kotzebue's] *Misanthropy and Remorse*.[16] Gottfried "annihilated", "foul putrefaction", "dry eyed", "thirst for revenge", "dagger", "the bosom of his rival", "heart-blood of his enemy", "cold as ice", "maddening pain", etc. (p. 156 and 157).

The element in these "Sorrows and Joys of a poor Theologian" that gives most pain to our unhappy student is the thought that she had "spurned him for the sake of the uncertain possession of earthly goods" (p. 157). Having been moved by the relevant theatrical feelings he finally rises to the following consolation:

"She was unworthy of you—and you still possess the pinions of genius that will bear you aloft high above this dark misery! And *when one day your fame encircles the globe* the false woman will find a judge in her own heart!—Who knows, perhaps one day in the years to come *her children* will seek me out to implore my aid and *I would not wish to miss that*" (p. 157).

Having, inevitably, enjoyed in advance the exquisite pleasure of "his future fame encircling the globe" he reveals himself to be a common philistinic cleric. He speculates that later on Elise's children will come to beg alms from the great poet—and this he would "not wish to miss". And why? Because Elise prefers a horse to the "future fame" of which he constantly dreams, because she prefers "earthly goods" to the farce he intends to perform with himself in the role of Heinrich von Ofterdingen. Old Hegel was quite right when he pointed out that a noble consciousness always transposes into a base one.[17]

"Bonn. Summer 1838–Summer 1843"
(Intrigue and Love)

Having furnished a caricature of Goethe in Italy, Gottfried now resolves on his return to produce Schiller's *Intrigue and Love*.[18] Though his heart is rent with Weltschmerz Gottfried feels "better than ever" physically (p. 167). His intention is "to establish literary fame for himself through his works" (p. 169), which does not prevent him from acquiring a cheaper fame without works later on when his "works" failed to do what was expected of them.

The "dark longing" which Gottfried always experiences when he pursues a woman finds expression in a remarkably rapid succession of engagements and promises of marriage. The promise of marriage is the classical method by which the strong man and the superior mind "of the future" seeks to conquer his beloved and bind her to him in reality. As soon as the poet catches sight of a little blue flower that might assist him in his efforts to become Heinrich von Ofterdingen, the gentle mists of emotion assume the firm shape of the student's dream of perfecting the ideal affinity by the addition of the bond of "duty". No sooner are the first greetings over than offers of marriage fly in all directions *à tort et à travers* towards every Daisy and Water Lily in sight. This bourgeois hunt puts in an even more revolting light the unprincipled tail-wagging coquetry with which Gottfried constantly opens his heart to reveal all "the torments of the great poet".

Thus after his return from Italy Gottfried naturally has to "promise" marriage yet again. The object of his passion on this occasion was directly chosen by his sister, the pietistic Johanna whose fanaticism has already been immortalised by the exclamations in Gottfried's diary.

"Bögehold had just recently announced his engagement to Miss Kinkel and Johanna who was more importunate than ever in her meddling in her brother's affairs of the heart now conceived the wish, for a number of reasons concerning the family, that Gottfried should *reciprocate* and marry Miss Sophie Bögehold, her fiancé's sister" (p. 172). It goes without saying that "Kinkel *could not but* feel drawn to a gentle girl. . . . And she was indeed a dear, innocent maiden" p.(173). "In the most tender fashion"—it goes without saying—"Kinkel asked for her hand which was joyfully promised him by her parents as soon as"—it goes without saying—"he had established himself in a job and was in a position to lead his bride to the home of—it goes without saying—a professor or a parson."

On this occasion our passionate student set down in elegant verses an account of that tendency towards marriage that forms such a constant ingredient of his adventures.

> *"Nach anders nichts trag' ich Verlangen*
> *Als nur nach einer weissen Hand!"*

> [Nought else can stir my passion
> So much as a white hand]

Everything else, eyes, lips, locks is dismissed as a mere "trifle".

> *"Das alles reizt nicht sein Verlangen*
> *Allein die kleine weisse Hand!"* (p. 174)

> [All these fail to stir his passion
> Nought does so but her small, white hand]

He describes the flirtation that he begins with Miss Sophie Bögehold at the command of "his meddling sister Johanna" and spurred on by the unquenchable longing for a hand, as "deep, firm and tranquil" (p. 175). Above all "it is the *religious* element that predominates in this new love" (p. 176).

In Gottfried's romances we often find the religious element alternating with the novelistic and theatrical element. Where he cannot devise dramatic effects to achieve new Siegwart situations he applies religious feelings to adorn these banal episodes with the patina of higher meaning. Siegwart becomes a pious Jung-Stilling[19] who had likewise received such miraculous strength from God that even though three women perished beneath his manly chest he was still able repeatedly to lead a new love to his home.

We come finally to the fateful catastrophe of this eventful life-history, to Stilling's meeting with *Johanna Mockel*, who had formerly borne the married name of Mathieux. Here Gottfried discovered a female Kinkel, his romantic *alter ego*. Only she was harder, smarter, less confused and thanks to her greater age she had left her youthful illusions behind her.

What Mockel had in common with Kinkel was the fact that her talents too had gone unrecognised by the world. She was repulsive and vulgar; her first marriage had been unhappy. She possessed musical talents but they were insufficient to enable her to make a name with her compositions or technical mastery. In Berlin her attempt to imitate the stale childhood antics of Bettina [von Arnim][20] had led to a fiasco. Her character had been soured by her experiences. Even though she shared with Kinkel the affectation of inflating the ordinary events of her life so as to invest them with a "more exalted, sacred meaning", owing to her more advanced age she nevertheless felt a *need* for love (according to Strodtmann) that was more pressing than her need for the "poetic" drivel that accompanies it. Whereas Kinkel was feminine in this respect, Mockel was masculine. Hence nothing could be more natural than for such a person to enter with joy into Kinkel's comedy of the misunderstood tender souls and to play it to a satisfying conclusion, i.e. to acknowledge Siegwart's fitness for the role of Heinrich von Ofterdingen and to arrange for him to discover that she was the "Blue Flower".

Kinkel, having been led to his third or fourth fiancée by his sister was now introduced into a new labyrinth of love by Mockel.

Gottfried now found himself in the "social swim", i.e. in one of those little circles consisting of the professors or other worthies of German university towns. Only in the lives of Teutonic, christian students can such societies form such a turning point. Mockel sang and was applauded. At table it was arranged that Gottfried should sit next to her and here the following scene took place:

" 'It must be a glorious feeling', Gottfried opined, 'to fly through the joyous world on the pinions of genius, admired by all'—'I should *say* so', Mockel exclaimed. 'I hear that you have a great gift for poetry. Perhaps people will scatter incense for you *also* . . . and I shall ask you then if you can be happy if you are not. . . .'—'If I am not?' Gottfried asked, as she paused" (p. 188).

The bait has been put out for our clumsy lyrical student.

Mockel then informed him that recently she had heard

"him preaching about the yearning of Christians to return to their faith and she had thought about how resolutely the handsome preacher must have abandoned the world if he could arouse a timid longing even in her for the harmless childhood slumber with which the echo of faith now lost had once surrounded her" (p. 189).

Gottfried was "enchanted" (p. 189) by such politeness. He was tremendously pleased to discover that "Mockel was unhappy" (*loc. cit.*). He immediately resolved "to devote his passionate enthusiasm for the faith of salvation at the hands of Jesus Christ to bringing back this sorrowing soul *too* into the fold" (*loc. cit.*). As Mockel was a Catholic the friendship was formed on the imaginary basis of the task of recovering a soul "in the service of the Almighty", a comedy in which Mockel too was willing to participate.

"In 1840 Kinkel was appointed as an assistant in the Protestant community in Cologne where he went every Sunday to preach" (p. 193).

This biographical comment may serve as an excuse for a brief discussion of Kinkel's position as a theologian. "In 1840" the critical movement had already made devastating inroads into the content of the Christian faith; with Bruno Bauer[21] science had reached the point of open conflict with the state. It is at this juncture that Kinkel makes his debut as a preacher. But as he lacks both the energy of the orthodox and the understanding that would enable him to see theology objectively, he comes to terms with Christianity on the level of lyrical and declamatory sentimentality à la Krummacher. That is to say, he presents a Christ who is a "friend and leader", he seeks to do away with formal aspects of Christianity that he proclaims to be "ugly", and for the content he substitutes a hollow phraseology. The device by means of which content is replaced by form and ideas by phrases has produced a host of declamatory priests in Germany whose tendencies naturally led them finally in the direction of [liberal] *democracy*. But whereas in theology at least a superficial knowledge is still essential here and there, in the democratic movement where an orotund but vacuous rhetoric, *nullité sonore*, makes intellect and an insight into realities completely superfluous, an empty phraseology came into its own. Kinkel whose theological studies had led to nothing beyond the making of sentimental extracts of Christianity in the manner of Clauren's popular novels, was in speech and in his writings the very epitome of the fake pulpit oratory that is sometimes described as "poetic prose" and which he now comically made the basis of his "poetic mission". This latter, moreover, did not consist in planting true laurels but only red rowan berries with which he beautified the highway of trivia. This same feebleness of character which attempts to overcome conflicts not by resolving their content but by clothing them in an attractive form is visible too in the way he lectures at the university. The struggle to abolish the old scholastic pedantry is sidestepped by means of a "hearty" attitude which turns the lecturer into a student and exalts the student placing him on an equal footing with the lecturer. This school then produced a whole generation of Strodtmanns, Schurzes and suchlike who were able to make use of their phraseology, their knowledge and their easily acquired "lofty mission" only in the democratic movement.

Kinkel's new love develops into the story of *Gockel, Hinkel und Gackeleia*.[22]

The year 1840 was a turning point in the history of Germany. On the one hand, the critical application of Hegel's philosophy to theology and politics had brought about a scientific revolution. On the other hand, the coronation of Frederick William IV saw the emergence of a bourgeois movement whose constitutional aspirations still possessed a wholly radical veneer, varying from the vague "political poetry" of the period to the new phenomenon of a daily press with revolutionary powers.

What was Gottfried doing during this period? Together with Mockel he founded the "Maybug" (*Maikäfer*) "a Journal for non-Philistines" (p. 209) and the Maybug Club. The aim of this paper was nothing more than "to provide a cheerful and enjoyable evening for a group of friends once a week and to give the participants the opportunity to present their works for criticism by a benevolent, artistically-minded audience" (pp. 209–10).

The actual purpose of the Maybug Club was to solve the riddle of the Blue Flower. The meetings took place in Mockel's house, where, surrounded by a group of insignificant students Mockel paraded as "Queen" (p. 210) and Kinkel as "Minister" (p. 225). Here our two misunderstood beautiful souls found it possible to make up for the "injustice the harsh world had done them" (p. 296); each could acknowledge the right of the other to the respective roles of Heinrich von Ofterdingen and the Blue Flower. Gottfried to whom the aping of other people's roles had become second nature must have felt happy to have created such a "theatre for connoisseurs" (p. 254). The farce itself acted as the prelude to practical developments:

"These evenings provided the opportunity to see Mockel also in the house of her parents" (p. 212).

Moreover, the Maybug Club copied also the Göttinger Hain[23] poets, only with the difference that the latter represented a stage in the development of German literature while the former remained on the level of an insignificant local caricature. The "merry Maybugs" Sebastian Longard, Leo Hasse, C. A. Schlönbach, etc., were, as the biographical apologia admits, pale, insipid, indolent, unimportant youths (pp. 211 and 298).

Naturally, Gottfried soon began to make "comparisons" (p. 221) between Mockel and his fiancée, but he had "had no time hitherto"— much against his usual habit—"to reflect at all about weddings and marriage" (p. 219). In a word, he stood like Buridan's ass between the two bundles of hay, unable to decide between them. With her greater maturity and very practical bent Mockel "clearly discerned the invisible bond" (p. 225); she resolved to give "chance or the will of God" (p. 229) a helping hand.

"At a time of day when Kinkel was usually prevented by his scientific labours from seeing Mockel, he one day went to visit her and as he quietly approached her room he heard the sound of a mournful song. Pausing to listen he heard this song:

> "*Du nahst! Und wie Morgenröte*
> *Bebt's über die Wangen mein, usw. usw.*
> *Viel namenlose Schmerzen:*
> *Wehe Du fühlst es nicht!*
>
> [You draw nigh! And like the dawn
> There trembles on my cheeks, etc. etc.
> Many a nameless pain.
> Alas, you feel them not!]

A long drawn-out, melancholy chord concluded her song and faded gradually in the breeze" (pp. 230 and 231).

Gottfried crept away unobserved, as he imagined, and having arrived home again he found the situation very interesting. He wrote a

large number of despairing sonnets in which he compared Mockel to
the Lorelei (p. 233). In order to escape from the Lorelei and to remain
true to Miss Sophie Bögehold he tried to obtain a post as a teacher in
Wiesbaden, but was rejected. This accident was compounded by a
further intervention by Fate which proved to be decisive. Not only was
the "sun striving to leave the sign of Virgo" (p. 236), but also Gottfried
and Mockel took a trip down the Rhine in a skiff; their skiff was over-
turned by an approaching steam-boat and Gottfried swam ashore
bearing Mockel.

> "As he drew towards the shore he felt her heart close to his and
> was suddenly overwhelmed by the feeling that only *this* woman
> would be able to make him happy" (p. 238).

On this occasion the experience that Gottfried has undergone is
from a real novel and not merely an imaginary one: it is to be found in
[Goethe's] *Elective Affinities*. This decided the matter; he broke off his
engagement to Sophie Bögehold.

First love, then the intrigue. In the name of the Presbytery Pastor
Engels protested to Gottfried that the marriage of a divorced Catholic
woman to a Protestant preacher was offensive. Gottfried replied by
appealing to the eternal rights of man and made the following points
with a good deal of unction.

> "1. It was no crime for him to have drunk coffee with the lady in
> Hirzekümpchen" (p. 249).
> "2. The matter is ambiguous as he had neither announced in
> public that he intended to marry the lady, nor that he did not intend
> to do so" (p. 251).
> "3. As far as faith is concerned, no-one can know what the future
> holds in store" (p. 250).
> "And with that out of the way, may I ask you to step inside and
> have a cup of coffee" (p. 251).

With this slogan Gottfried and Pastor Engels, who could not resist
such an invitation, left the stage. In this way, quietly and yet forcefully
Gottfried was able to resolve the conflict with the powers that be.

The following extract serves to illustrate the effect of the Maybug
Club on Gottfried:

"It was June 29, 1841. On this day the first anniversary of the Maybug Club was to be celebrated on a grand scale" (p. 253). "A shout as of one voice arose to decide who should carry off the prize. Modestly Gottfried bent his knee before the Queen who placed the inevitable laurel wreath on his glowing brow, while the setting sun cast its brightest rays over the transfigured countenance of the poet" (p. 285).

The solemn dedication of the imagined poetic fame of Heinrich von Ofterdingen is followed by the feelings and the wishes of the Blue Flower. That evening Mockel sang a Maybug anthem she had composed which ends with the following strophe symptomatic of the whole work:

"*Und was lernt man aus der Geschicht'?*
Maikäfer, flieg!
Wer alt ist kriegt kein Weiblein mehr,
Drum hör', bedenk' dich nicht zu sehr!
Maikäfer, flieg!

[And what's the moral of the tale?
Fly, Maybug, fly!
A man who's old will ne'er find wife,
So make haste, do not waste your life,
Fly, Maybug, fly!]

The ingenuous biographer remarks that "the invitation to marriage contained in the song was wholly free of any ulterior motives" (p. 255). Gottfried perceived the ulterior motives but "was anxious not to miss" the opportunity of being crowned for two further years before the whole Maybug Club and of being an object of passion. So he married Mockel on May 22, 1843 after she had become a member of the Protestant Church despite her lack of faith. This was done on the shabby pretext that "definite articles of faith are less important in the Protestant church than the *ethical* spirit" (p. 315).

Und das lernt man aus der Geschicht',
Traut keiner blauen Blume nicht!

[So that's the moral of the tale:
The Bluest Flower will soon grow stale.]

Gottfried had established the relationship with Mockel on the pretext of leading her out of her unfaith into the Protestant Church. Mockel now demanded the *Life of Jesus* by D. F. Strauss and lapsed into paganism, "while with heavy heart he followed her on the path of doubt and into the abysses of negation. Together with her he toiled through the labyrinthine jungle of modern philosophy" (p. 308).

He is driven into negation not by the development of philosophy which even at that time began to impinge on the masses but by the intervention of a chance emotional relationship.

What he brings with him out of the labyrinth is revealed in his diaries:

"I should like to see whether the mighty river flowing from Kant to Feuerbach will drive me out into—Pantheism!" (p. 308).

He writes just as if this particular river did not flow beyond pantheism, and as if Feuerbach were the last word in German philosophy!

"The corner-stone of my life", the diary goes on to say, "is not historical knowledge, but a coherent system, and the heart of theology is not ecclesiastical history but dogma" (ibid.).

He is clearly ignorant of the fact that the whole achievement of German philosophy lies in its dissolution of the coherent systems into historical knowledge and the heart of dogma into ecclesiastical history! —In these confessions the image of the counter-revolutionary democrat stands revealed in every detail. For such a person movement is nothing more than a means by which to arrive at a few irremovable eternal truths and then to subside into a slothful tranquillity.

However, Gottfried's apologetic book-keeping of his whole development will enable the reader to judge the intensity of the revolutionary impulse that lay concealed in the melodramatic hamming of this theologian.

II

This brings to a close the first Act of the drama of Kinkel's life and nothing worthy of mention then occurs before the outbreak of the February Revolution. The publishing house of Cotta accepted his poems but without offering him a royalty and most of the copies remained unsold until the celebrated stray bullet in Baden gave a poetic nimbus to the author and created a market for his products.

Incidentally, our biographer omits mention of one momentous fact. The self-confessed goal of Kinkel's desires was that he should die as an old theatre director: his ideal was a certain old Eisenhut who together with his troupe used to roam up and down the Rhine as a travelling Pickelhäring [clown] and who afterwards went mad.

Alongside his lectures with their rhetoric of the pulpit Gottfried also gave a number of theological and aesthetic performances in Cologne from time to time. When the February Revolution broke out, he concluded them with this prophetic utterance:

> "The thunder of battle reverberates over to us from Paris and opens a new and glorious era for Germany and the whole continent of Europe. The raging storm will be followed by Zephyr's breezes with their message of freedom. On this day is born the great, bountiful epoch of—*constitutional monarchy!*"

The constitutional monarchy expressed its thanks to Kinkel for this compliment by appointing him to a professorial chair. Such recognition could however not suffice for our *grand homme en herbe*. The constitutional monarchy showed no eagerness to cause his "fame to encircle the globe". Moreover, the laurels Freiligrath had collected for his recent political poems prevented our crowned Maybug poet from sleeping. Heinrich von Ofterdingen, therefore, resolved upon a swing to the left and became first a constitutional democrat and then a republican democrat (*honnête et modéré*). He set out to become a deputy but the May elections took him neither to Berlin nor to Frankfurt. Despite this initial setback he pursued his objective undismayed and it can truthfully be said that he did not spare himself. He wisely limited himself at first to his immediate environment. He founded the *Bonner Zeitung* [Bonn News], a modest local product distinguished only by the peculiar feebleness of its democratic rhetoric and the naiveté with which it aspired to save the nation. He elevated the Maybug Club to the rank of a democratic Students' Club and from this there duly flowed a host of disciples that bore the Master's renown into every corner of the district of Bonn, importuning every assembly with the fame of Professor Kinkel. He himself politicked with the grocers in their club, he extended a brotherly hand to the worthy manufacturers and even hawked the warm breath of freedom among the peasantry of Kindenich and Seelscheid. Above all he reserved his sympathy for the honourable caste of master craftsmen. He wept together with them over the decay of handicrafts, the monstrous effects of free competition, the modern dominance of capital and of machines. Together with them he devised plans to restore the guilds and to prevent the violation of guild regulations by the journeymen. So as to do everything of which he was capable he set down the results of his pub deliberations with the petty guild masters in the pamphlet entitled *Handicraft, save yourself!*

Lest there be any doubt as to Mr. Kinkel's position and to the significance of his little tract for Frankfurt and the nation he dedicated it to the "thirty members of the economic committee of the Frankfurt National Assembly".

Heinrich von Ofterdingen's researches into the "beauty" of the artisan class led him immediately to the discovery that "the whole artisan class is at present divided by a yawning chasm" (p. 5). This chasm consists in the fact that some artisans "frequent the clubs of the grocers and officials" (what progress!) and that others do not do this and also in the fact that some artisans are educated and others are not. Despite this chasm the author regards the artisans' clubs, the assemblies springing up everywhere in the beloved fatherland and the agitation for improving the state of handicrafts (reminiscent of the congresses à la Winkelblech[24] of 1848) as the portent of a happy future. To ensure that his own good advice should not be missing from this beneficent movement he devises his own programme of salvation.

He begins by asking how to eradicate the evil effects of *free competition* by restricting it but without eliminating it altogether. The solutions he proposes are these:

"A youth who lacks the requisite ability and maturity should be debarred by law from becoming a master" (p. 20).

"No master shall be permitted to have more than one apprentice" (p. 29).

"The course of instruction in a craft shall be concluded by an examination" (p. 30).

"The master of an apprentice must unfailingly attend the examination" (p. 31).

"On the question of maturity it should become mandatory that henceforth no apprentice may become a master before completion of his twenty-fifth year" (p. 42).

"As evidence of ability every candidate for the title of master should be required to pass a public examination" (p. 43).

"In this context it is of vital importance that the examination should be free" (p. 44). "All provincial masters of the same guild must likewise submit themselves to the same examination" (p. 55).

Friend Gottfried who is himself a political hawker desires to abolish the "travelling tradesman or hawker" in other, profane wares on the grounds of the dishonesty of such work. (p. 60.)

> "A manufacturer of craft goods desires to withdraw his assets from the business to his own advantage and, dishonestly, to the disadvantage of his creditors. Like all ambivalent things this pheno-menon too is described by a foreign word: it is called bankruptcy. He then quickly takes his finished products to a neighbouring town and sells them there to the highest bidder" (p. 64). These auctions— "in actual fact like a sort of garbage that our dear neighbour, Com-merce, disposes of in the garden of Handicraft"—must be abolished. (Would it not be much simpler, Friend Gottfried, to go to the root of the matter and abolish bankruptcy itself?).
> "Of course, the annual fairs are in a special position" (p. 65). "The law will have to be flexible so as to allow the various places to call an assembly of all the citizens to decide by majority vote (!) whether permanent annual fairs should be retained or abolished" (p. 68).

Gottfried now comes to the "vexed" question of the relationship between manufacture and machine industry and produces the following:

> "Let everyone *sell only those goods that he himself produces with his own hands.*" (p. 80.) "Because machines and manufacture have gone their own ways they have strayed from their true paths and now both are in a sorry plight." (p. 84).
> He wishes to unite them by getting artisans such as the bookbind-ders, to band together and maintain a machine.
> "As they only use the machine for themselves and when it is required they will be able to produce more cheaply than the factory owner" (p. 85). "Capital will be broken by association" (p. 84). (And associations will be broken by capital.)

He then generalises his ideas about the "purchase of a machine to rule lines, and to cut paper and cardboard" (p. 85) for the united certificated bookbinders of Bonn and conceives the notion of a "Machine-Chamber".

> "Confederations of the various guild masters must set up businesses everywhere, similar to the factories of individual businessmen though

on a smaller scale. These will work to order, exclusively for the benefit of local masters. They will not accept commissions from other employers" (p. 86).

What distinguishes these Machine Chambers is the fact that "a commercial management" will only "be needed initially" (*ibid*). "Every idea as novel as this one", Gottfried exclaims "ecstatically", "can only be put into practice when all the details have been thought out in the most sober, matter of fact way". He urges "each and every branch of manufacture to perform this analysis for itself"! (pp. 87, 88).

There follows a polemic against competition from the state in the shape of the labour performed by the inmates of prisons, reminiscences about a colony of criminals ("The creation of a human Siberia" (p. 102)), and finally an attack on the "so-called handicraft companies and handicraft commissions" in the armed forces. The aim here is to ease the burdens imposed by the army on the artisan classes by inducing the state to commission goods from the guild masters that it could itself produce more cheaply.

"This deals satisfactorily with the problems of competition" (p. 109).

Gottfried's second important point touches on the material aid due to the manufacturing classes from the state. Gottfried regards the state solely from the point of view of an official and hence arrives at the opinion that the easiest and surest way to help the artisan is by direct subsidy from the Treasury to erect trade halls and set up loan-funds. How the funds reach the Treasury in the first place is the "ugly" side of the problem and naturally enough, cannot be investigated here.

Lastly, our theologian inevitably lapses into the role of moral preacher. He reads the artisan class a moral lecture on self-help. He firstly condemns the "complaints about long-term borrowing and about discounts" (p. 136), and invites the artisan to inspect his own conscience: "Do you always fix the same, unchanging price, my friend, for every job of work that you undertake?" (p. 132). On this occasion he also warns the artisan against making extortionate demands on "wealthy Englishmen". "The whole root of the evil", according to the fantasies that inhabit Gottfried's mind, "is the system of annual accounts" (p. 139). This is followed by Jeremiads about the way in which the artisans carry on in the taverns and their wives indulge their love of finery (p. 140 ff.).

The means by which the artisan class is to better itself are "the corporation, the sickness fund and the artisans' court" (p. 146); and lastly, the workers' educational clubs (p. 153). Here is his closing statement about these educational clubs.

"And finally the union of song and oratory will create a bridge to *dramatic performances* and *the artisan theatre* which must constantly be kept in view as the ultimate objective of these aesthetic strivings. Only when the labouring classes learn once more how to move on the *stage* will their artistic education be complete" (pp. 174-175).

Gottfried has thus succeeded in changing the artisan into a comedian and has arrived back at his own situation.

This whole flirtation with the guild aspirations of the master craftsmen in Bonn did not fail to achieve a practical result. In return for the solemn promises to promote the cause of the guilds Gottfried's election as Member for Bonn in the Lower Chamber under the dictated constitution[25] was contrived. "From this moment on Gottfried felt happy."

He set off at once for Berlin and as he believed that it was the intention of the government to establish a permanent "corporation" of approved masters in the craft of legislation in the Lower Chamber, he acted as if he were to stay there for ever and even decided to send for his wife and child. But then the Chamber was dissolved and Friend Gottfried, bitterly disappointed, had to leave his parliamentary bliss and go back to Mockel.

Soon afterwards conflicts broke out between the Frankfurt Assembly and the German governments and this led to the upheavals in South Germany and on the Rhine. The Fatherland called and Gottfried obeyed. Siegburg was the site of the arsenal for the province and next to Bonn Siegburg was the place where Gottfried had sown the seed of freedom most frequently. He joined forces with his friend, Anneke, a former lieutenant and summoned all his loyal vassals to a march on Siegburg. They were to assemble at the rope ferry. More than a hundred were supposed to come but when after waiting a long time Gottfried counted the heads of the faithful there were barely thirty—and of these only three were students, to the undying shame of the Maybug Club! Undaunted, Gottfried and his band crossed the Rhine and marched towards Siegburg. The night was dark and it was drizzling. Suddenly the sound of horses' hooves could be heard behind our valiant heroes. They took cover at the side of the road, a patrol of lancers galloped by: miserable knaves had talked too freely and the

F

authorities had got wind of it. The march was now futile and had to be abandoned. The pain that Gottfried felt in his breast that night can only be compared with the torments he experienced when both Knapp and Chamisso declined to print the first flowering of his poetic talent in their magazines.

After this he could remain no longer in Bonn but surely the Palatinate would provide great scope for his activities? He went to Kaiserslautern and as he had to have a job he obtained a sinecure in the War Office (it is said that he was put in charge of naval affairs). But he continued to earn his living by hawking around his ideas about freedom and the people's paradise among the peasants of the region and it is said that his reception in a number of reactionary districts was anything but cordial. Despite these minor misfortunes Kinkel could be seen on every high-road, striding along purposefully, his rucksack on his back and from this point on he appears in all the newspapers accompanied by his rucksack.

But the upheavals in the Palatinate were quickly terminated and we discover Kinkel again in Karlsruhe where instead of the rucksack he carries a musket which now becomes his permanent emblem. This musket is said to have had a very *beautiful* aspect, i.e. a butt and stock made of mahogany and it was certainly an artistic, aesthetic musket; there was also an *ugly* side to it and this was the fact that Gottfried could neither load, nor see, nor shoot nor march. So much so that a friend asked him why he was going into battle at all. Whereupon Gottfried replied: Well, the fact is that I can't return to Bonn, I have to live!

In this way Gottfried joined the ranks of the warriors in the corps of the chivalrous Willich. As a number of his comrades in arms have reliably reported. Gottfried served as a common partisan, sharing all the vicissitudes of this company with humility. He was as merry and friendly in bad times as in good, but he was mostly engaged in maraud-ing. In Rastatt,[26] however, this unsullied witness to truth and justice was to undergo the test from which he would emerge unblemished and as a martyr to the plaudits of the whole German nation. The exact details of this exploit have never been established with any accuracy. All that is known is that a troop of partisans got lost in a skirmish and a few shots were fired on their flank. A bullet grazed Gottfried's head and he fell to the ground with the cry "I am dead". He was not in fact dead but his wound was serious enough to prevent him from retreating with the others. He was taken to a farm house where he turned to the

worthy Black Forest peasants with the words "Save me—I am Kinkel!"
Here he was discovered by the Prussians, who dragged him off into
Babylonian captivity.

III

With his capture a new epoch opened in Kinkel's life and at the same
time there began a new era in the history of German Philistinism. The
Maybug Club had scarcely heard the news of his capture than they
wrote to all the German papers that Kinkel, the great poet, was in
danger of being summarily shot and exhorting the German people,
especially the educated among them, and above all the women and
girls to give their all to save the life of the imprisoned poet. Kinkel
himself composed a poem at about this time, as we are told, in which
he compared himself to "Christ, his friend and teacher", adding: "My
blood is shed for you." From this point on his emblem is the lyre. In this
way Germany suddenly learned that Kinkel was a poet, a great poet
moreover, and from this moment on the mass of German Philistines
and aestheticising drivellers joined in the Farce of the Blue Flower put
on by our Heinrich von Ofterdingen.

In the meantime the Prussians brought him before a military tribunal. For the first time after a long interval he saw his opportunity to
try out one of those moving appeals to the tear ducts of his audience
which—according to Mockel—had brought him such applause earlier
on as an assistant preacher in Cologne. Cologne too was destined soon
to witness his most glorious performance in this sphere. He made a
speech in his own defence before the tribunal which thanks to the
indiscretion of a friend was unfortunately made available to the public
through the medium of the Berlin *Abendpost*. In this speech Kinkel
"repudiates any connection between his activities and the filth and the
dirt that, as I well know, has latterly attached itself to this revolution".

After this rabid revolutionary speech Kinkel was sentenced to
twenty years detention in a fortress. As an act of grace this was reduced
to prison with hard labour and he was removed to Naugard where he
was employed in spinning wool and so just as formerly he had appeared
with the emblem first of the rucksack, then the musket and then the
lyre, he now appears in association with the *spinning wheel*. We shall
see him later wandering over the ocean accompanied by the emblem of
the purse.

In the meantime a curious event took place in Germany. It is well known that the German Philistine is endowed by Nature with a beautiful soul. Now he found his most cherished illusions cruelly shattered by the hard blows of the year 1849. Not a single hope had become reality and even the fast-beating hearts of young men began to despair about the fate of the fatherland. Every heart yielded to a lachrymose torpor and the need began to be felt for a democratic Christ, for a real or imagined Sufferer who in his torments would bear the sins of the Philistine world with the patience of a lamb and whose Passion would epitomise in extreme form the unrestrained but chronic self-pity of the whole of Philistinism. The Maybug Club, with Mockel at its head, set out to satisfy this universal need. And indeed, who better fitted for the task of enacting this great Passion Farce than our captive passion flower, Kinkel at the Spinning Wheel, this sponge able to absorb endless floods of sentimental tears, who was in addition preacher, professor of fine arts, deputy, political colporteur, musketeer, newly discovered poet and old impresario all rolled into one? Kinkel was the man of the moment and as such he was immediately accepted by the German Philistines. Every paper abounded in anecdotes, vignettes, poems, reminiscences of the captive poet, his sufferings in prison were magnified a thousandfold and took on mythical stature; at least once a month his hair was reported to have gone grey; in every bourgeois meeting-place and at every tea party he was remembered with grief; the daughters of the educated classes sighed over his poems and old maids who knew what unrequited passion is wept freely in various cities at the thought of his shattered manhood. All other profane victims of the revolutionary movement, all who had been shot, who had fallen in battle or who had been imprisoned disappeared into naught beside this one sacrificial lamb, beside this one hero after the hearts of the Philistines male and female. For him alone did the rivers of tears flow, and indeed, he alone was able to respond to them in kind. In short, we have the perfect image, complete in every detail of the democratic Siegwart epoch which yielded in nothing to the literary Siegwart epoch of the preceding century and Siegwart-Kinkel never felt more at home in any role than in this one where he could seem great not because of what he did but because of what he did not do. He could seem great not by dint of his strength and his powers of resistance but through his weakness and spineless behaviour in a situation where his only task was to survive with decorum and sentiment. Mockel, however, was able and experienced enough to take practical advantage of the public's soft heart and she immediately organised a highly efficient industry. She caused all of Gottfried's published and unpublished works to be printed for they all suddenly became fashionable and were much in demand; she also found a market for her own life-experiences from the insect world, e.g., her *Story of a Firefly*; she employed the Maybug Strodtmann to assemble Gottfried's most secret diary-feelings and prostitute them to the public for a considerable sum of money; she organised collections of every kind and in general she displayed undeniable talent and great perseverance in converting the feelings of the educated public into hard cash. In addition she had the great satisfaction "of seeing the greatest men of Germany, such as Adolf Stahr, meeting daily in her own little room".

The climax of this whole Siegwart mania was to be reached at the Assizes in Cologne where Gottfried made a guest appearance early in 1850. This was the trial resulting from the attempted uprising in Siegburg and Kinkel was brought to Cologne for the occasion. As Gottfried's diaries play such a prominent part in this sketch it will be appropriate if we insert here an excerpt from the diary of an eyewitness.

"Kinkel's wife visited him in gaol. She welcomed him from behind the grill with verses; he replied, I understand, in hexameters; whereupon they both sank to their knees before each other and the prison inspector, an old sergeant-major, who was standing by wondered whether he was dealing with madmen or clowns. When asked later by the chief prosecutor about the content of their conversation he declared that the couple had indeed spoken German but that he could not make head nor tail of it. Whereupon Mrs. Kinkel is supposed to have retorted that a man who was so wholly innocent of art and literature should not be made an inspector."

Faced with the jury Kinkel wriggled his way out by acting the pure tear-jerker, the poetaster of the Siegwart period of the vintage of *Werther's Sufferings*.[27]

"Members of the Court, Gentlemen of the Jury—the blue eyes of my children—the green waters of the Rhine —it is no dishonour to shake the hand of the proletarian—the pallid lips of the prisoner—the peaceful air of one's home"—and similar crap: that was what the whole famous speech amounted to and the public, the jury, the prosecution and even the police shed their bitterest tears and the trial closed with a unanimous acquittal and a no less unanimous weeping and wailing. Kinkel is doubtless a dear, good man but he is also a repulsive mixture of religious, political and literary reminiscences."

It's enough to make you sick.

Fortunately this period of misery was soon terminated by the romantic liberation of Kinkel from Spandual gaol. His escape was a re-enactment of the story of Richard Lionheart and Blondel with the difference that this time it was Blondel who was in prison while Lionheart played on the barrel-organ outside and that Blondel was an ordinary music-hall minstrel and the lion was basically more like a rabbit. Lionheart was in fact the student Schurz from the Maybug Club, a little intriguer with great ambitions and limited achievements who was however intelligent enough to have seen through the "German Lamartine"! Not long after the escape student Schurz declared in Paris that he knew very well that Kinkel was no lumen mundi, whereas he, Schurz, and none other was destined to be the future president of the German Repubic. This mannikin, one of those students "in brown jackets and pale-blue overcoats" whom Gottfried had once followed with his gloomily flashing eyes succeeded in freeing Kinkel at the cost of sacrificing some poor devil of a warder who is now doing time elevated by the feeling of being a martyr for freedom—the freedom of Gottfried Kinkel.

IV

We next meet Kinkel again in London, and this time, thanks to his prison fame and the sentimentality of the German Philistines, he has become the greatest man in Germany. Mindful of his sublime mission Friend Gottfried was able to exploit all the advantages of the moment. His romantic escape gave new impetus to the Kinkel cult in Germany and he adroitly directed this onto a path that was not without beneficial material consequences. At the same time London provided the much venerated man with a new, complex arena in which to receive even greater acclaim. He did not hesitate: he would have to be the new lion of the season. With this in mind he refrained for the time being from all political activity and withdrew into the seclusion of his home in order to grow a beard, without which no prophet can succeed. After that he visited Dickens, the English liberal newspapers, the German businessmen in the City and especially the aesthetic Jews in that place. He was all things to all men: to one a poet, to another a patriot in general, professor of fine arts to a third, Christ to the fourth, the patiently suffering Odysseus to the fifth. To everyone, however, he appeared as the gentle, artistic, benevolent and humanitarian Gottfried. He did not rest until Dickens had eulogised him in the *Household Words*, until the *Illustrated News* had published his portrait. He induced the few Germans in London who had been involved in the Kinkel mania even at a distance to allow themselves to be invited to lectures on modern drama. Once he had organised them in this way tickets to these lectures flooded into the homes of the local German population. No running around, no advertisement, no charlatanism, no importunity was beneath him; in return, however, he did not go unrewarded. Gottfried sunned himself complacently in the mirror of his own fame and in the gigantic mirror of the Crystal Palace of the world. And we may say that he now felt tremendously content.

There was no lack of praise for his lectures (see *Kosmos*).

Kosmos: "Kinkel's Lectures"

"While looking once at Döbler's paintings of misty landscapes I was surprised by the whimsical question of whether it was possible to produce such chaotic creations in words, whether it was possible to utter misty images. It is no doubt unpleasant for the critic to have to confess that in this case his critical autonomy will vibrate against the galvanized nerves of an external reminiscence, as the fading sound of a dying note echoes in the strings. Nevertheless I would prefer to renounce any attempt at a bewigged and boring analysis of pedantic insensitivity than to deny that tone which the charming muse of the German refugee caused to resonate in my *sensibility*. This ground note of Kinkel's paintings, this sounding board of his chords is the sonorous, creative, formative and gradually shaping 'word'—'modern thought'. To 'judge' this thought is to lead truth out of the chaos of mendacious traditions, to constitute it as the indestructible property of the world and as such to place it under the protection of spiritually active, logical minorities who will educate the world leading it from a credulous ignorance to a state of more sceptical science. It is the task of the science of doubt to profane the mysticism of pious deceit, to undermine the absolutism of an atrophied tradition. Science must employ scepticism, that ceaselessly labouring guillotine of philosophy, to decapitate accepted authority and to lead the nations out of the misty regions of theocracy by means of revolution into the luscious meadows of democracy" (of nonsense). "The sustained, unflagging search in the annals of mankind and the understanding of man himself is the great task of all revolutionaries and this had been understood by that proscribed poet-rebel who on three recent Monday evenings uttered his subversive views before a bourgeois audience in the course of his lectures on the history of the modern theatre."   "A Worker"

It is generally claimed that this worker is a very close relation of Kinkel's—namely Mockel—as indeed seems likely from the use of such expressions as "sounding-board", "fading sound", "chords" and "galvanized nerves".

However, even this period of hard-earned pleasure was not to last forever. The Last Judgement on the existing world-order, the democratic day of judgement, namely the much celebrated May 1852[28] was drawing ever closer. In order to confront this day all booted and spurred Kinkel had to don his political lionskin once more: he had to make contact with the "Emigration".

So we come to the London "Emigration", this hotchpotch of former members of the Frankfurt Parliament, the Berlin National Assembly, and Chamber of Deputies, of gentlemen from the Baden Campagne, Gargantuas from the Comedy of the Imperial Constitution,[29] writers without a public, loudmouths from the democratic clubs and congresses, twelfth-rate journalists and so forth.

The heroes of the 1848 revolution in Germany had been on the point of coming to a sticky end when the victory of "tyranny" rescued them, swept them out of the country and made saints and martyrs of them. They were saved by the counter-revolution. The course of continental politics brought most of them to London which thus became their European centre. It is evident that something had to happen, something had to be arranged to remind the public daily of the existence of these world-liberators. At all costs it must not become obvious that the course of universal history might be able to proceed without the intervention of these mighty men. The more this refuse of mankind found itself hindered by its own impotence as much as by the prevailing situation from undertaking any real action, the more zealously did it indulge in spurious activity whose imagined deeds, imagined parties, imagined struggles and imagined interests have been so noisily trumpeted abroad by those involved. The less able they were to bring about a new revolution the more they discounted the importance of such an eventuality in their minds, while they concentrated on sharing out the plum jobs and enjoying the prospect of future power. The form taken by this self-important activity was that of a mutual insurance club of the heroes-to-be and the reciprocal guarantee of government posts.

V

The first attempt to create such an "organisation" took place as early as the Spring of 1850. A magniloquent "draft circular to German democrats" was hawked around London in manuscript form together with a "Covering Letter to the Leaders". It contained an exhortation to found a united democratic church. Its immediate aim was to form a Central Office to deal with the affairs of German *émigrés*, to set up a central administration for refugee problems, to start a printing press in London, and to unite all patriots against the common enemy. The Emigration would then become the centre of the internal revolutionary movement, the organisation of the Emigration would be the beginning of a comprehensive democratic organisation, the outstanding per-sonalities among the members of the Central Office would be paid salaries raised by taxes levied on the German people. This tax proposal seemed all the more appropriate as "the German Emigration had gone abroad not merely without a respectable hero but what is even worse, without common *assets*". It is no secret that the Hungarian, Polish and French committees already in existence provided the model for this "organisation" and the whole document is redolent of envy of the privileged position of these prominent allies.

The circular was the joint production of Messrs. Rudolph *Schramm* and Gustav *Struve*, behind whom lay concealed the merry figure of Mr. Arnold *Ruge*, a corresponding member living in Ostend at the time.

Mr. *Rudolph Schramm*—a rowdy, loudmouthed and extremely con-fused little manikin whose life-motto came from *Rameau's Nephew*: "I would rather be an impudent windbag than be nothing at all."

When at the height of his power, Mr. Camphausen[30] would gladly have given the young forward Crefelder an important post, had it been permissible to elevate a junior official. Thanks to bureaucratic etiquette Mr. Schramm found only the career of a democrat open to him. And in this profession he really did advance at one point to the post of President of the Democratic Club in Berlin and with the support of some left-wing Members of Parliament he became the Deputy for Striegau in the Berlin National Assembly. Here the normally so loquacious Schramm distinguished himself by his obstinate silence, which was accompanied, however, by an uninterrupted series of grunts. After the Assembly had been dissolved[31] our democratic man of the people wrote a pamphlet in support of a constitutional monarchy

F*

but this did not suffice to get him re-elected. Later, at the time of the Brentano government he appeared momentarily in Baden and there in the "Club for Resolute Progress" he became acquainted with Struve. On his arrival in London he declared his intention of withdrawing from all political activity for which reason he then published the circular referred to above. Essentially a bureaucrat Mr. Schramm imagined that his family relations qualified him to represent the radical bourgeiosie in exile and he did indeed present a fair caricature of the radical bourgeois.

Gustav Struve is one of the more important figures of the emigration. At the very first glimpse of his leathery appearance, his protuberant eyes with their sly, stupid expression, the matt gleam on his bald pate and his half Slav, half Kalmuck features one cannot doubt that one is in the presence of an unusual man. And this first impression is confirmed by his low, guttural voice, his oily manner of speaking and the air of solemn gravity he imparts to his gestures. To be just it must be said that faced with the greatly increased difficulties of distinguishing oneself these days, our Gustav at least made the effort to attract attention by using his diverse talents—he is part prophet, part speculator, part bunion healer—centring his activities on all kinds of peripheral matters and making propaganda for the strangest assortment of causes. For example, he was born a Russian but suddenly took it into his head to enthuse about the cause of German freedom after he had been employed in a minor capacity in the Russian embassy to the Federal Diet and had written a little pamphlet in defence of the Diet. Regarding his own skull as normal he suddenly developed an interest in phrenology and from then on he refused to trust anyone whose skull he had not yet felt and examined. He also gave up eating meat and preached the gospel of strict vegetarianism; he was, moreover, a weather-prophet, he inveighed against tobacco and was prominent in the interest of German Catholicism and water-cures. In harmony with his thorough-going hatred of scientific knowledge it was natural that he should be in favour of free universities in which the four faculties would be replaced by the study of phrenology, physiognomy, chiromancy and necromancy. It was also quite in character for him to insist that he must become a great writer simply because his mode of writing was the antithesis of everything that could be held to be stylistically acceptable.

In the early Forties Gustav had already invented the *Deutscher Zuschauer*, a little paper that he published in Mannheim, that he patented and that pursued him everywhere as an *idée fixe*. He also made the discovery at around this time that Rotteck's *History of the World* and the Rotteck-Welcker *Lexicon of Politics*, the two works that had been his Old and New Testaments, were out of date and in need of a new *democratic* edition. This revision Gustav undertook without delay and published an extract from it in advance under the title *The Basic Elements of Political Science*. He argued that the revision had become "an undeniable necessity since 1848 as the late-lamented Rotteck had not experienced the events of recent years".

In the meantime there broke out in Baden in quick succession the three "popular uprisings" that Gustav has placed in the very centre of the whole modern course of world history. Driven into exile by the very first of these revolts (Hecker's) and occupied with the task of publishing the *Deutscher Zuschauer* once again, this time from Basel, he was then dealt a hard blow by fate when the Mannheim publisher continued to print the *Deutscher Zuschauer* under a different editor. The battle between the true and the false *Deutscher Zuschauer* was so bitterly fought that neither paper survived. To compensate for this Gustav devised a constitution for the German Federal Republic in which Germany was to be divided into 24 republics, each with a president and two chambers; he appended a neat map on which the whole proposal could be clearly seen. In September 1848 the second insurrection began in which our Gustav acted as both Caesar and Socrates. He used the time granted him on German soil to issue serious warnings to the Black Forest Peasantry about the deleterious effects of smoking tobacco. In Lörrach he published his Moniteur with the title of *Government Organ—German Free State—Freedom, Prosperity, Education*. This publication contained *inter alia* the following decree:

"Article 1. The extra tax of 10 per cent on goods imported from Switzerland is hereby abolished; Article 2. *Christian Müller, the Customs Officer is to be given the task of implementing this measure.*"

He was accompanied in all his trials by his faithful Amalia who subsequently published a romantic account of them. She was also active in administering the oath to captured gendarmes, for it was her custom to fasten a red band around the arm of every one who swore allegiance to the German Free State and to give him a big kiss. Unfortunately Gustav and Amalia were taken prisoner and languished in gaol where the imperturbable Gustav at once resumed his republican translation of Rotteck's *History of the World* until he was liberated by the outbreak of the third insurrection. Gustav now became a member of a real provisional government and the mania for provisional governments was now added to his other *idées fixes*. As President of the War Council he hastened to introduce as much muddle as possible into his department and to recommend the "traitor" Mayerhofer for the post of Minister for War (vide Goegg, *Retrospect*, Paris 1850). Later he vainly aspired to the post of Foreign Minister and to have 60,000 Florins placed at his disposal. Mr. Brentano soon relieved Gustav of the burdens of government and Gustav now entered the "Club of Resolute Progress" from which he became leader of the opposition. He delighted above all in opposing the very measures of Brentano which he had hitherto supported. Even though the Club too was disbanded and Gustav had to flee to the Palatinate this disaster had its positive side for it enabled him to issue one further number of the inevitable *Deutscher Zuschauer* in Neustadt an der Haardt—this compensated Gustav for much undeserved suffering. A further satisfaction was that he was successful in a by-election in some remote corner of the uplands and was nominated member of the Baden Constituent Assembly which meant that he could now return in an official capacity. In this Assembly Gustav only distinguished himself by the following three proposals that he put forward in Freiburg: (1) On June 28th: everyone who enters into dealings with the enemy should be declared a traitor. (2) On June 30th: a new provisional government should be formed in which Struve would have a seat and a vote. (3) On the same day that the previous motion was defeated he proposed that as the defeat at Rastatt had rendered all resistance futile the uplands should be spared the terrors of war and that therefore all officials and soldiers should receive ten days' wages and members of the Assembly should receive ten days' expenses together with travelling costs after which they should all repair to Switzerland to the accompaniment of trumpets and drums. When this proposal too was rejected Gustav set out for Switzerland on his own and having been driven from thence by James Fazy's stick he retreated to London where he at once came to the fore with yet another discovery, namely the *Six scourges of mankind*. These six scourges were: the princes, the nobles, the priests, the bureaucracy, the standing army, mammon and bedbugs. The spirit in which Gustav interpreted the lamented Rotteck can be gauged from the further discovery that mammon was the invention of Louis Philippe. Gustav preached the gospel of the six scourges in the *Deutsche Londoner Zeitung* [German London News] which belonged to the ex-Duke of Brunswick. He was amply rewarded for this activity and in return he gratefully bowed to the ducal censorship. So much for Gustav's relations with the first scourge, the princes. As for his relationship with the nobles, the second scourge, our moral and religious republican had visiting cards printed on which he figured as "Baron von Struve". If his relations with the remaining scourges were less amicable this cannot be his fault. Gustav then made use of his leisure time in London to devise a republican calendar in which the saints were replaced by right-minded men and the names "Gustav" and "Amalia" were particularly prominent. The months were designated by German equivalents of those in the calendar of the French Republic and there were a number of other common-places for the common good. For the rest, the remaining *idées fixes* made their appearance again in London: Gustav made haste to revive the *Deutscher Zuschauer* and the Club of Resolute Progress and to form a provisional government. On all these matters he found himself of one mind with Schramm and in this way the circular came into being.

The third member of the alliance, the great *Arnold Ruge* with his air of a sergeant-major living in hopes of civilian employment outshines in glory the whole of the emigration. It cannot be said that this noble man commends himself by his notably handsome exterior; Paris acquaintances were wont to sum up his Pomeranian–Slav features with the word "ferret-face" (*figure de fouine*). Arnold Ruge, the son of peasants of the isle of Rügen, had endured seven years in Prussian prisons for democratic agitation. He embraced Hegelian philosophy as soon as he had realised that once he had leafed through Hegel's *Encyclopaedia* he could dispense with the study of all other science. He also developed the principle (described in a Novelle and which he attempted to practise on his friends—poor Georg Herwegh can vouch for the truth of this), of profiting from marriage and he early acquired a "substantial property" in this manner.

Despite his Hegelian phrases and his substantial property he did not advance beyond the post of porter to German philosophy. In the *Hallische Jahrbücher* [Halle Annals] and the *Deutsche Jahrbücher* [German Annals] it was his task to announce and to trumpet the names of the great philosophers of the future and he showed that he was not without talent in exploiting them for his own purposes. Unfortunately, the period of philosophical anarchy soon supervened, that period when science no longer had a universally acknowledged king, when Strauss, Bruno Bauer and Feuerbach fought among themselves and when the most diverse alien elements began to disrupt the simplicity of classical doctrine. Ruge looked on helplessly, he no longer knew which path to take; his Hegelian categories had always operated in a vacuum, now they ran completely amok and he suddenly felt the need for a mighty movement in which exact thought and writing were not indispensable.

Ruge played the same role in the *Hallische Jahrbücher* as the late bookseller Nicolai had done in the old *Berliner Monatsschrift* [Berlin Monthly Magazine]. Like the latter his ambition was to print the works of others and in so doing, to derive material advantage and also to quarry literary sustenance for the effusions of his own brain. The only difference was that in this literary digestive process with its inevitable end product Ruge went much further than did his model in rewriting his collaborators' articles. Moreover, Ruge was not the porter of German Enlightenment, he was the Nicolai of modern German philosophy and thus was able to conceal the natural banality of his genius behind a thick hedge of speculative jargon. Like Nicolai he fought valiantly against *Romanticism* because Hegel had demolished it philosophically in the *Aesthetics* and Heine had done the same thing from the point of view of literature in *The Romantic School*. Unlike Hegel he agreed with Nicolai in arrogating to himself the right as an anti-Romantic to set up a vulgar Philistinism and above all his own Philistinic self as an ideal of perfection. With this in mind and so as to defeat the enemy on his own ground Ruge went in for making verses. No Dutchman could have achieved the dull flatness of these poems which Ruge hurled so challengingly into the face of Romanticism.

And in general our Pomeranian thinker did not really feel at ease in Hegelian philosophy. Able as he was in detecting contradictions he was all the more feeble in resolving them and he had a very understandable horror of dialectics. The upshot was that the crudest possible contradictions dwelt peaceably together in his dogmatic brain and that his powers of understanding, never very agile, were nowhere more at home than in such mixed company. It is not unknown for him to read simultaneously two articles by two different writers and to conflate them into a single new product without noticing that they had been written from two opposing viewpoints. Always riding firmly between his own contradictions he sought to extricate himself from condemnation by the theorists by declaring his faulty theory to be "practical", while at the same time he would disarm the practical by interpreting his practical clumsiness and inconsequentiality as theoretical expertise. He would end by sanctifying his own entanglement in insoluble contradictions, his chaotically uncritical faith in popular slogans by regarding them as proof that he was a man of "principle".

Before we go on to concern ourselves with the further career of our Maurice of Saxony, as he liked to style himself in his intimate circle or friends, we would point to two qualities which made their appearance already in the *Jahrbücher*. The first is his *mania for manifestos*. No sooner had someone hatched a novel opinion that Ruge believed to have a future than he would issue a manifesto. As no-one reproaches him with ever having given birth to an original thought of his own, such manifestos were always suitable opportunity to claim this novel idea as his own property in a more or less declamatory fashion. This would be followed by the attempt to form a party, a "mass" which would stand behind him and to whom he could act as sergeant-major. We shall see later to what unbelievable heights of perfection Ruge had developed the art of fabricating manifestos, proclamations and pronunciamentos. The second quality is the particular *diligence* in which Arnold excels. As he does not care to study overmuch, or as he puts it "to transfer ideas from one library into another", he prefers "to gain his knowledge fresh from life". He means by this to note down conscientiously every evening all the witty, novel or bright ideas that he has read, heard or just picked up during the day. As opportunity arises these materials are then made to contribute to Ruge's daily stint which he labours at just as conscientiously as at his other bodily needs. It is this that his admirers refer to when they say that he cannot hold his ink. The subject of his daily literary production is a matter of complete indifference; what is vital is that Ruge should be able to immerse every possible topic in that wonderful stylistic sauce that goes with everything just like the English who enjoy their Soyer's relish or Worcester Sauce equally with fish, fowl, cutlets or anything else. This daily stylistic diarrhoea he likes to designate the "all-pervading beautiful form" and he regards it as adequate grounds for passing himself off as an artist.

Contented as Ruge was to be the Swiss guard of German philosophy he still had a secret sorrow gnawing at his innermost vitals. He had not written a single large book and had daily to envy the happy Bruno Bauer who had published 18 fat volumes while still a young man. To reduce the discrepancy Ruge had one and the same essay printed three times in one and the same volume under different titles and then brought out the same volume in a number of different formats. In this way Arnold Ruge's *Complete Works* came into being and even today he derives much pleasure from counting them every morning volume by volume as they stand there neatly bound in his library, whereupon he exclaims joyfully: "And anyway, Bruno Bauer is a man without principles!"

Even though Arnold did not manage to comprehend the Hegelian system of philosophy, he did succeed in representing one Hegelian category in his own person. He was the very incarnation of the "honest consciousness" and was strengthened in this when he made the pleasant discovery in the *Phenomenology*—a book that was otherwise closed to him and bound with seven seals—that the honest consciousness "always has pleasure in itself". Though he wears his integrity on his sleeve the honest consciousness uses it to conceal the petty malice and crotchetiness of the Philistine; he has the right to allow himself every kind of base action because he knows that his baseness springs from honest motives. His very stupidity becomes a virtue because it is an irrefutable proof that he stands up for his principles. Despite every *arrière pensée* he is firmly convinced of his own integrity and however base or filthy an intended act may be it does not prevent him from appearing sincere and trusting. Beneath the halo of good intentions all the petty meannesses of the citizen become transformed into as many virtues; sordid self-interest appears as an innocent babe when dressed up to look like a piece of self-sacrifice; cowardice appears disguised as a higher form of courage, baseness becomes magnanimity, and the coarse manners of the peasant become ennobled, and indeed trans-figured into the signs of decency and good humour. This is the gutter into which the contradictions of philosophy, democracy and the cliché industry all pour; such a man is moreover richly endowed with all the vices, the mean and petty qualities, with the slyness and the stupidity, the greed and the clumsiness, the servility and the arrogance, the untrustworthiness and the bonhomie of the emancipated serf, the peasant; Philistine and ideologist, atheist and slogan worshipper, absolute ignoramus and absolute philosopher all in one—that is Arnold Ruge as Hegel foretold him in 1806.

After the *Deutsche Jahrbücher* were suppressed Ruge transported his family to Paris in a carriage specially designed for the purpose. Here, his unlucky star brought him into contact with *Heine* who honoured him as the man who "had translated Hegel into Pomeranian". Heine asked him whether Prutz was not a pseudonym of his which Ruge could deny in good conscience. However, it was not possible to make Heine believe that anyone but Arnold was the author of Prutz's poems. Heine also discovered very soon that even though Ruge had no talent he knew very well how to give the appearance of being a man of character. Thus it came about that Friend Arnold gave Heine the idea for his *Atta Troll*. If Ruge was not able to immortalise his sojourn in Paris by writing a great work he at least deserves our thanks for the one Heine produced for him. In gratitude the poet wrote for him this well-known epitaph:

> *Atta Troll, Tendenzbär; sittlich*
> *Religiös; als Gatte brünstig;*
> *Durch Verführtsein von dem Zeitgeist*
> *Waldursprünglich Sansculotte;*
>
> *Sehr schlecht tanzend, doch Gesinnung*
> *Tragend in der zott'gen Hochbrust;*
> *Manchmal auch gestunken habend;*
> *Kein Talent, doch ein Charakter!*

> [Atta Troll, reforming bear,
> Pure and pious; a passionate husband,
> By the Zeitgeist led astray
> A backwoods sansculotte,
>
> Dances badly but ideals
> Dwell within his shaggy breast
> Often stinking very strongly—
> Talent none, but Character]

In Paris our Arnold experienced the misfortune of becoming involved with the Communists. He published articles by Marx and Engels in the *Deutsch-Französische Jahrbücher* that contained views running directly counter to those he had himself announced in the Preface, an accident to which the *Augsburger Allgemeine Zeitung* drew his attention but which he bore with philosophical resignation.

To overcome an innate social awkwardness Ruge has collected a small number of curious anecdotes that could be used on any occasion. He calls these anecdotes jokes. His preoccupation with these jokes, sustained over many years, finally led to the transformation of all events, situations and circumstances into a series of pleasant or unpleasant, good or bad, important or trivial, interesting or boring jokes. The Paris upheavals, the many new impressions, socialism, politics, the Palais-Royal, the cheapness of the oysters—all these things wrought so powerfully on the mind of this unhappy wretch that his head went round and round in a permanent and incurable whirl of jokes and Paris itself became an unlimited storehouse of jokes. One of the brightest of these

jokes was the idea of using wood shavings to make coats for the proletariat and in general he had a foible for industrial jokes for which he
could never find enough share-holders.

When the better known Germans were expelled from France Ruge
contrived to avoid this fate by presenting himself to the minister,
Duchâtel, as a *savant sérieux*. He evidently had in mind the scholar in
Paul de Kock's *Amant de la lune*, who established himself as a *savant* by
means of an original device for propelling corks through the air.
Shortly afterwards Arnold went to Switzerland where he joined forces
with a former Dutch NCO, Cologne writer and Prussian tax sub-
inspector, called *Heinzen*. Both were soon bound together by the bonds
of the most intimate friendship. Heinzen learnt philosophy from Ruge,
Ruge learnt politics from Heinzen. From this time on we detect in Ruge
a growing necessity to appear as a philosopher par excellence only
among the coarser elements of the German movement, a fate that led
him down and down until at last he was accepted as a philosopher only
by non-conformist parsons (Dulon), German catholic parsons (Ronge)
and Fanny Lewald. At the same time anarchy was growing apace in
German philosophy. Stirner's *The Self and its Own*, Stein's *Socialism,
Communism*, etc., all recent intruders, drove Ruge's sense of humour to
breaking-point: a great leap must be ventured. So Ruge escaped into
humanism, the slogan with which all Confusionists in Germany from
Reuchlin to Herder have covered up their embarrassment. This slogan
seemed all the more appropriate as Feuerbach had only recently "re-
discovered man" and Arnold fastened on to it with such desperation
that he has not let go of it to this day. But while still in Switzerland
Arnold made yet another, incomparably greater discovery. This was
that "the ego by *appearing frequently* before the public proves itself a
character". From this point on a new field of activity opened for Arnold.
He now erected the most shameless meddling and interfering into a
principle. Ruge had to poke his nose into everything. No hen could
lay an egg without Ruge "commenting on the reason underlying the
event". Contact had to be maintained at all cost with every obscure
local paper where there was a chance of making frequent appearances.
He wrote no newspaper articles without signing his name and, where
possible, mentioning himself. The principle of the frequent appearance
had to be extended to every article; an article had first to appear in
letter form in the European papers (and after Heinzen's emigration, in
the American papers also), it was then reprinted as a pamphlet and
appeared again finally in the collected works.

Thus equipped Ruge could now return to Leipzig to obtain definitive recognition of his *character*. But once arrived all was not a bed of roses. His old friend Wigand, the bookseller, had very successfully replaced him in the role of Nicolai and as no other post was vacant Ruge fell into gloomy reflections on the transitoriness of all jokes. This was his situation when the German Revolution broke out.

For him too it came in the hour of need. The mighty movement in which even the clumsiest could easily swim with the current had finally got underway and Ruge went to Berlin where he intended to fish in troubled waters. As a *revolution* had just broken out he felt that it would be appropriate for him to come forward with proposals for *reform*. So he founded a paper with that name. The pre-revolutionary *Réforme* of Paris had been the most untalented, illiterate and boring paper in France. The Berlin *Reform* demonstrated that it was possible to surpass its French model and that one need not blush at offering German public such an incredible journal even in the "metropolis of intelligence". On the assumption that Ruge's defective grasp of style contained the best guarantee for the profound content lying behind and beneath it Arnold was elected to the Frankfurt Parliament as Member for Breslau. Here he saw his chance as editor of the democratic Left-wing to come forward with an absurd *manifesto*. Apart from that he distinguished himself only by his passion for issuing *manifestos for European People's Congresses*, and hastened to add his voice to the general wish that Prussia should be absorbed into Germany. Later, on his return to Berlin he demanded that Germany should be swallowed up by Prussia and Frankfurt by Berlin and when he finally decided to become a peer of Saxony he proposed that Prussia and Germany should both be swallowed up by Dresden.

His parliamentary activity brought him no laurels other than the fact that his own party despaired at so much folly. *At the same time* his *Reform* was going downhill, a situation that could only be remedied, as he thought, by his personal presence in Berlin. As an "honest consciousness" it goes without saying that he also discovered an urgent political reason for taking such a step and in fact he demanded that the whole of the Left should accompany him there. Naturally, they refused and Ruge went to Berlin alone. Once there, he discovered that modern conflicts can best be resolved by the "Dessau method" as he termed the small state, a model of constitutional democracy. Then during the siege [of Vienna] he again drew up a manifesto in which General

Wrangel was exhorted to march against Windischgraetz and free Vienna. He even obtained the approval of the democratic Congress for this curious document by pointing out that the type had been set up and that it was already being printed. Finally, when Berlin itself came under siege, Ruge went to Manteuffel and made proposals concerning the *Reform*, which were, however, rejected. Manteuffel told him that he wished all opposition papers were like the *Reform*, the *Neue Preussische Zeitung*[32] was much more dangerous to him—an utterance which the naïve Ruge, with a tone of triumphant pride, hastened to report through the length and breadth of Germany. Arnold became an enthusiastic advocate of *passive resistance* which he himself put into practice by leaving his paper, editors and everything in the lurch and running away. Active flight is evidently the most resolute form of passive resistance. The counter-revolution had arrived and Ruge fled before it all the way from Berlin to London without stopping.

At the time of the May uprising in Dresden[33] Arnold placed himself at the head of the movement in Leipzig together with his friend Otto Wigand and the city council. He and his allies issued a vigorous manifesto to the citizens of Dresden urging them to fight bravely; Ruge, Wigand and the city fathers, it went on, were sitting watching in Leipzig and whoever did not desert himself would not be deserted by Heaven. Scarcely had the manifesto been published than our brave Arnold took to his heels and fled to Karlsruhe.

In Karlsruhe he felt unsafe even though the Baden troops were standing on the Neckar and hostilities were a long way from breaking out. He asked Brentano to send him to Paris as ambassador. Brentano permitted himself the joke of giving him the post for 12 hours and then revoking it just when Ruge was about to depart. Undaunted, Ruge still went to Paris together with Schütz and Blind, the official representatives of the Brentano government, and once there made such a spectacle of himself that his former editor announced in the official *Karlsruhe Zeitung* that Mr. Ruge was not in Paris in any official capacity but merely "on his own initiative". Having once been taken along by Schütz and Blind to see Ledru-Rollin Ruge suddenly interrupted the diplomatic negotiations with a terrible diatribe against the Germans in the presence of the Frenchmen so that his colleagues finally had to withdraw discomfited and compromised. June 13th[34] came and dealt our Arnold such a severe blow that he took to his heels and did not pause to take breath again until he found himself in London, on free British soil. Referring to this flight later he compared himself to Demosthenes.

In London Ruge first attempted to pass himself off as the Baden provisional ambassador. He then tried to gain acceptance in the English press as a great German writer and thinker but was turned away on the grounds that the English were too materialistic ever to understand German philosophy. He was also asked about his works—a request which Ruge could answer only with a sigh while the image of Bruno Bauer once again rose up before his eyes. For even his Collected Works, what were they but reprints of pamphlets? And they were not even pamphlets but merely newspaper articles in pamphlet form, and basically they were not even newspaper articles but only the muddled fruits of his reading. Action was necessary and so Ruge wrote two articles for the *Leader* in which under the pretext of an analysis of German democracy he declared that in Germany *"humanism"* was the order of the day as represented by Ludwig Feuerbach and Arnold Ruge, the author of the following works: (1) *The Religion of our Age*, (2) *Democracy and Socialism*, (3) *Philosophy and the Revolution.* These three epoch-making works which have not appeared in the bookshops to this day are, it goes without saying, nothing more than new titles arbitrarily applied to old essays of Ruge's. Simultaneously he resumed his daily stints when for his own edification, for the benefit of the German public and to the horror of Mr. Brüggemann[35] he began to retranslate articles into German that had somehow got out of the *Kölnische Zeitung* and into the *Morning Advertiser*. Not exactly burdened with laurels he withdrew to Ostend where he found the leisure necessary to his preparations for the role of universal sage, the *Confusius of the German Emigration.*

Just as Gustav was the vegetable and Gottfried the sensibility of the German petty-bourgeois Philistine, Arnold is representative of its *understanding* or rather its *non-understanding.* Unlike Arnold Winkelried[36] he does not open up a path to freedom [der Freiheit eine Gasse]; he is in his own person the gutter of freedom [der Freiheit eine Gosse]; Ruge stands in the German revolution like the notices seen at the corner of certain streets: It is permitted to pass water here.

We return at last to our circular with its covering letter. It fell flat and the first attempt to create a united democratic church came to nought. Schramm and Gustav later declared that failure was due solely to the circumstance that Ruge could neither speak French nor write German. But then the heroes again set to work.

Che ciascun oltra moda era possente,
Come udirete nel canto seguente.

[For puissant were they all beyond compare,
As in our next canto you shall hear.][37]

VI

Together with Gustav, Rodomonte Heinzen had arrived in London
from Switzerland. Karl Heinzen had for many years made a living
from his threat to destroy "tyranny" in Germany. After the outbreak of
the February Revolution he went so far as to attempt, with unheard-of
courage, to inspect German soil from the vantage point of Schuster
Island [near Basle]. He then betook himself to Switzerland where from
the safety of Geneva he again thundered against the "tyrants and oppressors of the people" and took the opportunity to declare that
"Kossuth is a great man, but Kossuth has forgotten about explosive
silver". His horror of bloodshed was such that it turned him into the
alchemist of the revolution. He dreamt of an explosive substance that
would blast the whole European reaction into the air in a trice without
its users even getting their fingers burnt. He had a particular aversion
to walking amid a shower of bullets and in general to conventional
warfare in which principles are no defence against bullets. Under the
government of Brentano he risked a revolutionary visit to Karlsruhe.
As he did not receive the reward he thought due to him for his heroic
deeds he resolved to edit the *Moniteur*[38] of that "traitor" Brentano.
But as the Prussians advanced he declared that Heinzen would not "let
himself be shot" for that traitor Brentano. Under the pretext of forming
an élite corps where political principles and military organisation would
mutually complement each other, i.e. where military cowardice would
pass for political courage, his constant search for the ideal free corps
made him retrace his steps until he had regained the familiar territory
of Switzerland. *Sophie's Journey from Memel to Saxony*[39] was a good
deal more bloody than Heinzen's revolutionary expedition. On his
arrival in Switzerland he declared that there were no longer any real
men in Germany, that the authentic explosive silver had not yet been
discovered, that the war was not being conducted on revolutionary
principles but in the normal fashion with powder and lead, and that he
intended to revolutionise in Switzerland as Germany was a lost cause.
In the secluded idyll of Switzerland and with the tortured dialect they

speak there it was easy for Rodomonte to pass for a German writer and even for a dangerous man. He achieved his aim. He was expelled and dispatched to London at Federal expense. Rodomonte Heinzen had not directly participated in the European revolutions; but, undeniably, he had moved about extensively on their behalf. When the February Revolution broke out he took up a collection of "revolutionary money" in New York, hastened to the aid of his country and advanced as far as the Swiss border. When the March Club's[40] revolution collapsed he retired from Switzerland to beyond the Channel at the expense of the Swiss Federal Council. He had the satisfaction of making the revolution pay for his advance and the counter-revolution for his retreat.

At every turn in the Italian epics of chivalry we encounter mighty, broad-shouldered giants armed with colossal staves who despite the fact that they lash about them wildly and make a frightening din in battle, never manage to kill their foes but only to destroy the trees in the vicinity. Mr. Heinzen is such an Ariostian giant in political literature. Endowed by nature with a churlish figure and huge masses of flesh he interpreted these gifts to mean that he was destined to be a great man. His weighty physical appearance determines his whole literary posture which is physical through and through. His opponents are always small, mere dwarfs, who can barely reach his ankles and whom he can survey with his kneecap. When, however, he should indeed make a physical appearance, our *uomo membruto* takes refuge in literature or in the courts. Thus scarcely had he reached the safety of English soil than he wrote a tract on moral courage. Or again, our giant allowed a certain Mr. Richter to thrash him so frequently and so thoroughly in New York that the magistrate, who at first only imposed insignificant fines relented and in recognition of Heinzen's doggedness he sentenced the dwarf Richter to pay 200 dollars damages. The natural complement to this great physique so healthy in every fibre is the *healthy commonsense* which Heinzen ascribes to himself in the highest possible degree. It is inevitable that a man with such commonsense will turn out to be a natural genius who has learnt nothing, a barbarian innocent of literature and science. By virtue of his commonsense (which he also calls his "perspicacity" and which allows him to tell Kossuth that he has "advanced to the extreme frontiers of thought"), he learns only from hearsay or the newspapers. He is therefore always behind the times and always wears the coat that literature has cast off some years previously, while rejecting as immoral and reprehensible the new modern dress he cannot find his way into. But when he has once assimilated a thing his faith in it is unshakable; it transforms itself into something that has grown naturally, that is self-evident, that everyone must immediately agree to and that only malicious, stupid or sophisticated persons will pretend not to believe. Such a robust body and healthy commonsense must of course have also some honest, down-to-earth principles and he even shows to advantage when he takes the craze for principles to extremes. In this field Heinzen is second to none. He draws attention to his principles at every opportunity, every argument is met by an appeal to principle, everyone who fails to understand him or whom he does not understand is demolished by the argument that he has no real principles, his insincerity and pure ill-will are such that he would deny that day was day and night night. To deal with these base disciples of Ahriman he summons up his muse, indignation; he curses, rages, boasts, preaches, and foaming at the mouth he roars out the most tragicomical imprecations. He demonstrates what can be achieved in the field of literary invective by a man to whom Börne's[40] wit and literary talent are equally alien. As the muse is, so is the style. An eternal bludgeon, but a commonplace bludgeon with knots that are not even original or sharp. Only when he encounters science does he feel momentarily at a loss. He is then like that Billingsgate fishwife with whom O'Connell became involved in a shouting match and whom he silenced by replying to a long string of insults: "You are all that and worse: you are an isosceles triangle, you are a parallelepiped".

From the earlier history of Mr. Heinzen mention should be made of the fact that he was in the Dutch colonies where he advanced not indeed to the rank of general but to that of NCO, a slight for which he later on always treated the Dutch as a nation without principles. Later we find him back in Cologne as a sub-inspector of taxes and in this capacity he wrote a comedy in which his healthy commonsense vainly strove to satirise the philosophy of Hegel. He was more at home in the gossip columns of the *Kölnische Zeitung*, in the feuilleton where he let fall some weighty words about the quarrels in the Cologne Carnival Club, the institute from which all the great men of Cologne have graduated. His own sufferings and those of his father, a forester, in his conflicts with superiors assumed the proportions of events of universal significance, as easily happens when the man of healthy commonsense contemplates his little personal problems. He gives an account of them in his *Prussian Bureaucracy*, a book much inferior to Venedey's[42] and containing nothing more than the complaints of a petty official against the higher authorities. The book involved him in a trial and although the worst he had to fear was six months in gaol he thought his head was in danger and fled to Brussels. From here he demanded that the Prussian government should not only grant him a safe conduct but also that they should suspend the whole French legal system and give him a jury trial for an ordinary offence. The Prussian government issued a warrant for his arrest; he replied with a "warrant" against the Prussian government which contained *inter alia* a sermon on moral resistance and constitutional monarchy and condemned revolution as immoral and jesuitical. From Brussels he went to Switzerland. Here, as we saw above, he met Friend Arnold and from him he learnt not only his philosophy but also a very useful method of self-enrichment. Just as Arnold sought to assimilate the ideas of his opponents in the course of polemicising against them, so Heinzen learned to acquire ideas new to him by reviling them. Hardly had he become an atheist than with all the zeal of the proselyte he immediately plunged into a furious polemic against poor old Follen because the latter saw no reason to become an atheist in his old age. Having had his nose rubbed in the Swiss Federal Republic our healthy commonsense developed to the point where it desired to introduce the Federal Republic into Germany too. The same commonsense came to the conclusion that this could not be done without a revolution and so Heinzen became a revolutionary. He then began a trade in pamphlets which in the coarsest tones of the Swiss peasant preached immediate revolution and death to the rulers from whom all the evils of the world stem. He sought out committees in Germany who would drum up the cost of printing and distributing these pamphlets and this led naturally to the growth of a begging industry on a large scale in the course of which the party workers were first exploited and then reviled. Old Itzstein could tell a story or two about that. These pamphlets gave Heinzen a great reputation among itinerant German wine salesmen who praised him everywhere as a bonny little fighter.

From Switzerland he went to America. Here, although his Swiss rustic style enabled him to pass as a genuine poet he nevertheless managed to ride the New York *Schnellpost* to death in no time at all

Having returned to Europe in the wake of the February revolution he sent despatches to the *Mannheimer Zeitung* announcing the arrival of the great Heinzen and he also published a pamphlet to revenge himself on Lamartine who together with his whole government had refused to acknowledge him as an official representative of the American Germans. He still did not wish to go to Prussia as he still feared for his head despite the March Revolution and the general amnesty. He would wait until the nation summoned him. As this did not happen he resolved to stand in absentia for the Hamburg constituency to the Frankfurt Parliament: his hope was that he would compensate for being a bad speaker by the loudness of his voice—but he lost the election.

Arriving in London after the collapse of the Baden uprising he fell into a rage with the young people who knew nothing of this great man of *before* the revolution and of *after* the revolution, and who caused him to sink into oblivion. He had always been nothing more than *l'homme de la veille* or *l'homme du lendemain*, he was never *l'homme du jour* or even *de la journée*. As the authentic exploding silver had still not been discovered new weapons had to be found to combat the reaction. He called for two million heads so that he could be a dictator and wade up to the ankles in blood—shed by others. His real aim was, of course, to create a scandal; the reaction had brought him to London at its own expense, by means of an expulsion order from England it would now, so Heinzen hoped, expedite him gratis to New York. The coup failed and its only consequence was that the radical French papers called him a fool who shouted for two million heads only because he had never risked his own. To complete the picture it should be pointed out that his bloodthirsty article had been published in the *Deutsche Londoner Zeitung* owned by the ex-Duke of Brunswick—in return for a cash payment, of course.

Gustav and Heinzen had admired each other for a considerable time. Heinzen praised Gustav as a sage and Gustav praised Heinzen as a fighter. Heinzen had scarcely been able to wait for the end of the European revolution so that he could put an end to the "ruinous disunity in the democratic German *emigration*" and to re-open his pre-revolutionary business. He called for discussion of a draft programme of the German Revolutionary Party. This programme was distinguished by the invention of a special ministry "to cater for the all-important need for public playgrounds, battlegrounds" (minus hail of bullets) "and gardens", and was notable also for the article abolishing "the privileges of the male sex especially in marriage" (and also in thrusting manoeuvres [Stosstaktik] in war, see Clausewitz). This programme was actually no more than a diplomatic note from Heinzen to Gustav as no-one else was clamouring for it. And instead of the hoped for unification it brought about the immediate separation of the two warriors. Heinzen had demanded that during the "revolutionary transition period" there should be a single dictator who would moreover be a Prussian and, to preclude all misunderstandings, he added: "No soldier can qualify as dictator." Gustav, on the other hand, argued for a triumvirate comprising two Badeners and himself. Moreover, Gustav found that Heinzen had included in his prematurely published programme an "idea" stolen from him. This put an end to the second attempt at unification and Heinzen, denied recognition by the whole world, receded into obscurity until, in Autumn 1850, he found English soil too hot for him and sailed off to New York.

VII

Gustav and the Colony of Renunciation

After the indefatigable Gustav had made an unsuccessful attempt to establish a *Central Refugee Committee* together with Friedrich Bobzin, Habegg, Oswald, Rosenblum, Cohnheim, Grunich and other "outstanding" men, he made his way towards Yorkshire. For here, so he believed, a magic garden would flower and in it, unlike the garden of Alcine,[43] virtue would rule instead of vice. An old Englishman with a sense of humour who had been bored by Gustav's theories took him at his word and gave him a few acres of moor in Yorkshire on the express condition that he would there found a "colony of renunciation", a colony in which the consumption of meat, tobacco and spirits would be strictly prohibited, only a vegetarian diet would be permitted and where every colonist would be obliged to read a chapter from Struve's book on Constitutional Law at his morning prayers. Moreover, the colony was to be self-supporting. Accompanied by his Amalia, by Schnauffer, his Swabian canary and by a few other good men and true, Gustav placed his trust in God and went to found the "Colony of Renunciation". Of the colony it must be reported that it contained little prosperity, much culture and unlimited freedom to be bored and to grow thin. One fine morning Gustav uncovered a dreadful plot. His companions who did not share Gustav's ruminant constitution had resolved behind his back to slaughter the old cow, the only one and one whose milk provided the chief source of income of the "Colony of Renunciation". Gustav wrung his hands and shed bitter tears at this betrayal of a fellow creature. He indignantly dissolved the colony and decided to become a "wet" Quaker[44] if he were unable to revive the

Deutscher Zuschauer or to establish a "provisional government" in London.

VIII

Arnold, who was anything but content in his retreat in Ostend and who longed for a "frequent appearance" before the public, heard of Gustav's misfortune. He resolved to return to England at once and by climbing on Gustav's shoulders, to hoist himself into the pentarchy of European democracy. For in the meantime the European Central Committee[45] had been formed consisting of Mazzini, Ledru-Rollin and Darasz, Mazzini of course was the soul of the enterprise. Ruge thought he could smell a vacant position. In his *Proscrit* Mazzini had indeed introduced General Ernst Haug, his own invention, as the German associate but for decency's sake it was not possible to nominate such a completely unknown person onto the Central Committee. Ruge was not unaware of the fact that Gustav had had dealings with Mazzini in Switzerland. He himself was acquainted with Ledru-Rollin but unfortunately Ledru-Rollin was not acquainted with him. So Arnold took up residence in Brighton and flattered and cajoled the unsuspecting Gustav, promised to help him found a *Deutscher Zuschauer* in London and even to undertake as a joint venture the democratic publication of the Rotteck–Welcker *Lexicon of Politics* with Ruge paying the costs. At the same time he introduced Gustav as a great man and collaborator into the local German paper which in accordance with his principles he always had on tap (this time the blow fell on the *Bremer Tages–Chronik* of the nonconformist parson Dulon). One good deed deserves another: Gustav presented Arnold to Mazzini. As Arnold's French was wholly incomprehensible there was nothing to prevent him from introducing himself to Mazzini as the greatest man in Germany and above all as her greatest "thinker". The canny Italian idealist at once realised that Arnold was the man he was looking for, the *homme sans conséquence* who would provide the German countersignature of his anti-papal Bulls. Thus Arnold Ruge became the fifth wheel on the state coach of European democracy. When an Alsatian asked Ledru what on earth possessed him to make an ally of such a *bête*, Ledru replied brusquely: "He is Mazzini's man." When Mazzini was asked why he became involved with Ledru, a man bereft of all ideas, he answered slyly: "I took him for that very reason." Mazzini himself had every reason to avoid people with ideas. But Arnold Ruge saw his wildest dreams come true and for the moment he even forgot Bruno Bauer.

When the time came for him to sign Mazzini's first manifesto he sadly recalled the days when he had presented himself to Professor Leo in Halle and old Follen in Switzerland as a Trinitarian on one occasion and as a humanist atheist on another. This time he had to declare himself for *God* and against the princes. However, Arnold's philosophic conscience had been enfeebled by his association with Dulon and other parsons among whom he passed for a philosopher. Even in his best days Arnold could not entirely suppress a certain foible for religion in general and moreover his "honest consciousness" kept on whispering to him: Sign, Arnold! Paris vaut bien une messe. One does not become fifth wheel on the coach of the provisional government of Europe in partibus for nothing. Reflect, Arnold! all you have to do is sign a manifesto every two weeks, and as a member of the German Parliament, in the company of the greatest men in all Europe. And bathed in perspiration Arnold signs. A curious joke, he murmurs. Ce n'est que le premier pas qui coûte. He had copied this last sentence into his notebook the previous night. However, Arnold had not come to the end of his trials. The European Central Committee had issued a series of manifestos to Europe, to the French, the Italians, the Poles and the Wallachians and now, following the great battle at Bronzell,[46] it was *Germany's* turn. In his draft Mazzini attacked the Germans for their lack of cosmopolitan spirit, and in particular, for their arrogant treatment of Italian salami vendors, organ-grinders, confectioners, dormouse tamers and mouse–trap sellers. Taken aback Arnold confessed that it was true. He went further. He declared his readiness to cede the Austrian Tirol and Istria to Mazzini. But this was not enough. He had not only to appeal to the conscience of the German people, but also to attack them where they were most vulnerable. Arnold received instructions that this time he was to have an opinion, as he represented the German element. He felt like the student Jobs.[47] He scratched himself thoughtfully behind his ear and after long reflection he stuttered: "Since the age of Tacitus the voices of German bards and baritones can be heard. In winter they kindle fires on all the mountains so as to warm their feet." The bards, the baritones and fires on all the mountains! That will put a bomb under German freedom! thought Mazzini with a grin. The bards, baritones, fires on all the mountains and German freedom to boot went into the manifesto as a sop for the German nation. To his astonishment Arnold had passed the examination and understood for the first time with what little wisdom the world is governed. From that moment on he despised Bruno Bauer more than ever for all his eighteen hefty tomes written while he was still young.

While Arnold in the wake of the European Central Committee was signing *warlike* manifestoes with God, for Mazzini and against the princes, the *peace movement* was raging not only in England, under the aegis of Cobden, but even beyond the North Sea. So that in Frankfurt/ Main the Yankee swindler, Elihu Burritt together with Cobden, Jaup, Girardin and the Red Indian Ka–gi–ga–gi–wa–wa–be–ta organised a Peace Congress. Our Arnold was just itching to be able to make one of his "frequent appearances" and to give birth to a manifesto. So he proclaimed himself the corresponding member of the Frankfurt Assembly and sent over an extremely confused Peace Manifesto translated out of Cobden's speeches into his own speculative Pomeranian. Various Germans drew Arnold's attention to the contradiction between his warlike attitude in the Central Committee and his peaceful Quaker- ism. He would reply: "Well, there you have the contradictions. That's the dialectic for you. In my youth I studied Hegel." His "honest consciousness" was eased by the thought that Mazzini knew no German and that it was not hard to pull the wool over his eyes.

Moreover, his relationship with Mazzini promised to become even more secure thanks to the protection of *Harro Harring* who had just landed in Hull. For with Harring a new and highly symptomatic character steps onto the stage.

IX

The great drama of the democratic emigration of 1848–52 had been preceded by a prelude eighteen years previously: the democratic emigration of 1830–31. Even though with the passage of time most of the players had disappeared from the stage there still remained a few noble ruins who, stoically indifferent to the course of history and their own lack of success, continued their activities as agitators, devised comprehensive plans, formed provisional governments and hurled proclamations into the world in every direction. It is obvious that these experienced swindlers were infinitely superior to the younger genera- tion in business know-how. It was this very know-how acquired through eighteen years practice in conspiring, scheming, intriguing, pro-claiming, duping, showing off and pushing oneself to the fore that gave Mr. Mazzini the cheek and the assurance to install himself as the Central Committee of European democracy supported only by three straw men of much smaller experience in such matters.

No one was more favoured by circumstances to become the very type of the *émigré* agitator than our friend *Harro Harring*. And indeed he did become the prototype whom all our heroes of the Exile, all the Arnolds, Gustavs and Gottfrieds strove more or less consciously and with varying success to emulate. They may even equal him if circumstances are not unfavourable, but they will hardly surpass him.

Harro who like Caesar has himself described his own great deeds (London 1852) was born on the "Cimbrian peninsula" and belongs to that visionary North Frisian race which has already been shown by Dr. Clement to have produced all the great nations of the world.

"Already in early youth" he attempted to "set the seal of action upon his enthusiasm for the cause of the peoples" by going to *Greece* in 1821. We see how Friend Harro had an early premonition of his mission to be everywhere where confusion reigned. Later on "a strange fate led him to the source of absolutism, to the vicinity of the Czar and he had seen through the Jesuitism of constitutional monarchy in *Poland*".

So Harro fought for freedom in Poland also. But "the crisis in the history of Europe following the fall of Warsaw greatly perplexed him", and his perplexity led him to the idea of "the democracy of nations", which he at once "documented in the work: *The Nations*, Strasbourg, March 1832". It is worth remarking that this work was almost quoted at the Hambacher Fest.[48] At the same time he published his "republican poems: *Blutstropfen* [Drops of Blood]; *The History of King Saul or the Monarchy*; *Male voices on Germany's Freedom*" and edited the journal *Deutschland* in Strasbourg. All these and even his future writings had the unexpected good fortune to be banned by the Federal Diet on November 4, 1831. This was the only thing he still lacked, only now did he achieve real importance and also the martyr's crown. So that he could exclaim "My writings were everywhere well received and echoed loudly in the hearts of the people. They were mostly distributed gratis. In the case of some of them I did not even receive enough to cover the costs of printing."

But new honours still awaited him. In 1831 Mr. Welcker had vainly attempted in a long letter "to convert him to the *vertical horizon* of constitutional monarchy". And now, in January 1832, there came a visit from Mr. Malten, a well-known Prussian agent abroad, who proposed that he should enter Prussian service. What double recognition this was—and from the enemy too! Enough, Malten's offer "triggered off the idea that in the face of this dynastic treachery he should give birth to the concept of Scandinavian nationality", and "from that time on at least the *word* Scandinavia was reborn after having been forgotten for centuries".

In this manner our North Frisian from South Jutland who did not know himself whether he was a German or a Dane acquired at least an imaginary nationality whose first consequence was that the men of Hambach would have nothing to do with him.

With all these events behind him Harro's fortune was made. Veteran of freedom in Greece and Poland, the inventor of "democracy of nations", re-discoverer of the word "Scandinavia", poet acknowledged by the ban of the Federal Diet, thinker and journalist, marytr, a great man esteemed even by his enemies, a man whose allegiance constitutionalists, absolutists and republicans vied with each other to possess and, with all that, empty-headed and confused enough to believe in his own greatness—what then was needed to make his happiness complete? But Harro was a conscientious man and as his fame grew so did the demands which he made upon himself. What was missing was a great work that would present in an entertaining and popular form the great doctrines of freedom, the idea of democracy, and of nationality and all the sublime struggles for freedom on the part of the youthful Europe arising before his very eyes. None but a poet and thinker of the very first rank could produce such a work and none but Harro could be this man. Thus arose the first three plays of the "dramatic cycle" *The People*, of which there were twelve parts in all, one of them in Danish, a labour to which the author devoted ten years of his life. Unfortunately eleven of these twelve parts have "hitherto remained in manuscript".

However, this dallying with the muse was not to last forever.

"In the winter of 1832–1833 a movement was prepared in Germany—which was brought to a tragic end in the skirmish in Frankfurt. I was entrusted with the task of taking the fortress (?) in Kehl on the night of 6 April. Men and weapons were at the ready."

Unfortunately it all came to nothing and Harro had to retire to the depths of France where he wrote his *Words of a Man*. From there he was summoned to Switzerland by the Poles arming themselves for their march on Savoy. Here he became "attached to their General Staff", wrote a further two parts of his dramatic cycle *The People*, and made the acquaintance of Mazzini in Geneva. The whole band of fire–eaters consisting of Polish, French, German, Italian and Swiss adventurers under the command of the noble Ramorino then made their famous attack on Savoy.[49] In this campaign our Harro "discovered the value of his life and strength". But as the other freedom fighters felt "the value of their lives" no less than Harro and no doubt had just as few illusions about their "strength" the exploit ended badly and they returned to Switzerland beaten, dishevelled and in disarray.

This campaign was all that was needed to give our band of emigrant knights a complete insight into the terror they inspired in the tyrants. As long as the aftermath of the July Revolution could still be felt in isolated insurrections in France, Germany or Italy, as long as they felt someone or other standing behind them our *émigré* heroes felt themselves to be but atoms in the seething masses—more or less privileged, prominent atoms, to be sure, but in the last analysis they were still atoms. But as these insurrections gradually grew feebler, as the great mass of "lackeys", of the "half–hearted" and the "men of little faith" retired from the putschist swindles and as our knights felt increasingly lonely, so did their self-esteem grow in proportion. If the whole of Europe became craven, stupid and selfish, how could our trusty heroes fail to grow in their own estimation, for were they not the priests who kept the sacred fires of hatred for all tyrants burning in their breasts and who maintained the traditions of virtue and love of freedom for a more vigorous generation yet to come! If they too deserted the flag the tyrants would be safe for ever. So like the democrats of 1848 they saw in every defeat a guarantee of future victory and they gradually transformed themselves more and more into itinerant Don Quixotes with dubious sources of income. Once arrived at this point they could plan their greatest act of heroism, the foundation of "Young Europe" whose Charter of Brotherhood was drawn up by Mazzini and signed in Berne on 15 April 1834. Harro appears in it as

> "initiator of the Central Committee, adoptive member of Young Germany and Young Italy and also as representative of the Scandinavian branch" which he "still represents today".

The date of the Charter of Brotherhood marks for Harro the great

G

epoch from which calculations are made forwards and backwards, thus replacing the birth of Christ. It is the highpoint of his life. He was co-dictator of Europe in partibus and although the world knew nothing of him he was one of the most dangerous men alive. No one stood behind him but his many unpublished works, a few German artisans in Switzerland and a dozen political speculators who had seen better days—but for that very reason he could claim that all the people of the world were on his side. For it is the fate of all great men not to be recognised by their own age whereas the future belongs to them. And Harro had taken care of the future—he had it in black and white in his bag in the form of the Charter of Brotherhood.

But now began Harro's decline. His first sorrow was that "Young Germany split off from Young Europe in 1836". But Germany was duly punished for that. Because of the split *nothing had been prepared for a national movement in Germany early in 1848*" and this is why everything ended so miserably.

But a much greater sorrow for Harro was the growth of communism. We learn from him that the founder of communism was none other than

> "the cynic Johannes Müller from Berlin, the author of a very interest-ing pamphlet on Prussian policy, Altenburg 1831". Müller went to England where "the only available opening for him was in Smith-field Market where he had to tend swine at the crack of dawn".

Communism soon began to spread among the German artisans in France and Switzerland and it became a very dangerous enemy for Harro as it cut off the only market for his writings. This was due to the "indirect censorship of communism" from which poor Harro has suffered to this very day and indeed it is now worse than ever as he sadly confesses and "as the fate of my drama *The Dynasty* proves". This indirect communist censorship even succeeded in expelling Harro from Europe and so he went to Rio de Janeiro (in 1840) where he lived for a time as a painter. "Using his time conscientiously here as every-where" he brought out a new work: "*Poems of a Scandinavian* (2000 copies) which has been distributed so widely among sea-faring people as to have become an oceanic best-seller".

However, his "scrupulous sense of obligation towards Young Europe" unfortunately led him to retun to the Old World.

He "hastened to Mazzini in London and soon perceived the danger that threatened the cause of the peoples from communism".

New deeds awaited him. The Bandiera brothers[50] were preparing for their expedition to Italy. To support them and to divert the forces of despotism Harro "returned to South America where in union with Garibaldi he dedicated himself to furthering the idea of a United States of South America".

But the despots had got wind of his mission and Harro took to his heels. He sailed to New York.

"During the voyage I was very active intellectually and wrote among other things a drama: *The Power of Ideas*, which belonged to the dramatic cycle *The People*—this too has remained in MS. up to now!"

From South America he brought with him to New York a programme from a group alleged to be affiliated with *Humanidad*.

The news of the February Revolution inspired him to produce a pamphlet in French, *La France réveillée* and while embarking for Europe "I documented my love for my country once again in some poems, *Scandinavia*".

He went to Schleswig-Holstein. Here, after an absence of twenty-seven years, he "discovered an unheard of conceptual confusion in the sphere of international law, democracy, republicanism socialism and communism, a chaos which lay like rotting hay and straw in the Augean stables of party factions and national hatred".

No wonder, for his "political writings" like his "whole striving and activities since 1831 had remained alien and unknown in those frontier provinces of my home country".

The Augustenburg Party[51] had suppressed him for eighteen years by means of a conspiracy of silence. To deal with this he girt on a sabre, a rifle, four pistols and six daggers and called for the formation of a free corps, but in vain. After various adventures he finally arrived in Hull. Here he hastened to issue two circulars to the peoples of Schleswig-Holstein, Scandinavia and Germany and even sent a note, as has been reported, to two communists in London with this message: "Five thousand workers in Norway send you fraternal greetings through me."

Despite this curious appeal he soon became a sleeping partner of the European Central Committee again, thanks to the Charter of Brotherhood, and he also became "nightwatchman and employee of a young firm of brokers in Gravesend on the Thames where my task was to drum up trade among ships' captains in nine different languages until

I was accused of fraud, a thing which the philosopher Johannes Müller was at least spared in his capacity as swineherd".

Harro summarised his action-packed life as follows:

> "It can easily be calculated that apart from my poems I have given away more than 18,000 copies of my writings in German (varying from 10 shillings to 3 Marks in price, and hence amounting to around 25,000 Marks in toto) to the democratic movement. I have never even been reimbursed for the printing costs, let alone received any profit for myself."

With this we bring the adventures of our demagogic Hidalgo from the South Jutland Mancha to a close. In Greece and Brazil, on the Vistula and La Plata, in Schleswig-Holstein and in New York, in London and in Switzerland: the representative of Young Europe and of the South American *Humanidad*, painter, nightwatchman and employee, peddler of his own writings; among Poles one day and gauchos the next, and ship's captains the day after that; unacknowledged, abandoned, ignored but everywhere an itinerant knight of freedom with a thoroughgoing dislike of ordinary bourgeois hard work—our hero at all times in all countries and in all circumstances remains himself; with the same confusion, the same meddlesome pretensions, the same faith in himself. He will always defy the world and never cease to say, write and print that since 1831 he has been the mainspring of world history.

X

Despite his unexpected successes hitherto Arnold had not yet arrived at the goal of his labours. As Germany's representative by the grace of Mazzini, he was under the obligation on the one hand to obtain confirmation of his appointment at least by the German emigration and, on the other hand, to present the Central Committee with people who respected his leadership. He did indeed claim that in Germany "there was a clearly defined part of the people behind him" but this hind portion could scarcely inspire much confidence in Mazzini and Ledru as long as they could see nothing but the Ruge front portion. Suffice it to say that Arnold had to look around among the *émigrés* for a "clearly defined" tail.

At about this time Gottfried Kinkel came to London and together with him or soon afterwards a number of other exiles partly from France, partly from Switzerland and Belgium: Schurz, Strodtmann, Oppenheim, Schimmelpfennig, Techow, etc. These new arrivals some of whom had already tried their hand at forming provisional governments in Switzerland, infused new life into the London emigration and for Arnold the moment seemed more favourable than ever. At the same time Heinzen again took over the *Schnellpost* in New York and so Arnold could now make his "frequent appearances" on the other side of the ocean and not just in the local Bremen paper. Should Arnold ever find his Strodtmann the latter would surely declare the monthly numbers of the *Schnellpost* from the beginning of 1851 on to be a priceless source of information. One has to see this infinitely feeble mixture of gossip, silliness and nastiness, this ant-like self-importance with which Arnold deposits his dung, for otherwise one would not believe it. While Heinzen portrays Arnold as a European Great Power, Arnold treats Heinzen as an American newspaper oracle. He tells him the secrets of European diplomacy and in particular the latest events in the history of world emigration. Arnold sometimes figures as the anonymous correspondent in London and Paris in order to keep the American public informed of some of the great Arnold's fashionable movements.

"Once again Arnold Ruge has the communists by the throat" — "Arnold Ruge *yesterday* (dated from Paris so that the dating gives the old joker away) made an excursion from Brighton to London." And again: "Arnold Ruge to Karl Heinzen: Dear Friend and Editor .... Mazzini sends his greetings ... Ledru-Rollin *gives his permission* to translate his pamphlet on the June 13th" and so on.

A letter from America has this comment to make:

> "As I see from Ruge's letters in the *Schnellpost* Heinzen must be writing Ruge (privately) all sorts of funny stories about the importance of his paper in America, while Ruge seems to act as if he were a major European government. Whenever Ruge imparts a momentous piece of information to Heinzen he never omits to add: You can ask other newspapers to reprint this. As if they would hesitate to print news regardless of Ruge's authorisation. Incidentally, I have never seen these momentous reports actually appear anywhere else despite Ruge's advice and permission."

Father Ruge employed both this paper and the *Bremer Tages-Chronik* to win over new arrivals by flattery: Kinkel is here now, the patriot and poet of genius; Strodtmann, a great writer; Schurz, a young man as amiable as he is bold, and a whole array of distinguished revolutionary warriors.

Meanwhile in contrast to the Mazzini Committee a *plebeian* European Committee was formed with the support of the "inferior refugees" and the *émigré* dregs of the various European nations. At the time of the battle of Bronzell this committee had issued a manifesto that included the following outstanding German signatories: Gebert, Majer, Dietz, Schärttner, Schapper, Willich. This document was couched in peculiar French and contained the information that at that moment (10 November 1850) the Holy Alliance of Tyrants had assembled 1,330,000 soldiers backed by another 700,000 armed lackeys in reserve; that "the German papers and the Committee's own contacts" had revealed the secret intentions of the Warsaw Conferences[52] and that these were to massacre all the republicans of Europe. This was followed by the inevitable call to arms. This "manifeste-Faneron-Caperon-Gouté" as it was described by the *Patrie* (to whom they sent it) was overwhelmed with ridicule by the reactionary press. The *Patrie* called it "the manifesto of the dii minorum gentium, written without chic, without style and equipped with only the most banal clichés, 'serpents', 'sicaires' and 'égorgements' ".

The *Indépendence Belge* states that it was written by the most obscure soldiers of democracy, poor devils who had sent it to their correspondent in London even though their paper was conservative. Greatly as they longed to get into print, they would nevertheless not publish the names of the signatories as a punishment. Despite their attempts to beg from the reaction these noble people did not manage to obtain recognition as dangerous conspirators.

The establishment of this rival firm spurred Arnold on to even greater efforts. Together with Struve, Kinkel, R. Schramm and Bucher, etc. he tried to found a *Volksfreund*, or, if Gustav were to insist, a *Deutscher Zuschauer*. But the plan fell through. Partly because our "good-humoured" Gottfried demanded payment in cash whereas Arnold shared Hansemann's view that in money matters there is no room for good humour. Arnold's particular aim was to impose a levy on the Reading Circle, a club of German watchmakers, well-paid workers and petty bourgeois, but in this too he was frustrated.

But soon there arose another opportunity for Arnold to make one of his "frequent appearances". Ledru and his supporters among the French *émigrés* could not let 24 February (1851)[53] pass without celebrating a "Fraternal Feast" of the nations of Europe. In fact only the French and the Germans attended. Mazzini did not come and excused himself by letter: Gottfried who was present went home fuming because his mute presence failed to produce the magical effect he expected; Arnold lived to see the day when his friend Ledru pretended not to know him and became so confused when he arose to speak that he kept quiet about the French speech he had prepared and which had been approved in high places; he just stammered a few words in German and retreated precipitately, exclaiming: *À la restauration de la révolution!* to the accompaniment of a general shaking of heads.

On the same day a rival banquet took place under the auspices of the competing committee referred to above. Annoyed that the Mazzini–Ledru committee had not invited him to join them from the beginning Louis Blanc took himself off to the refugee mob, declaring that "the aristocracy of talent must also be abolished". The whole lower emigration was thus assembled. The chivalrous Willich presided. The hall was festooned with flags and the walls were emblazoned with the names of the greatest men of the people: Waldeck between Garibaldi and Kossuth, Jacoby between Blanqui and Cabet, Robert Blum between Barbès and Robespierre. That coquettish ape Louis Blanc read out in a whining voice an address from his old Eeyore brothers, the future peers of the social republic, the delegates of the Luxemburg of 1848. Willich read out an address from Switzerland the signatures to which had partly been collected under false pretences. Later he was indiscreet enough to publish the address, which resulted in the mass expulsion of the signatories. From Germany no message had arrived. Then speeches. Despite the eternal brotherhood boredom could be seen on every face.

The banquet gave rise to a highly edifying scandal which like the heroic deeds of the European central mob-committee, unfolded within the pages of the counter-revolutionary press. It had struck observers as very strange that during the banquet a certain Barthélemy should have given an extremely grandiose eulogy of *Blanqui* in the presence of Louis Blanc. The puzzle was now elucidated. The *Patrie* printed a toast that Blanqui had sent from Belle-Île in response to a request from the orator at the banquet. In the toast he aimed some rough blows at the whole provisional government of 1848 and at Louis Blanc in particular. The *Patrie* expressed astonishment that this toast had been suppressed in the course of the banquet. Louis Blanc at once wrote to

The Times declaring that Blanqui was an abominable intriguer and had never sent such a toast to the Banquet committee. The committee consisting of Messrs, Blanc, Willich, Landolphe, Schapper, Barthélemy and Vidil, announced simultaneously in the *Patrie* that they had never received the toast. The *Patrie*, however, did not allow the declaration to be printed until they had made inquiries of M. Antoine, Blanqui's brother-in-law, who had given them the text of the toast. Beneath the declaration of the Banquet committee they printed M. Antoine's reply: he had sent the toast to Barthélemy, one of the signatories of the declaration and had received an acknowledgement from him. Whereupon Mr. Barthélemy was forced to admit that it was true that he had lied. He had indeed received the toast but had thought it unsuitable and so had not informed the committee of it. But before this, behind Barthélemy's back his co-signatory, the French ex-captain Vidil had also written to the *Patrie* saying that his honour as a soldier and his sense of truth compelled him to confess that not only he but also Louis Blanc, Willich and all the other signatories of the first declaration had lied. The committee had consisted of 13 members and not 6. They had all seen Blanqui's toast, they had discussed it and after a long debate agreed to suppress it by a majority of 7 votes to 6. He had been one who had voted *in favour* of reading it in public.

It is easy to imagine the joy of the *Patrie* when it received Barthélemy's declaration after Vidil's letter. They printed it with this preface:

"We have often asked ourselves, and it is a difficult question to answer, whether the demagogues are notable more for their stupidity or their boastfulness. A fourth letter from London has increased our perplexity. There they are, we do not know how many poor wretches, who are so tormented by the longing to write and to see their names published in the *reactionary* press that they are undeterred even by the prospect of infinite humiliation and mortification. What do they care for the laughter and the indignation of the public—the *Journal des Débats*, the *Assemblée nationale* and the *Patrie* will find space for their stylistic exercises; to achieve this no cost to the cause of cosmopolitan democracy can be too high. . . . In the name of literary commiseration we include the following letter from 'Citizen' Barthélemy—it is a novel, and, we hope, the last proof of the authenticity of Blanqui's famous toast whose existence they first all denied and now fight among themselves for the right to acknowledge."

XI

"The actual force of events", to use one of Arnold's all-pervading beautiful forms, now took the following course. On 24 February, Ruge had compromised himself and the German *émigrés* in the presence of foreigners. Hence the few *émigrés* who still felt inclined to go along with him felt insecure and without any support. Arnold put the blame on the division in the emigration and pressed harder than ever for unity. Compromised as he was, he still reached eagerly for the chance to compromise himself further.

Hence the *Anniversary of the March revolution in Vienna* was used to give a German banquet. The chivalrous Willich declined the invitation; as he belonged to "citizen" Louis Blanc he could not collaborate with "citizen" Ruge who belonged to "citizen" Ledru. Likewise the ex-deputies Reichenbach, Schramm, Bucher, etc., recoiled from Ruge's presence. Not counting the silent guests there appeared Mazzini, Ruge, Struve, Tausenau, Haug, Ronge and Kinkel—all of whom spoke.

Ruge filled the role of "the complete fool" as even his friends admitted. The German public was however to experience even greater things. Tausenau's clowning, Struve's croaking, Haug's meanderings, Ronge's litanies turned the whole audience to stone and the majority drifted away even before that flower of rhetoric, Jeremiah-Kinkel, who had been saved for the dessert, could begin his speech. "In the name of the martyrs" for the martyrs, Gottfried spoke as a martyr and uttered lachrymose words of reconciliation to all "from the simple defender of the constitution down to the red republican". At the same time as all these republicans, and even red republicans, like Kinkel, groaned away in this fashion, they also knelt down before the English constitution in humble adoration, a contradiction to which the Morning Chronicle politely drew their attention the following morning.

The same evening Ruge saw the fulfilment of his desires as can be seen from a proclamation whose most brilliant sections we offer here:

"To the Germans!

Brothers and friends in Germany! We, the undersigned, constitute at present and until such time as you decide differently, *the committee for German affairs*" (irrespective which affairs).

"The Central Committee of the European democratic movement has sent us Arnold *Ruge*, the Baden revolution has sent Gustav
G*

Struve, the Viennese revolution has sent us Ernst Haug, the religious movement has sent us Johannes Ronge and prison has sent us Gottfried Kinkel; we have invited the social-democratic workers to send a representative to our midst.

"German brothers! Events have deprived you of your freedom . . . we know that you are incapable of abandoning your freedom for ever and we have omitted nothing" (in the way of committees and manifestoes) "that might accelerate your recovery of it.

"When we . . . when we gave our guarantee and our support to the Mazzini loan, when we . . . when we invoked the Holy Alliance of peoples against the unholy alliance of their oppressors, we only did, as you know, what you wished with all your hearts to see done. . . . The tyrants have been arraigned before the universal court of mankind in the great trial of freedom" (and with Arnold as public prosecutor, the "tyrants" can sleep in peace) ". . . arson, murder, pillaging, hunger and bankruptcy will soon be widespread throughout Germany.

"You have the example of France before your eyes—Smouldering with fury it is more united than ever in its determination to liberate itself" (I ask you, who on earth could have foreseen the 2 December!) —look at Hungary, even the Croats have been converted" (thanks to the *Deutscher Zuschauer* and Ruge's wood-shaving coats)—"and believe us, for we know, when we say that Poland is immortal" (Mr. Darasz confided this piece of information to them under solemn oath of secrecy).

"Force against force—that is the justice that is being prepared. And we shall leave nothing undone to bring into being a *more effective provisional government*" (aha!) "than the Vorparlament[54] and a more potent arm of the people than the National Assembly" (see below what these gentlemen brought into being when they attempted to lead each other by the nose).

"Our draft proposals concerning the finances and the press" (Articles 1 and 2 of the strong provisional government—the Customs Officer, Christian Müller, is to be given the task of implementing this measure) "shall be presented separately. We wish only to say that every purchase for the Italian Loan will be of immediate benefit to our Committee and to our cause and that for the moment you can help in a practical way above all by ensuring a *liberal supply of money*. We shall then *know how to translate this money into public opinion and public violence.* (With Arnold as translator) ". . . We say to you: *Subscribe 10 million Francs and we shall liberate the Continent!*

"Germans, remember . . ." (that you sing baritone and light fires on the mountains) ". . . lend us your thoughts" (which we need almost as badly as your money), "your purse" (yes, don't forget that) "and your arm! We expect your zeal to increase with the intensity of your sufferings and that the Committee shall be adequately strengthened for the hour of decision by your present contributions." (If not, they would have to resort to spirituous liquor which would be against Gustav's principles.)

"All democrats are *instructed* to publicise our appeal" (the Customs Officer, Christian Müller, will take care of the rest).

"London, 13 March 1851

The Committee for German Affairs
Arnold Ruge, Gustav Struve,
Ernst Haug, Johannes Ronge,
Gottfried Kinkel"

Our readers are now acquainted with Gottfried, they are also acquainted with Gustav; Arnold's "frequent appearances" have likewise been repeated often enough. So there remain but two members of the "effective provisional government" whom we have still to introduce.

Johannes *Ronge* or Johannes Kurzweg as he likes to be known in his intimate circle, is certainly not the author of the Book of *Revelations*. There is nothing mysterious about him, he is banal, hackneyed, as insipid as water, luke-warm dish-water. As is well known Johannes became famous when he refused to permit the Holy Mantle[55] in Trier to intercede for him—though it is wholly unimportant who intercedes for Johannes. When Johannes first made his appearance the elderly Paulus[56] expressed his regrets that Hegel was dead as he would no longer be able to regard *him* as shallow were he alive and he added that the late lamented Krug was lucky to be dead as he thereby escaped the danger of acquiring a reputation for profundity. Johannes is one of those phenomena often met with in history who only begin to understand a movement centuries after its rise and fall and who then like children reproduce the content of the movement as if it had just been discovered, regurgitating it in the most feeble, colourless and philistinic manner imaginable. Such craftsmanship does not last very long and soon our Johannes found himself in a daily deteriorating situation in Germany. His watered-down version of the Enlightenment went out of fashion and Johannes made a pilgrimage to England where we see him reappear, without any notable success, as the rival of Padre Gavazzi.[57] The ungainly, sallow, tedious village parson naturally paled by the side of the fiery, histrionic Italian monk and the English bet heavily that this arid Johannes could not be the man who had set the deep-thinking German nation in motion. But he was consoled by Arnold Ruge who found that the German-Catholicism of our Johannes was remarkably similar to his own brand of atheism.

Ludwig von Hauck had been a captain of engineers in the Imperial Austrian army, then co-editor of the *Constitution* in Vienna, later still leader of a battalion in the Viennese National Guard, where he defended the Burgtor against the Imperial army on October 30 with great courage, abandoning his post only after all was lost. He escaped to Hungary, joined up with Bem's army in Siebenbürgen where in consequence of his valour he advanced to the rank of colonel in the general staff. After Görgy surrendered at Vilagos Ludwig Hauck was taken prisoner and died like a hero on one of the many gallows that the Austrians erected in Hungary to avenge their repeated defeats and to express their fury at the protection Russia had extended and which they so bitterly resented. In London Haug was long thought to be the incarcerated Hauck, an officer, who had so distinguished himself in the Hungarian campaign. However, it now seems to be established that he is not the late Hauck. Just as he was unable to prevent Mazzini from improvising him into a general after the fall of Rome, so too he could do nothing to stop Arnold Ruge from transforming him into the representative of the Viennese revolution and a member of the strong provisional government. Later he gave aesthetic lectures about the economic foundations of the cosmogony of universal history from a geological standpoint and with musical accompaniment. Among the *émigrés* this melancholic man is known as "the poor wretch", or as the French say, "*la bonne bête*".

Arnold could not believe his good fortune. He had a manifesto, a strong provisional government, a loan of ten million francs and even a homunculus to produce a weekly magazine with the modest title *Kosmos*, edited by General Haug.

The manifesto came and went unread. The *Kosmos* died of malnutrition in the third number, the money failed to roll in, the provisional government dissolved into its components once more.

At first, the *Kosmos* contained advertisements for Kinkel's lectures, for the worthy Willich's appeals for money for the Schleswig-Holstein refugees and for Göhringer's saloon. It contained further a lampoon by Arnold. The old joker invented a certain hospitable friend called Müller in Germany whose guest, Schulze, he pretended to be. Müller expresses astonishment at what he reads in the papers about English hospitality;

he fears that all this "sybaritism" may distract Schulze from his "affairs of state"—but he does not grudge him this as when Schulze returns to Germany he will be so overwhelmed by state affairs that he will have to deny himself the pleasures of Müller's hospitality. Finally, Müller exclaims: "Surely it was not the traitor Radowitz, but Mazzini, Ledru-Rollin, Citizen Willich, Kinkel and yourself" (Arnold Ruge) "who were invited to Windsor Castle?"

If after all this the *Kosmos* folded up after the third issue the failure could not be put down to lack of publicity, for at every possible English meeting the speakers would find it pressed into their hands with the urgent request to recommend it as they would find their own principles specially represented in it.

Scarcely had the subscriptions for the ten-million-Franc loan been opened than the rumour went around that a list of contributors to a fund to dispatch Struve (and Amalia) to America, was circulating in the City.

> "When the Committee resolved to publish a German weekly with Haug as editor, Struve protested as he wanted the post of editor for himself and wished the journal to bear the title *Deutscher Zuschauer*. Having protested he resolved to go to America."

Thus far the report in the *Deutsche Schnellpost* of New York. It remains silent about the fact (and Heinzen had his reasons for this) that as Gustav was a collaborator on the Duke of Brunswick's *Deutscher Londoner Zeitung* Mazzini had struck his name off the list of the German Committee. Gustav soon acclimatised his *Deutscher Zuschauer* in New York. But soon after came the news from over the ocean: "Gustav's *Zuschauer* is dead." As he says, this was not for the lack of subscribers, nor because he had no leisure for writing but simply because of a dearth of *paying* subscribers. However, the democratic revision of Rotteck's *Universal History* could not be postponed any longer, so great was the need for it, and as he had already begun it 15 years previously he would give the subscribers a corresponding number of issues of the *Universal History* instead of the *Deutscher Zuschauer*. He would have to request payment in advance for this to which in the circumstances no one could object. As long as Gustav had remained on this side of the Atlantic Heinzen regarded him along with Ruge as the greatest man in Europe. Scarcely had he reached the other side than a great scandal arose between them.

Gustav writes:

"When on 6 June in Karlsruhe Heinzen saw that cannon was being brought up he left for Strasbourg with female companions."

Whereupon Heinzen called Gustav "a soothsayer".

Arnold was busy broadcasting the virtues of the *Kosmos* in the journal of his faithful disciple Heinzen, when it failed to appear, and at about the time when the strong provisional government was disintegrating Rodomonte–Heinzen was busy proclaiming "military obedience" towards it in his journal. Heinzen is famous for his love of the military in peacetime.

"Shortly after Struve's departure *Kinkel* too resigned from the Committee which was thereby reduced to impotence." (*Deutsche Schnellpost*, No. 23.)

With this the strong provisional government dwindled still further and only Messrs. Ruge, Ronge, and Haug remained in it. Even Arnold realised that with this Trinity nothing at all could be brought into existence, let alone a cosmos. Nevertheless through all the permutations, variations and combinations it remained the nucleus of all his subsequent attempts to form committees. An indefatigable man, he saw no reason to throw in his hand; after all his aim was merely to do something that would have the appearance of action, the semblance of profound political schemes, something that, above all, would provide matter for self-important consultations, frequent appearances and complacent gossip.

As for Gottfried, his dramatic lectures for respectable city merchants did not allow him to compromise himself. But on the other hand it was altogether too evident that the purpose of the manifesto of March 13 was none other than to provide support for the place Arnold had usurped in the European Central Committee. Even Gottfried could not fail to realise this: but it was not in his interest to grant Ruge such recognition. So it came to pass that shortly after the manifesto had been published, the *Kölnische Zeitung* printed a declaration by that *dama acerba*, Mockel. Her husband, she wrote, had not signed the appeal, he was not interested in public loans and had resigned from the newly-formed committee. Whereupon Arnold gossiped in the New York *Schnellpost* to the effect that Kinkel had been prevented by illness from signing the manifesto, but he gave his approval, the plan to issue it had been conceived in his room, he had himself taken responsibility for despatching a number of copies to Germany and he only left the committee because it elected General Haug president in preference to himself. Arnold accompanied this declaration with angry attacks on Kinkel's vanity, calling him "absolute martyr" and "the Beckerath of the democrats" and affirming his suspicions of Mrs. Johanna Kinkel who had access to such prohibited journals as the *Kölnische Zeitung*.

In the meantime, Arnold's seed had not fallen on stony soil. Kinkel's "beautiful soul" resolved to turn the tables on his rivals and to raise the treasure of revolution alone. Johanna's statement dissociating him from this hare-brained scheme had scarcely appeared in the *Kölnische Zeitung* when Gottfried launched his own appeal in the transatlantic papers with the comment that the money should be sent to the man "who inspires the most confidence". And who could this man be but Gottfried Kinkel? For the time being he demanded an advance payment of £500 sterling with which to manufacture revolutionary paper money. Ruge, not to be outdone, had the *Schnellpost* declare that he was the treasurer of the Democratic Central Committee and that Mazzini notes were already available and could be purchased from him. Whoever wished to lose £500 sterling would do better to take the available notes than to speculate in something that did not even exist. And Rodomonte–Heinzen roared that unless Mr. Kinkel abandoned his manoeuvres he would be branded publicly as an "enemy of the revolution". Gottfried had counter-articles published in the *New-Yorker Staatszeitung*, the direct rival of the *Schnellpost*. In this way full-scale hostilities were in progress on the other side of the Atlantic while kisses of Judas were still being exchanged in this side.

By issuing an appeal for a national loan in his own name Gottfried had shocked the democratic rank and file, as he soon realised. To make good his blunder he now declared that "this appeal for money, for a German national loan did not proceed from him. In all likelihood what had happened was that some all too zealous friends in America had made free with his name."

This declaration provoked the following answer from Dr. Wiss in the *Schnellpost*:

"It is generally known that the appeal to agitate for a German Loan was sent to me *by Gottfried Kinkel with the urgent request* to publicise it in all the German newspapers and I am ready and willing to show this letter to anyone who is in doubt on this point. If Kinkel has now really alleged the contrary the only honourable course for him to pursue is to retract his statements publicly and to publish my correspondence with him from which it will become plain to the Party that I was quite independent and certainly that I did not exhibit 'an excess of zeal'. Should he not have been guilty of these allegations it was Kinkel's duty to denounce the journalist responsible for printing them as an evil slanderer, or if there had been a misunderstanding, as an irresponsible and unscrupulous gossip. For my part I am unable to believe Kinkel capable of such unmitigated perfidy. Dr. C. Wiss." (Weekly supplement of the *Deutsche Schnellpost*.)

What was Kinkel to do? Once again he thrust his *aspra donzella* into the breach, he denounced Mockel as the "irresponsible, unscrupulous gossip", he claimed that his wife had promoted the loan behind his back. It cannot be denied that this tactic was highly "aesthetic".

Thus did Gottfried sway like a reed, now advancing, now retreating, now launching a project, now dissociating himself from it, always tacking to adjust to the wind of popularity. While he officially allowed the aesthetic bourgeoisie to fête and feast him in London as the martyr of the Revolution behind the backs of the same people he indulged in forbidden commerce with the mob of the Emigration as represented by Willich. While living in circumstances that could be described as luxurious in comparison with his modest situation in Bonn, he wrote to St. Louis that he was living as befitted the "representative of poverty". In this way he behaved towards the bourgeoisie as etiquette required, while at the same time he deferred humbly to the taste of the proletariat. But as a man whose imagination far outweighed his understanding he could not help falling into the bad manners and the arrogant postures of the parvenu and this alienated many a pompous bonhomme from him. Wholly characteristic of him was the article on the Great Exhibition that he wrote for *Kosmos*. He admired nothing so much as the giant mirror that was exhibited in the Crystal Palace. The objective world reduces itself to a mirror, the subjective world to a cliché. Under the pretext of seeing only the beautiful side of things he aestheticises everything and this process he designates poetry, self-sacrifice or religion, as the occasion demands. Fundamentally, everything is used to exalt himself. It is inevitable that in practice the ugly side should make its appearance, as imagination turns into lies and enthusiasm into baseness. In any case it was to be expected that Gottfried would soon cast off his lion's skin when he fell into the hands of old, experienced clowns like Gustav and Arnold.

XII

The Great Industrial Exhibition inaugurated a new epoch in the Emigration. The great throng of German Philistines that flooded into London during the summer, felt ill at ease in the bustle of the great Crystal Palace and in the even larger town of London with its noise, its din and its clamour. And when the toil and the labour of the day, the dutiful inspection of the Exhibition and the other sights had been completed in the sweat of his brow, the German Philistine could recover at his ease with Schärttner at the Hanau or Göhringer at the Star, with their beery cosiness, their smoke-filled fug and their public-house politics. Here "the whole of the fatherland could be seen" and in addition all the greatest men of Germany could be seen gratis. There they all sat, the members of parliament, the deputies of Chambers, the generals, the Club orators of the halcyon days of 1848 and 1849, they smoked their pipes just like ordinary people and debated the loftiest interests of the fatherland day after day, in public and with unshakeable dignity. This was the place where for the price of a few bottles of extremely cheap wine the German citizen could discover exactly what went on at the most secret meetings of the European cabinets. This was the place where he could learn to within a minute when "it would all start". In the meantime one bottle after another was started and all the Parties went home unsteadily but strengthened in the knowledge that they had made their contribution to the salvation of the fatherland. Never has the Emigration drunk more and cheaper than during the period when the solvent masses of German Philistines were in London.

The true organisation of the Emigration was in fact this *tavern organisation* presided over by Silenus–Schärttner in Long Acre which experienced its heyday thanks to the Exhibition. Here the true Central Committee sat in perpetual session. All other committees, organisations, party-formations were just trimmings, the patriotic arabesques of this primeval German tavern society of idlers.

In addition the Emigration was strengthened numerically at the time by the arrival of Messrs. Meyen, Faucher, Sigel, Goegg and Fickler, etc.

Meyen was a little porcupine who had come into the world without any quills and who under the name Poinsinet, was once described by Goethe in this way:

"In literature, as in society, one often encounters such curious little manikins. Endowed with some small talent they endeavour always to claim the attention of the public and as they can easily be seen through by all they are the source of much amusement. However, they always manage to profit sufficiently. They live, produce, are mentioned everywhere and are even accorded a favourable reception. Their failures do not disconcert them; they regard them as exceptional and look to the future for greater success. Poinsinet is a figure of this sort in the French literary world. It goes almost beyond belief to see what has been done with him, how he has been fooled and mystified and even his sad death by drowning in Spain does not diminish the ridiculous impression made by his life, just as a frog made of fireworks does not attain to dignity by concluding a lengthy series of sputters with a loud bang."[58]

Writers contemporary with him pass on the following information: Eduard Meyen belonged to the "Resolute" group which represented the Berliner intelligentsia as against the mass stupidity of the rest of Germany. He too had a Maybug Club in Berlin with his friends Mügge, Klein, Zabel, Buhl etc. Each of these maybugs sat on his own little leaf [*Blättchen*—"leaf" and "newspaper"]. Eduard Meyen's paper was called the *Mannheimer Abendblättchen* and here, every week, after enormous efforts, he deposited a small green turd of correspondence. Our Maybug really did progress to the point where he was *about* to publish a monthly periodical; contributions from various people landed on his desk, the publisher waited but the whole project collapsed because Eduard after eight months in cold sweat declared that he could not finish the prospectus. As Eduard took all his childish activities seriously he was widely regarded in Berlin after the March Revolution as a man who meant business. In London he worked together with Faucher on a German edition of the *Illustrated London News* under the editorship and censorship of an old woman who had known some German twenty years before, but he was discarded as useless after he had attempted with great tenacity to insert a profound article about sculpture that he had had published ten years previously in Berlin. But when, later on, the Kinkel–emigration made him their secretary he realised that he was really a practical *homme d'état* and he announced in a lithographed leaflet that he had arrived at the "tranquillity of a point of view". After his death a whole heap of titles for future projects will be found among his papers.

Conjointly with Meyen we must necessarily consider *Oppenheim*, his co-editor and co-secretary. It has been claimed that Oppenheim is not so much a man as an allegorical figure: the goddess of boredom it is reported, came down to Frankfurt on Main and assumed the shape of this son of a Jewish jeweller. When Voltaire wrote: "*Tous les genres sont bons, excepté le genre ennuyeux*", he must have had a premonition of our Heinrich Bernhard Oppenheim. We prefer Oppenheim the writer to Oppenheim the orator. His writings may be avoided, but his spoken delivery—*c'est impossible*. The pythagorean metempsychosis may have some foundation in reality but the name borne by Heinrich Bernhard Oppenheim in former ages can no longer be discovered as no man ever made a name for himself through being an unbearable chatterbox. His life may be epitomised by its three climactic moments: Arnold Ruge's editor—Brentano's editor—Kinkel's editor.

The third member of the trio is Mr. Julius Faucher. He is one of those Berlin Huguenots who know how to exploit their minor talent with great commercial adroitness. He made his public debut as the Lieutenant Pistol of the Free Trade Party in which capacity he was employed by Hamburg commercial interests to make propaganda. During the revolutionary disturbances they allowed him to preach free trade in the apparently chaotic form of anarchism. When this ceased to be relevant to the times he was dismissed and, together with Meyen, he became joint editor of the Berlin *Abendpost*. Under the pretence of wishing to abolish the state and introduce anarchy he refrained from dangerous opposition towards the existing government and when, later on, the paper failed because it could no longer afford the deposit, the *Neue Preussische Zeitung* commiserated with Faucher, the only able writer among the democrats. This cosy relationship with the *Neue Preussische Zeitung* soon became so intimate that Faucher began to act as its correspondent in London. Faucher's activity in the London Emigration did not last long; his free trade inclined him towards commerce where he found his true calling, to which he returned with great energy and in which he achieved wonders never seen before: namely a price-list that assesses goods according to a completely sliding scale. As is well known, the *Breslauer Zeitung* was indiscreet enough to inform the general public of this document.

This three-star constellation of the Berlin intelligentsia can be contrasted with the three-star constellation of wholesome South German principles: Sigel, Fickler, Goegg. Franz Sigel, whom his friend Goegg describes as a short, beardless man, bearing a strong resemblance to Napoleon, is, again according to Goegg, "a hero", "a man of the future", "above all a genius, intellectually creative and constantly hatching new plans".

Between ourselves, General Siegel is a young Baden lieutenant of principle and ambition. He read in an account of the campaigns of the French Revolution that the step from sub-lieutenant to supreme general is mere child's play and from that moment on this little beardless man firmly believed that Franz Sigel must become supreme commander in a revolutionary army. His wish was granted thanks to the Baden insurrection of 1849 and a popularity with the army arising from a confusion of names. The battles he fought on the Neckar and did not fight in the Black Forest are well known; his retreat to Switzerland has been praised even by the enemy as a timely and correct manoeuvre. His military plans here bear witness to his study of the [French] Revolutionary Wars. In order to remain faithful to the revolutionary tradition Hero Sigel, ignoring the enemy and operational and withdrawal lines and similar bagatelles, went conscientiously from one Moreau position to the next. And if he did not manage to parody Moreau's campaigns[59] in every detail, if he crossed the Rhine at Eglichau and not at Paradies, this was the fault of the enemy who was too ignorant to appreciate such a learned manoeuvre. In his orders of the day and in his instructions Sigel emerges as a preacher and if he has an inferior style to Napoleon, he has more principle. Later, he concerned himself with devising a handbook for revolutionary officers in all branches of warfare from which we are in a position to offer the following important extract:

"an officer of the revolution must carry the following articles according to regulations: 1 head-covering and cap, 1 sabre with belt, 1 black, red and yellow[60] camel-hair sash, 2 pairs of black leather gloves, 2 battle coats, 1 cloak, 1 pair cloth trousers, 1 tie, 2 pairs of boots or shoes, 1 black leather travelling case—12″ wide, 10″ high, 4″ deep, 6 shirts, 3 pairs of underpants, 8 pairs of socks, 6 handkerchiefs, 2 towels, 1 washing and shaving kit, 1 writing implement, 1 writing tablet with letters patent, 1 clothes brush, 1 copy of service regulations".

Joseph *Fickler—*

"the model of a decent, resolute, imperturbably tenacious man of the people whom the people of the whole Baden upland and the Lake District supported as one man and whose struggles and sufferings over many years had earned him a popularity approaching that of Brentano" (according to the testimony of his friend Goegg).

As befits a decent, resolute, imperturbably tenacious man of the people, Joseph Fickler has a fleshy full-moon face, a fat craw and a paunch to match. The only fact known about his early life is that he earned a livelihood with the aid of a carving from the 15th century and with relics relating to the Council of Constance. He allowed travellers and foreign art-lovers to inspect these curiosities in exchange for money and incidentally sold them "antique" souvenirs of which Fickler, as he loved to relate, would constantly make up a new supply in all their authentic "antiquity".

His only deeds during the Revolution were firstly his arrest by Mathy[61] after the Vorparlament, and, second, his arrest by Römer in Stuttgart in June 1849. Thanks to these arrests he was happily deprived of the opportunity to compromise himself. The Württemberg Democrats deposited 1000 guilders as bail for him, whereupon Fickler went to Thurgau incognito and to the great distress of his guarantors no more was heard of him. It is undeniable that he successfully translated the feelings and opinions of the lakeside peasants into printers' ink in his *Lake journals*; for the rest he shares the opinion of his friend Ruge that much study makes you stupid and for this reason he warned his friend Goegg not to visit the library of the British Museum.

Amandus Goegg, lovable, as his name indicates, is no great orator, but "an unassuming citizen whose noble and modest bearing earns him the friendship of people everywhere" (*Westamerikanische Blätter*). From sheer nobility Goegg became a member of the provisional government in Baden, where, as he admits, he could do nothing against Brentano and in all modesty he assumed the title of Dictator. No one denies that his achievements as Finance Minister were modest. In all modesty he proclaimed the "Social-democratic Republic" in Donaueschingen the day before the final retreat to Switzerland actually took place, although it had been decreed before. In all modesty he later declared (See *Janus* by Heinzen, 1852) that the Paris proletariat had lost on December 2 because it did not possess his own Franco-Badenese democratic experience nor the insights available elsewhere in the frenchified Germany of the South. Anyone who desires further proofs of Goegg's modesty and of the existence of a "Goegg Party" will find them in the book *The Baden Revolution in Retrospect*. Paris 1850, written by himself. A fitting climax to his modesty came in a public meeting in Cincinnati when he declared that "reputable men came to him after the bankruptcy of the Baden Revolution and had announced that in that revolution men of all the German tribes had taken an active part. It was therefore to be regarded as a German matter just as the Rome uprising was of concern to the whole of Italy. As he was the man who had held out they said that he must become the *German Mazzini*. His modesty compelled him to refuse."

Why? A man who was once "dictator" and who to cap it all, is the bosom friend of "Napoleon" Sigel, could surely also become the "German Mazzini".

Once the Emigration was augmented by these and similar, less noteworthy arrivals, it could proceed to those mighty battles that the reader shall learn of in the next canto.

XIII

Chi mi dara la voce e le parole,
E un proferir magnanimo e profondo!
Che mai cosa piu fiera sotto il sole
Non fu veduta in tutto quanto il mondo;
L'altre battaglie fur rose e viole,
Al raccontar di questa mi confondo;
Perche il valor, e'l pregio della terra
A fronte son condotti in questa guerra

(Boiardo, *Orlando Inamorato*, Canto 27)

[Now who will give me words and who the tongue,
To sing of such brave deeds in sonorous sounds!
For ne'er was strife upon this earth begun
More proudly fought on bloodier battle grounds;
Compared to this all other wars are roses
To tell of it my lyric art confounds
For on this earth there ne'er was seen such glory
Or noble valour bright as in this story]

The latest fashionable arrivals had made up the full complement of the Emigration and the time had now come for a more comprehensive "organisation", to round it off upwards to a full dozen. As might have been expected these attempts degenerated into bitter feuds. The paper war conducted in the transatlantic journals now reached its climax. The privations of individuals, intrigues, plots, self-praise—the heroes spent their energies in such paltry activities. But the Emigration did have one achievement to its credit: a history of its own, lying outside world history, with its own political pettifoggery running parallel to public affairs. And the very fact that they fought each other so bitterly led each to believe in the importance of the other. Beneath the façade of all these strivings and conflicts lay the speculation in democratic party funds, "the Holy Grail", and this transformed these transcendental rivalries, these disputes about the Emperor's beard, into ordinary quarrels among fools. Anyone who wishes to pursue the study of this great war between the frogs and the mice will find all the decisive original documents in the *New-Yorker Schnellpost*, the New York *Deutsche Zeitung*, the *Allgemeine Deutsche Zeitung* and the *Staatszeitung*, in the Baltimore *Correspondent*, in the *Wecker* [Clarion] and in other German–American papers. However, this display of alleged connections and imagined conspiracies, this whole hue and cry raised by the *émigrés* was not without serious consequences. It provided the governments with the pretext they needed to arrest all sorts of people in Germany, to suppress the indigenous movements and to use these wretched strawmen in London as scarecrows with which to frighten the German middle classes. Far from constituting any danger to existing circumstances these heroes of the exile wished only that everything should die down in Germany so that their voice might be heard the better and that the general level of thought should decline so far that even men of their stature might appear outstanding.

The newly-arrived South German *bonhommes*, lacking in any definite commitment, found themselves in an excellent position to mediate between the various cliques and, at the same time, to gather the mass of *émigrés* around the leaders as a kind of chorus. Their sturdy sense of duty impelled them not to forgo this opportunity.

At the same time, however, they could already see Ledru-Rollin where he saw himself, namely in the chair of the president of France. As the most important neighbours of France it was vital for them to obtain recognition from the provisional government of France as the provisional overlords of Germany. Sigel especially wished to see his supreme command guaranteed by Ledru. But the way to Ledru led over Arnold's corpse. However, they were still impressed by Arnold's *persona* and he still passed as the philosophical Northern Light who would illumine their South German twilight. So they turned to Ruge.

On the opposing side stood in the first instance *Kinkel* with his more immediate entourage — Schurz, Strodtmann, Schimmelpfennig, Techow etc.; then came the former deputies and members of parliament, led by *Reichenbach* with Meyen and Oppenheim as the representatives of literature; and, lastly, Willich with his host which, however, remained in the background. The roles were distributed as follows: Kinkel playing a passion-flower represented the German Philistines in general; Reichenbach playing a Count represented the bourgeoisie; Willich, playing Willich represented the proletariat.

The first thing to say about August *Willich* is that Gustav always felt secretly mistrustful of him because of his pointed skull signifying that the enormous overgrowth of self-esteem had stunted all other qualities.

A German Philistine who once caught sight of ex-Lieutenant Willich in a London pub snatched up his hat and fled exclaiming: My God, he looks just like Jesus Christ! In order to increase the similarity Willich became a carpenter for a while before the Revolution. Later on he emerged as a partisan leader in the campaign in Baden and the Palatinate.

The partisan leader, a descendant of the old Italian condottiere is a peculiar phenomenon of more recent wars, especially in Germany. The partisan leader, accustomed to act on his own initiative, is reluctant to subordinate himself to a more general command. His men owe their allegiance only to him, but he is likewise wholly dependent on them. For this reason the discipline in a free corps is somewhat arbitrary; according to circumstances it may be savagely strict, but mostly it is extremely lax. The partisan leader cannot always act the martinet, he must often flatter his men and win them over individually with the aid of physical caresses; the normal military practices are of little use here and boldness must be supplemented by other qualities if the leader is to retain the respect of his subordinates. If he is not noble he must at least have a noble consciousness to be complemented as always by cunning, the talent for intrigue and a covert practical baseness. In this way he not only wins over his soldiers but also bribes the inhabitants, surprises the enemy and contrives matters so that even his opponents acknowledge his strength of character. But all this does not suffice to hold together a free corps whose members either come from the Lumpenproletariat or are soon assimilated into it. What is needed in addition is a higher ideal. The partisan leader must therefore have a nucleus of *idées fixes*, he must be a man of principle in permanent pursuit of his mission to redeem the world. By means of sermons at the front and sustained didactic propaganda he must impart a consciousness of this higher ideal to every man individually and in this way he will transform the whole troop into sons within the faith. If this higher ideal is tinged with philosophy or mysticism or anything that surpasses normal understanding, if it is something Hegelian by nature (as was the case with the ideas that General Willisen[62] tried to infuse into the Prussian army), then so much the better. For this ensures that the noble consciousness will enter into each and every partisan and the deeds of the whole corps thereby attain to a speculative consecration which exalts them far above the level of ordinary unreflecting courage and in any case the fame of such an army depends less on its achievements than on its messianic calling. The strength of a corps can only be enhanced if all the warriors are made to swear an oath that they will not survive the destruction of the cause for which they are fighting and would prefer to be massacred to the last man beneath the apple tree on the frontier while singing a hymn. Of course, such a corps and such a leader inevitably feel degraded by contact with ordinary profane soldiers and they will make every effort either to keep at a distance from the army or else to shake off the society of the uncircumcised. They hate nothing more than a large army and a large war where their cunning buttressed by spiritual faith can achieve little if the normal rules of war are disregarded. The partisan leader must then be a crusader in the full sense of the word, he must be Peter the Hermit and Walther von Habenichts[63] rolled into one. Faced with the heterogeneous elements and the informal mode of life of his corps he must always uphold virtue. He must not allow his men to drink him under the table and so he must only drink in solitude, for instance at night in bed. If it should happen to him, as it might to any fallible human being, that he find himself returning to barracks late at night after inordinate indulgence in the pleasures of this life, he will take care not to enter through the main gate, but to go round the side and climb over the wall to avoid giving offence. Feminine charms should leave him cold, but it will make a good impression if he, like Cromwell, takes his NCOs or a tailor's apprentice into his bed from time to time. In general he cannot lead too strict and ascetic a life. Behind the *cavalieri della ventura* in his corps stand the *cavalieri del dente*[64] who live mainly from requisitions and free quarters to all of which Walther von Habenichts has to turn a blind eye so that Peter the Hermit has always to be at hand with the consolation that such unpleasant measures contribute to the salvation of the nation and so are in the interest of the victims themselves.

All the qualities that the partisan leader must possess in wartime re-appear in peacetime in a modified form but one that can scarcely be regarded as an improvement. Above all else he must preserve the core of the regiment for later on and hence keep his recruiting officers in a state of constant activity. The core consisting of the remnants of the free corps and the general mob of *émigrés* is put into barracks either at government expense (as in Besançon) or by some other means. The consecration in the service of an ideal must not be lacking and it is provided by a barracks-communism that ascribes a higher significance to the custom of holding ordinary civic actions in contempt. As this communist barracks is no longer subject to the articles of war, but only to the moral authority and the dictates of self-sacrifice, it is inevitable that quarrels should break out over the communal funds. From these disputes moral authority does not always emerge unscathed. If there is an artisans' club anywhere in the vicinity it can be employed as a recruiting base and the artisans are given the prospect of a jolly life full of adventures in exchange for the oppressive work of the present. By pointing to the higher ethical significance of the barracks for the future of the proletariat, it is even possible to induce the club to make financial contributions. In both the barracks and the club the sermonis-ing and the patriarchal and gossipy style of personal relations will not fail to impress. Even in peacetime the partisan does not lose his indis-pensable assurance and just as in wartime every setback spurred him on to proclaim victory on the morrow, so now he is for ever expounding on the moral certainty and the philosophical inevitability with which "*it*" will start to happen within the next fortnight. As he must needs have an enemy and as the noble man is necessarily opposed by the ignoble ones he discovers in them a raging hostility towards himself, he imagines that they hate him merely because of his well-deserved popularity and would gladly poison him or stab him. With this in mind he resolves always to conceal a long dagger beneath his pillow. Just as the partisan leader in war will never succeed unless he assumes that the population reveres him, likewise in peace he will not indeed manage to form any lasting political groupings but he will constantly suppose them to exist and from this all sorts of strange mystifications can arise. The talent for requisitioning and obtaining free quarters appears again in the form of a cosy parasitism. By contrast, the strict asceticism of our Orlando, like everything that is good and great, is subject to terrible temptations in times of peace. Boiardo says in Canto 24:

Turpin behauptet, dass der Graf von Brava
Jungfräulich war auf Lebenszeit und keusch.
Glaubt ihr davon, was euch beliebt, ihr Herren—

[Turpin claims that the Count of Brava
Was virginal and chaste his whole life long.
Of that you may believe, Sirs, what you will—]

But we also learn that later on Count Brava lost his reason at the sight
of the beautiful Angelica and Astolf had to go to the moon to recover
it for him, as Master Lodovico Ariosto so charmingly narrates. Our
modern Orlando, however, mistook himself for the poet who tells
how he, too, loved so greatly that he lost his reason and tried to find it
with his lips and hands on the bosom of his Angelica and was thrown
out of the house for his pains.

In politics the partisan leader will display his superiority in all matters
of tactics. In conformity with the notion of a partisan he will go from
one party to the next. Petty intrigues, sordid hole-and-corner activities,
the occasional lie, morally outraged perfidy will be the natural symp-
toms of the noble consciousness. His faith in his mission and in the
higher meaning of his words and deeds will induce him to declare
emphatically: "I never lie!" The *idées fixes* become a splendid cloak
for his secret treachery and cause the simpletons of the Emigration,
who have no ideas *at all*, to conclude that he, the man of fixed ideas, is
simply a fool. And our worthy slyboots could desire nothing better.

Don Quixote and Sancho Panza rolled into one, as much in love with
his knapsack as with his *idées fixes*, with the free provisions of the
itinerant knight as much as with renown, Willich is the man of the
duodecimal[65] war and the microscopic intrigue. He conceals his
cunning beneath the mask of character. His real future lies in the prairies
of the Rio Grande del Norte.

Concerning the relations between the two wings of the Emigration
we have described, a letter from Mr. Goegg in the *Deutsche Schnellpost*
in New York is very revealing:

"They (the South Germans) resolved to bolster up the reputation
of the *moribund* central committee by attempting to unite with the
other factions. But there is little prospect of success for this well-
intentioned idea. Kinkel continues to intrigue, has formed a committee consisting of his rescuer, his biographer and a number of
Prussian lieutenants. Their aim is to work together in secret, to
expand, if possible to gain possession of the democratic funds, and

then suddenly tear off their mask and appear publicly as the powerful Kinkel party. This is neither honest nor just nor sensible!"

The "honesty" of the intentions of the South Germans can be seen from the following letter from Mr. Sigel to the same newspaper:

"If we, the few men with *honourable* intentions, have *in part* resorted to conspiracies, this is due to the need to protect ourselves against the terrible perfidy and the presumptuousness of Kinkel and his colleagues and to show them that they are not born to rule. *Our chief aim* was to force Kinkel to come to a large meeting in order to prove to him and to what he calls his close political friends that not all that glitters is gold. The devil take the instrument" (i.e. Schurz), "and the devil take the singer too"[66] (i.e. Kinkel). (Weekly edition of the *New-Yorker Deutsche Zeitung*, September 24 1851).

The strange constitution of the two factions that rebuke each other for being "north" and "south" can be seen from the fact that at the head of the South German elements stood the "mind" of Ruge, while at the head of the North German side were the "feelings" of Kinkel.

In order to understand the great struggle that was now waged we must waste a few words on the diplomacy of these two world-shaking parties.

Arnold (and his henchmen likewise) was concerned above all to form a "closed" society with the official *appearance* of "revolutionary activity". This society would then give birth to his beloved "Committee for German Affairs" and this committee would then propel Ruge into the European Central Committee. Arnold had been indefatigable in his efforts to realise this aim since the summer of 1850. He had hoped that the South Germans would provide "that happy medium where he could dominate in comfort". The official establishment of the Emigration and the formation of committees was the necessary policy of Arnold and his allies.

Kinkel and his cohorts, on the other hand, had to try and undermine everything that could legitimise the position Ruge had usurped in the European Central Committee. In reply to his appeal for an advance of £500 sterling Kinkel had received the promise of some money from New Orleans, whereupon he had formed a *secret finance committee* together with Willich, Schimmelpfennig, Reichenbach, Techow and Schurz, etc. They reasoned: once we have the money we shall have the Emigration; once we have the Emigration we shall also have the government in Germany. Their aim, therefore, was to occupy the whole Emigration with formal meetings but to undermine any attempt at setting up an official society that went beyond a "loose organisation" and above all to undermine all proposals to form committees. This would delay the enemy faction, block their activities and enable them to manoeuvre behind their backs.

Both parties, i.e. all the "distinguished men" had one thing in common: they both led the mass of *émigrés* by the nose, they concealed from them their real objectives, used them as mere tools and dropped them as soon as they had served their purpose.

Let us take a look at these democratic Machiavellis, Talleyrands and Metternichs and take note of their actions.

Scene 1. July 14, 1851.—After a "private understanding with Kinkel to make common cause" had fallen through, Ruge, Goegg, Sigel, Fickler and Ronge invited the distinguished men of all shades of opinion to a meeting in Fickler's home on July 14th. Twenty-six people appeared. Fickler proposed that a "private circle" of German refugees should be formed and this in turn would give birth to a "business committee for the advancement of revolutionary objectives". This was opposed mainly by Kinkel and six of his supporters. After a violent debate lasting several hours Fickler's motion was passed (16 votes to 10). Kinkel and the minority declared themselves unable to participate any further and took their departure.

Scene 2. July 20th.—The above majority constituted itself as a society. Joined, among others, by Tausenau, who had been introduced by Fickler.

If Ronge was the Luther and Kinkel the Melanchton then Tausenau is the Abraham a Sancta Clara[67] of the German democrats. If the two augurs in Cicero could not look each other in the face without laughing then Mr. Tausenau cannot catch sight of his own earnest features in the mirror without bursting into laughter. If Ruge had discovered in the Badeners people whom *he* impressed, Fate now had its revenge when it introduced him to the Austrian Tausenau, a man who impressed *him*.

At the suggestion of Goegg and Tausenau the negotiations were postponed in order to try once again to bring about a union with Kinkel's faction.

Scene 3. July 27th.—Session in the Cranbourne Hotel. The "distinguished" Emigration there to a man. Kinkel's group appeared but not with the intention of joining the society already in existence; on the contrary, they pressed for the formation of an "open discussion club *without* a business committee and without *definite objectives*". Schurz who acted as Kinkel's mentor throughout all these parliamentary negotiations, proposed:

> "The present company should form itself into a private political society with the name German Emigré Club and should accept as new members other citizens from among the German refugees on the nomination of a member and after a majority vote in favour."

Passed unanimously. The society resolved to meet every Friday.

> "The passing of this motion was welcomed with general applause and with the cry: 'Long live the German republic! ! !' Everyone felt that they had done their duty by being generally open-minded and that they had achieved something positive serving the cause of revolution." (Goegg, Weekly edition of the *Deutsche Schnellpost*, August 20, 1851.)

Eduard Meyen was so delighted with this success that he waxed ecstatic in his lithographed report:

> "The whole Emigration now form a coherent phalanx up to and including Bucher and with the sole exception of the incorrigible Marx clique."

This same notice of Meyen's can be found also in the *Berliner lithographische Korrespondenz*.

In this way, thanks to a general open-mindedness and to the accompaniment of three cheers for the German Republic the great Emigré Club which was to hold such inspiring meetings and which was to dissolve in satisfaction a few weeks after Kinkel's departure for America, came into being. Its dissolution did not of course prevent it from playing an important part as a living entity in America.

Scene 4. August 1st.—Second meeting in the Cranbourne Hotel.

> "Unfortunately we must already report today that the expectations raised by the formation of this club have been sadly disappointed." (Goegg, *loc. cit.*, August 27th.)

Kinkel introduced six Prussian refugees and six Prussian visitors to the Great Exhibition into the club without obtaining a majority decision. *Damm**★** (President, former president of the Baden Constituent Assembly) expressed his astonishment at this treacherous infringement of the statutes.

Kinkel explained: "The Club is only a *loosely* organised society with no other purpose than for people to get to know each other and to have discussions that are open to everyone. It is therefore desirable for visitors to be admitted to the Club in large numbers."

Student Schurz attempted to cover up quickly for the Professor's lack of tact by moving an amendment to permit the admission of visitors. Motion passed. Abraham a Sancta Clara Tausenau rose and put the two following motions with a perfectly straight face:

"1. A commission (*the* committee) 'should be set up to report weekly on current affairs, particularly in Germany. These reports are to be preserved in the archive of the Club and published at an appropriate time. 2. There should be a commission (*the* committee) to deposit in the archive all possible details concerning violations of the law and acts of cruelty towards the supporters of democracy committed by the servants of the reaction during the last three years and at the present time.'

"Reichenbach opposed this vigorously: 'He saw suspicious motives lurking behind these seemingly harmless proposals and also the wish to use the election of the members of this commission as a device to give the Club an official character not desired by himself or his friends.'

"Schimmelpfennig and Schurz: 'These commissions could arrogate powers unto themselves that might be of a conspiratorial nature and gradually lead to an *official* committee.'

"Meyen: 'I want words, not deeds.' "

According to Goegg's account the majority seemed inclined to accept the motion; Machiavelli Schurz proposed an adjournment. Abraham a Sancta Clara Tausenau agreed to the proposal so as not to seem unfriendly. Kinkel expressed the opinion that the vote should be postponed until the next meeting chiefly because his supporters were in the minority that evening and so he and his friends would be

★ "Damm is here!"
"Who is here?"
"Damm is here!"
"Who?"
"Damm, Damm, surely you know Damm?"

unable in the circumstances to regard the vote as "binding *on their conscience*". Adjournment agreed.

Scene 5. August 8th.—Third meeting in the Cranbourne Hotel. Discussion of the Tausenau motions.—Ignoring the agreement, Kinkel/ Willich had brought along the "rank and file refugees", *le menu peuple*, so as to "bind their consciences" this time.—Schurz moved an amendment proposing voluntary lectures on current affairs and in accordance with a previous arrangement Meyen immediately volunteered to speak on Prussia, Schurz on France, Oppenheim on England and Kinkel on America and the future (since his immediate future lay in America). Tausenau's proposals were rejected. He declared movingly that his only wish was to sacrifice his just anger on the altar of the nation and to remain within the bosom of his allies. But the Ruge/ Fickler contingent at once assumed the outraged indignation of beautiful souls who have been swindled.

Intermezzo.—Kinkel had finally received £160 sterling from New Orleans and together with other distinguished heroes he had set about investing it for the revolution. The Ruge/Fickler faction, already embittered by the recent vote, now learned of this. They had no time to lose, action was essential. They founded a new cesspool and concealed its foul stagnation under the name of the *Agitation Club*. Its members were Tausenau, Frank, Goegg, Sigel, Hertle, Ronge, Haug, Fickler and Ruge. The Club immediately announced in the English press:

> "Its aims are not to discuss but to work, it would produce not words but deeds and above all it appeals to likeminded comrades to make donations. The Agitation Club appoints Tausenau to be its executive leader and its foreign minister. It also recognises Ruge's position in the European Central Committee" (as Imperial Administrator)[68] "as well as his previous activity on behalf of and in the name of the German people."

The new combination does not conceal the original constellation: Ruge, Ronge and Haug. After the struggles and the efforts of so many years Ruge had finally reached his goal: he was acknowledged to be the fifth wheel on the central carriage of democracy and had a clearly—all too clearly—defined part of the people behind him, consisting of eight men in all. But even this pleasure was poisoned for him as his recognition was purchased at the cost of an indirect slight and was agreed to only on the condition imposed by the peasant Fickler that Ruge should henceforth cease to "broadcast his rubbish to the whole world".

The coarse Fickler regarded as "distinguished" only those writings by Ruge which he had not read and did not need to read.

Scene 6. August 22nd.—The Cranbourne Hotel. Firstly, there was a "diplomatic masterstroke" (vide Goegg) on the part of Schurz: he proposed the formation of a general refugee committee to comprise six members taken from the different factions together with five co-opted members of the already existing refugee committee of the Willich Artisan Club. (This would have given the Kinkel/Willich wing a permanent majority). Agreed. The elections were carried out but rejected by the members of the Rugean part of the state, which meant the complete collapse of the diplomatic master stroke. How seriously this refugee committee was meant to be taken can be seen from the fact that four days later Willich resigned from the committee of artisans and refugees which had only had a nominal existence for a long time, following upon repeated, wholly disrespectful revolts on the part of the "rank and file refugees" which had made the dissolution of the committee an inevitability.—Interpellation concerning the emergence in public of the Agitation Club. Motion: that the Emigré Club should have nothing to do with the Agitation Club and should publicly dissociate itself from all its actions. Furious attacks on the "Agitators" Goegg and Sigel junior (i.e. senior, see below, p. 228) in their presence. Rudolph Schramm declared that his old friend Ruge was a minion of Mazzini and a "gossipy old woman". Tu quoque, Brute! Goegg retorted, not as a great orator but as an honest citizen and he launched a bitter attack on the ambiguous, slack, perfidious, unctuous Kinkel.

> "It is irresponsible to prevent those who wish to work from doing so, but these people want a fictitious, inactive union that they can use as a cover for certain purposes."

When Goegg referred to the public announcement about the Agitator Club in the English papers Kinkel arose majestically and said that "He already controlled the whole American press and had taken steps to ensure his control of the French press too."

The motion of the German faction was passed and provoked a declaration from the "Agitators" that the members of their club could no longer remain within the Emigré Club.

Thus arose the terrible gulf between the Emigré Club and the Agitators' Club which gapes through the whole history of the modern world.

H

The most curious fact about it is that both creatures only survived until their separation and now they vegetate in the Kaulbachian[69] battle of the ghosts that still rages in German–American meetings and papers and no doubt will continue to rage to the end of time.

The whole session was all the more stormy as the undisciplined Schramm went so far as to attack Willich, claiming that the *Emigré* Club degraded itself by its connections with that knight. The chairman, who happened to be the timorous Meyen, had already lost control several times in despair. But the debate about the Agitators' Club and the resignation of its members brought the tumult to a climax. To the accompaniment of shouts, drumming, crashes, threats and raging the edifying meeting went on until 2 a.m. when the landlord turned off the gas and so plunged the heated antagonists into darkness. This brought all plans to save the nation to an abrupt end.

At the end of August the chivalrous Willich and the cosy Kinkel made an attempt to smash the Agitators' Club by putting a proposal to the worthy Fickler.

"He should join with them and their closer political friends in forming a Finance Committee to manage the money that had come in from New Orleans. This committee should continue to function until it is superseded by a general finance committee of *the* revolution. However, the acceptance of this offer would imply the dissolution of all German revolutionary and agitatorial societies that had existed hitherto."

The worthy Fickler rejected the idea of this "imposed, secret and irresponsible committee" with indignation.

"How", he exclaimed, "can a mere finance committee hope to unite all the revolutionary parties around it? The money that has arrived and that is still to come can never suffice to persuade the widely divergent strands of the democrats to sacrifice their autonomy."

Thus instead of achieving the hoped-for destruction of the opposition this attempted seduction enabled Tausenau to declare that the breach between the two mighty parties of Emigration and Agitation had become irreparable.

XIV

To show how pleasantly the war was waged between Emigration and Agitation we append here a few excerpts from the German–American papers.

Agitation.

Ruge declared that Kinkel was an "agent of the Prince of Prussia".

Another agitator discovered that the outstanding men of the Emigré Club consisted of "Pastor Kinkel together with three Prussian lieutenants, two mediocre Berlin literati and one student".

Sigel wrote: "It cannot be denied that Willich has gained some support. But when a man has been a preacher for three years and only tells people what they wish to hear, he would have to be very stupid not to be able to win some of them over. The Kinkelites are attempting to take these supporters over. The Willich supporters are whoring with the Kinkel supporters."

A fourth agitator declared that Kinkel's supporters are "idolators".

Tausenau gave this description of the Emigré Club.

"Divergent interests beneath the mask of conciliatoriness, the systematic gerrymandering of majorities, the emergence of unknown quantities as organising party leaders, attempts to impose a secret finance committee and all the other slippery manoeuvres with which *immature politicians* of all ages have tried to control the fates of their country in exile, while the first glow of the revolution disperses all such vanities like a morning mist."

Lastly, Rodomonte–Heinzen announced that the only reputable refugees in England personally known to him were Ruge, Goegg, Fickler and Sigel. The members of the Emigré Club were "egoists, royalists and communists". Kinkel was "an incurably vain fool and an aristocratic adventurer", Meyen, Oppenheim and Willich, etc. were people "who do not even come up to his, Heinzen's, knee and as for Ruge, they do not even reach to his ankle". (New York *Schnellpost, New-Yorker Deutsche Zeitung, Wecker*, etc. 1851.)

Emigration

"What is the purpose of an imposed committee, that stands firmly in mid-air, that confers authority on itself without consulting the people whom it claims to represent or asking them whether they wish to be represented by such people?"—"Everyone who knows Ruge, knows that the mania for proclamations is his incurable disease."—"In parliament Ruge did not even acquire the influence of a Simon of Trier or a Raveaux."[70]—"Where revolutionary energy in action, talent for organisation, discretion or reticence are necessary, Ruge is downright dangerous because he cannot hold his tongue, he cannot hold his ink and always claims that he represents everybody. When Ruge meets Mazzini and Ledru-Rollin this is translated into Rugean and published in all the papers as: Germany, France and Italy have banded together fraternally to serve the revolution."—"This pretentious imposition of a committee, this boastful inactivity determined Ruge's most intimate and intelligent friends, such as Oppenheim, Meyen and Schramm to join forces with other men." "Behind Ruge there is no clearly defined section of the people, but only a clearly outlined pigtail of peace."—"How many hundreds of people ask themselves daily who is this Tausenau and there is no one, no one who can give an answer. Here and there you can find a Viennese who will assure you that he is one of those democrats with whom the reaction used to reproach the Viennese democrats so as to put them in a bad light. But that is the concern of the Viennese. At any rate Tausenau is an unknown quantity, and whether he is a quantity of any kind is even more dubious."

"Let us take a look at these worthy men who regard everyone else as an immature politician. Sigel, the supreme commander. If anyone ever asks the muse of history how such an insipid nonentity was given the supreme command she will be completely at a loss for a reply. Sigel is only his brother's brother. His brother became a popular officer as a result of his critical remarks about the government, remarks which had been provoked by his frequent arrests for disorderly behaviour. The younger Sigel thought this reason enough in the early confusion prevailing at the outbreak of revolution to proclaim himself supreme commander and minister of war. The Baden artillery which had often proved its worth had plenty of older and more experienced officers who should have taken precedence over this young milksop Lieutenant Sigel, and they were more than a little indignant when they had to obey an unknown man whose inexperience was only matched by his incompetence. But there was Brentano, who was so mindless and treacherous as to permit anything that might ruin the revolution . . . . The total incapacity that Sigel displayed during the whole Baden campaign . . . . It is worthy of note that Sigel left the bravest soldiers of the republican army in the lurch in Rastatt and in the Black Forest without the reinforcements he had *promised* while he himself drove around Zürich with the epaulettes and the carriage of Prince von Fürstenberg and paraded as an interesting unfortunate supreme commander. This is the true magnitude of this mature politician who, understandably proud of his earlier heroic deeds, imposed himself as supreme commander for a second time, on this occasion in the Agitators' Club. This is the great hero, the brother of his brother."

"It is really laughable when such people" (as the Agitators) "reproach others with half-heartedness, for they are *political nonentities* who are neither half nor whole."—"Personal ambition is the whole secret of their fundamental position."—"As a club the Agitators' Club has meaning only as a private institution, like a literary circle or a billiard club, and therefore it has no claim to be taken into consideration or given a voice."—"You have cast the dice! Let the uninitiated be initiated so that they may judge for themselves what kind of people you are!" — (Baltimore *Correspondent*.)

It must be confessed that in their understanding of each other these gentlemen have almost achieved an understanding of themselves.

XV

In the meantime the secret finance committee of the "Emigrés" had elected an executive committee consisting of Kinkel, Willich and Reichenbach and it now resolved to take serious measures in connection with the German loan. As reported in the New York *Schnellpost*, the *New-Yorker Deutsche Zeitung* and the Baltimore *Correspondent* at the end of 1851, Student Schurz was sent on a mission to France, Belgium and Switzerland where he sought out all old, forgotten, dead and missing parliamentarians, Reichregents, deputies and other distinguished men, right down to the late lamented Raveaux, to get them to guarantee the loan. The forgotten wretches hastened to give their guarantee. For what else was the guarantee of the loan if not a mutual guarantee of government posts in partibus; and in the same way Messrs. Kinkel, Willich and Reichenbach obtained by this means guarantees of *their* future prospects. And these sorrowing bonhommes in Switzerland were so obsessed with "organisation" and the guarantee of future posts that they had long before worked out a plan by which government posts would be awarded according to seniority—which produced a terrible scandal about who were to have Nos. 1, 2 and 3. Suffice it to say that Student Schurz brought back the guarantee in his pocket and so they all went to work. Some days earlier Kinkel had, it is true, promised in another meeting with the "Agitators" that he would not go ahead with a loan without them. For that very reason he departed taking the signatures of the guarantors and *carte blanche* from Reichenbach and Willich—ostensibly to find customers for his aesthetic lectures in the north of England, but in reality to go to Liverpool and embark for New York where he hoped to play Parzival and to discover the *Holy Grail*, the gold of the democratic parties.

And now begins that sweet-sounding, strange, magniloquent, fabulous, true and adventurous history of the great battles fought on both sides of the Atlantic Ocean between the Emigrés and the Agitators. It was a war waged with renewed bitterness and with indefatigable zeal. In it we witness Gottfried's crusade in the course of which he contends with Kossuth and after great labours and indescribable temptations he finally returns home with the Grail in the bag.

> *Or bei signori, io vi lascio al presente,*
> *E se voi tornerete in questo loco,*
> *Diro questa battaglia dov'io lasso*
> *Ch'un altra no fu mai di tal fracasso.*
> (*Boiardo*, Bk I, Canto 26)

[And there, kind Sirs, I leave you for the present,
If one day you return unto this place
I'll give you further news of this great war
So full of mighty deeds ne'er done before.]

1. Written between May and June 1852. First published in 1930 by the Marx-Engels Institute in Moscow in Vol. 5 of the *Marx–Engels Archive*. This edition was in Russian translation; the first edition of the German original had to wait for the German *Werke* Vol. 8, of 1960.
2. Klopstock's *Messias*.
3. *Siegwart: Eine Klostergeschichte* by Miller appeared in 1776 and is typical of the sentimental trend in literature at the time.
4. Goethe, *Faust* I. *Faust's Study*. Translated by Louis Macneice and E. L. Stahl.
5. *Ibid.*
6. A reference to the Confessions of a beautiful soul which occur in Goethe's novel *Wilhelm Meister's Apprenticeship* and which epitomise the cult of sentiment.
7. Wagner was the naïve assistant of Faust.
8. Wolfram von Eschenbach and Gottfried von Strasbourg were the two chief exponents of the courtly epic in Germany. Their principal works were *Parzival* (Wolfram) and *Tristan* (Gottfried).
9. Platen (1796–1835) was a neo-classical poet who attacked both the Romantics and the Philistines; essentially second-rate he was himself the object of a notoriously violent satire by Heine.
10. Chamisso, the well-known author of *Peter Schlemihl* also published the *Deutscher Musenalmanach* which appeared in Leipzig from 1833 to 1839. Albert Knapp was the editor of *Christoterpe. Ein Taschenbuch für christliche Leser, Heidelberg* 1833–53.
11. The supreme Hindu deity Shiva was also known as Mahadeva. In the form used by Marx, Mahadöh, there is an echo of Goethe's poem *Der Gott und die Bajadere*.
12. The conflict between duty and inclination is seen by the mature Schiller as central to tragedy.
13. Christian Heinrich Spiess (1755–99), Heinrich Clauren (1771–1854), and Karl Gottlob Cramer (1758–1817) were all writers of popular novels or adventure stories.
14. *Heinrich von Ofterdingen* by Novalis was a paradigmatic work of the German Romantic school. The hero—modelled on a mediaeval poet of that name—spends his life in a search for the "blue flower" which becomes a symbol of that infinite romantic longing for the ideal, poetic realm removed from that of reality.
15. The concluding lines of Goethe's *Zahme Xenien* in which he makes fun of Pustkuchen's *Wanderjahre*, a work parasitic on his own Wilhem Meister and one which was for a while thought to be from his own pen. Goethe's own Italian Journey marks a decisive change in his career.
16. Kotzebue was an immensely popular writer of superficial melodramas.
17. Hegel, *The Phenomenology of Mind*, Berlin 1832, pp. 392 ff.
18. Schiller's *Kabale und Liebe* was one of the chief works of the German Storm and Stress period.
19. Johann Heinrich Jung-Stilling (1740–1817) a sentimental, pietistic writer.
20. Bettina von Arnim had managed to captivate the aging Goethe while she

was herself scarcely more than a precocious child. Her publication of Goethe's *Briefwechsel mit einem Kinde* brought her a certain notoriety.
21. The critical movement, i.e. the Young Hegelians, Strauss, Bruno Bauer and Feuerbach.
22. Tale by Clemens Brentano, one of the chief exponents of German Romanticism.
23. The Göttinger Hain poets (Hölty and Voss were the most important) were active from 1772 to 1774. Influenced by Klopstock and Bürger they played an important role in the formation of German literature before subsiding into philistinism.
24. The reference is to the artisans' congresses that took place in various towns in Germany in 1848 and which produced programmes for restoring the guilds to their former prosperity in accordance with Winkelblech's utopian theories.
25. The dictated constitution was introduced by Frederick William IV on December 5, 1848. The Lower Chamber met on February 26, 1849, but was dissolved by the government on April 27, 1849.
26. The battle of Rastatt took place on June 29 & 30, 1849. The defeat of the democratic forces at the hands of the Prussian troops marked the end of the Baden campagne.
27. The reference is to Goethe's celebrated novel, *The Sufferings of Young Werther*.
28. May 1852, i.e. the French presidential election which the democratic movement and especially the *émigrés* hoped would inaugurate a new democratic epoch.
29. I.e. the campagne for the Imperial Constitution whose defeat at Rastatt ended the revolutionary struggles.
30. The Camphausen Ministry in Prussia lasted from March to June 1848.
31. The Prussian Assembly was dissolved in November 1848.
32. The *Neue Preussische Zeitung* also known as the "Kreuzzeitung" was founded in June 1848. It was the organ of the extreme right-wing court camarilla. As such it opposed Manteuffel's more moderate conservatism.
33. The Dresden Uprising lasted from May 3 to May 8, 1849. It broke out when the King of Saxony refused to recognise the Imperial Constitution. The insurrection was led by Bakunin and Samuel Tzschirner and involved workers and artisans. Hence an appeal to the bourgeois democrats of Leipzig went unheeded.
34. The reference is to June 13, 1849, when Louis Napoleon defeated a challenge to his power by Ledru-Rollin and the Montagne. The influence of the Montagne was now broken and Ledru and others fled into exile.
35. Brüggemann was chief editor of the *Kölnische Zeitung*, 1846–1855.
36. Arnold Winkelried was the half-legendary popular hero of the Swiss war of liberation against the Habsburgs. According to tradition he opened the attack in the decisive battle of Sempach (1386) with the cry "Der Freiheit eine Gasse!"
37. Boiardo, *L'Orlando inamorato*, canto 17.
38. I.e. the *Karlsruher Zeitung*.
39. A popular sentimental novel by J. T. Hermes.
40. The March Clubs were the branches, existing in various German cities of the

Central March Club, that had been founded in November 1848 by members of the Frankfurt Left. They were frequently attacked by Marx and Engels in the *Neue Rheinische Zeitung* for their failure to take action.

41. Ludwig Börne was the founder of modern polemical German literature. Widely read in his day he exercised a profound influence on the style of Engels and perhaps also Marx. He is now unjustly neglected.

42. Jakob Venedey, *Preussen und Preussentum*. Mannheim 1839.

43. Alcina figures both in the *Orlando furioso* of Ariosto and the *Orlando Inamorato* of Boiardo.

44. The "wet" Quakers were a reformist trend within the movement in the Twenties of the last century.

45. See Note 3 to the "Revelations".

46. Bronzell was the site of an unimportant skirmish between Prussian and Austrian troops on November 8, 1850. It resulted from the claims of both sides to have the sole right to intervene in the affairs of Hesse and to crush an uprising there. Austria received diplomatic support from Russia and so Prussia had to yield. The agreement then reached at Olmütz effectively consolidated the Reaction.

47. I.e. in *Die Jobsiade. Ein komisches Heldengedicht* by K. A. Kortum.

48. The Hambacher Fest was a political demonstration by South German liberals and radicals in the castle of Hambach (in the Bavarian Palatinate) on May 27, 1832. It resulted in the complete abolition of the freedom of the press and association.

49. The invasion of Savoy was organised by Mazzini and took place in 1834. A detachment of *émigrés* of various nationalities marched on Savoy under the leadership of Ramorino, but was defeated by Piedmontese troops.

50. In June 1844 the Bandiera brothers, who were members of a secret conspiratorial organisation, landed on the Calabrian coast with the intention of sparking off an insurrection against the Neapolitan Bourbons and the Austrian yoke. They were betrayed by one of their number, taken prisoner and shot.

51. The Dukes of Augustenburg were a branch of the Holstein Ducal House. Their denial of the claims of the Danish kings to Schleswig-Holstein was a factor in German Danish relations and the complicated Schleswig-Holstein Question.

52. At the Warsaw Conference in October 1850 which was attended by Russia, Austria and Prussia the attempt was made to force Prussia to abandon all plans to unite Germany under its own hegemony.

53. The anniversary of the abdication of Louis Philippe on February 24, 1848.

54. The Vorparlament met in Frankfurt from March 31 and April 4, 1848, pending the election of an all-German Assembly and the formulation of a definitive constitution. It was moderate, i.e. constitutionalist and monarchist in character.

55. A famous relic in Trier, said to be the seamless coat of Christ for which the soldiers at the Crucifixion cast lots (see John 19, 23).

56. Paulus was a Protestant theologian, Wilhelm Traugott Krug was Kant's successor in the Königsberg chair of philosophy.

57. Alessandro Gavazzi was an Italian priest who took part in the Revolution of

H*

1848–49 in Italy. After the defeat of the Revolution he emigrated to England, agitated against the Catholic Church and the temporal power of the Pope. Later a supporter of Garibaldi.

58. Goethe, *Anmerkungen über Personen und Gegenstände, deren im dem Dialog "Rameau's Neffe" erwähnt wird.*

59. Jean-Victor Moreau, a general in the French Revolutionary army; as commander of the Rhine Moselle Army he gained fame with a brilliantly conducted retreat in face of superior enemy forces in 1797.

60. Black, red and yellow or gold were the colours of the revolutionaries in 1848.

61. Both Mathy and Römer were liberals in the Frankfurt National Assembly. Römer was also prime minister of Württemberg (1848–49).

62. The reference is to Willesen's book *Theorie des grossen Krieges angewendet auf den russisch-polnischen Feldzug von 1831* (1840) in which he based the science of war on abstract propositions rather than on the observable facts.

63. Both Peter the Hermit and Walther von Habenichts were peasant leaders in the First Crusade.

64. *Cavalieri della ventura* and *cavalieri del dente* are, respectively, "knights of fortune" and "knights of the knapsack".

65. The duodecimal, i.e. petty, war.

66. Goethe, *Faust* I.

67. Abraham a Sancta Clara (1664–1709) was Court preacher in Vienna. He is known for his biting satires.

68. Imperial Administrator (*Reichsverweser*) is a reference to the appointment of Archduke Johann to this post in 1848. It points to both the grandeur and the meaninglessness of Ruge's office.

69. Kaulbach's painting, the Battle of the Huns, shows the ghosts of the warriors who fell on the Catalaunian Plains in A.D. 451 continuing to fight.

70. Luwig Simon was a lawyer from Trier who became a left-wing member of the Frankfurt National Assembly; Franz Raveaux was one of the leaders of the Left-Centre in the Vorparlament and National Assembly; later he joined the provisional government in Baden. Both emigrated after the collapse of the revolution.

APPENDIX A

ADDRESS OF THE CENTRAL COMMITTEE
TO THE COMMUNIST LEAGUE
March, 1850

Brothers! In the two revolutionary years 1848–49 the League proved itself in double fashion: first, in that its members energetically took part in the movement in all places, that in the press, on the barricades and on the battlefields, they stood in the front ranks of the only decidedly revolutionary class, the proletariat. The League further proved itself in that its conception of the movement as laid down in the circulars of the congresses and of the Central Committee of 1847 as well as in the *Communist Manifesto* turned out to be the only correct one, that the expectations expressed in those documents were completely fulfilled and the conception of present day social conditions, previously propagated only in secret by the League, is now on everyone's lips and is openly preached in the market places. At the same time the former firm organisation of the League was considerably slackened. A large part of the members who directly participated in the revolutionary movement believed the time for secret societies to have gone by and public activities alone sufficient. The individual circles and communities allowed their connections with the Central Committee to become loose and gradually dormant. Consequently, while the democratic party, the party of the petty bourgeoisie, organised itself more and more in Germany, the workers' party lost its only firm foothold, remained organised at the most in separate localities for local purposes and in the general movement thus came completely under the domination and leadership of the petty-bourgeois democrats. An end must be put to this state of affairs, the independence of the workers must be restored. The Central Committee realised this necessity and therefore already in the winter of 1848–49 it sent an emissary, Josef Moll, to Germany for the reorganisation of the League. Moll's mission, however, was without lasting effect, partly because the German workers at that time had not acquired sufficient experience and partly because it was interrupted by the insurrection of the previous May. Moll himself took up the musket, entered the Baden-Palatinate army and fell on July 19th in the encounter at the Murg. The League lost in him one of its oldest, most active and most trustworthy members, one who had been active in all the congresses and Central Committees and even prior to this had carried out a series of missions with great success. After the defeat of the revolutionary parties of Germany and France in July 1849, almost all the members of the Central Committee came together again in London, replenished their numbers with new revolutionary forces and set about the reorganisation of the League with renewed zeal.

Reorganisation can only be carried out by an emissary, and the Central

Committee considers it extremely important that the emissary should leave precisely at this moment when a new revolution is impending, when the workers' party, therefore, must act in the most organised, most unanimous and most independent fashion possible if it is not to be exploited and taken in tow again by the bourgeoisie as in 1848.

Brothers! We told you as early as 1848 that the German liberal bourgeois would soon come to power and would immediately turn their newly acquired power against the workers. You have seen how this has been fulfilled. In fact it was the bourgeois who, immediately after the March movement of 1848, took possession of the state power and used this power to force back at once the workers, their allies in the struggle, into their former oppressed position. Though the bourgeoisie was not able to accomplish this without uniting with the feudal party, which had been disposed of in March, without finally even surrendering power once again to this feudal absolutist party, still it has secured conditions for itself which, in the long run, owing to the financial embarrass-ment of the government, would place power in its hands, and would safeguard all its interests, if it were possible for the revolutionary movement to assume already now a so-called peaceful development. The bourgeoisie, in order to safeguard its rule, would not even need to make itself obnoxious by violent measures against the people, since all such violent steps have already been taken by the feudal counter-revolution. Developments, however, will not take this peaceful course. On the contrary, the revolution, which will accelerate this development, is near at hand, whether it will be called forth by an indepen-dent uprising of the French proletariat or by an invasion of the Holy Alliance against the revolutionary Babylon.

And the role, this so treacherous role which the German liberal bourgeois played in 1848 against the people, will in the impending revolution be taken over by the democratic petty bourgeois, who at present occupy the same position in the opposition as the liberal bourgeois before 1848. This party, the demo-cratic party, which is far more dangerous to the workers than the previous liberal one, consists of three elements:

I. Of the most advanced sections of the big bourgeoisie, which pursue the aim of the immediate complete overthrow of feudalism and absolutism. This faction is represented by the one-time Berlin compromisers, by the tax resisters.

II. Of the democratic-constitutional petty bourgeois, whose main aim during the previous movement was the establishment of a more or less democratic federal state as striven for by their representatives, the Lefts in the Frankfurt Assembly, and later by the Stuttgart parliament, and by themselves in the campaign for the Reich Constitution.

III. Of the republican petty bourgeois, whose ideal is a German federative republic after the manner of Switzerland, and who now call themselves Red and social-democratic because they cherish the pious wish of abolishing the pressure of big capital on small capital, of the big bourgeois on the small bourgeois. The representatives of this faction were the members of the democratic congress and committees, the leaders of the democratic associations, the editors of the democratic newspapers.

Now, after their defeat, all these factions call themselves Republicans or Reds, just as the republican petty bourgeois in France now call themselves Socialists. Where, as in Württemberg, Bavaria, etc., they still find opportuntiy to pursue their aims constitutionally, they seize the occasion to retain their old phrases and to prove by deeds that they have not changed in the least. It is evident, moreover, that the altered name of this party does not make the slightest difference in its attitude to the workers, but merely proves that they are now obliged to turn against the bourgeoisie, which is united with absolutism, and to seek support in the proletariat.

The petty-bourgeois democratic party in Germany is very powerful; it comprises not only the great majority of the bourgeois inhabitants of the towns, the small people in industry and trade and the guild masters; it numbers among its followers also the peasants and the rural proletariat, in so far as the latter has not yet found a support in the independent urban proletariat.

The relation of the revolutionary workers' party to the petty-bourgeois democrats is this: it marches together with them against the faction which it aims at overthrowing, it opposes them in everything whereby they seek to consolidate their position in their own interests.

Far from desiring to revolutionise all society for the revolutionary proletarians, the democratic petty bourgeois strive for a change in social conditions by means of which existing society will be made as tolerable and comfortable as possible for them. Hence they demand above all diminution of state expenditure by a curtailment of the bureaucracy and shifting the chief taxes on to the big landowners and bourgeois. Further, they demand the abolition of the pressure of big capital on small, through public credit institutions and laws against usury, by which means it will be possible for them and the peasants to obtain advances, on favourable conditions, from the state instead of from the capitalists; they also demand the establishment of bourgeois property relations in the countryside by the complete abolition of feudalism. To accomplish all this they need a democratic state structure, either constitutional or republican, that will give them and their allies, the peasants, a majority; also a democratic communal structure that will give them direct control over communal property and over a series of functions now performed by the bureaucrats.

The domination and speedy increase of capital is further to be counteracted partly by restricting the right of inheritance and partly by transferring as many jobs of work as possible to the state. As far as the workers are concerned, it remains certain above all that they are to remain wage-workers as before; the democratic petty bourgeois only desire better wages and a more secure existence for the workers and hope to achieve this through partial employment by the state and through charity measures; in short, they hope to bribe the workers by more or less concealed alms and to break their revolutionary potency by making their position tolerable for the moment. The demands of the petty-bourgeois democracy here summarised are not put forward by all of its factions at the same time, and only a very few members of them consider that these demands constitute definite aims in their entirety. The further separate individuals or factions among them go, the more of these demands will they make their own, and those few who see their own programme in what has been outlined above might believe that thereby they have put forward the utmost that can be demanded from the revolution. But these demands can in nowise suffice for the party of the proletariat. While the democratic petty bourgeois wish to bring the revolution to a conclusion as quickly as possible, and with the achievement, at most, of the above demands, it is our interest and our task to make the revolution permanent, until all more or less possessing classes have been forced out of their position of dominance, until the proletariat has conquered state power, and the association of proletarians, not only in one country but in all the dominant countries of the world, has advanced so far that competition among the proletarians of these countries has ceased and that at least the decisive productive forces are concentrated in the hands of the proletarians. For us the issue cannot be the alteration of private property but only its annihilation, not the smoothing over of class antagonisms but the abolition of classes, not the improvement of existing society but the foundation of a new one. That, during the further development of the revolution, the petty-bourgeois democracy will for a moment obtain predominating influence in Germany is not open to doubt. The question, therefore, arises as to what the attitude of the proletariat of the League will be in relation to it:

1. During the continuance of the present conditions where the petty-bourgeois democrats are likewise oppressed;

2. In the next revolutionary struggle, which will give them the upper hand;

3. After this struggle, during the period of preponderance over the overthrown classes and the proletariat.

1. At the present moment, when the democratic petty bourgois are everywhere oppressed, they preach in general unity and reconciliation to the proletariat, they offer it their hand and strive for the establishment of a large opposition party which will embrace all shades of opinion in the democratic party, that is, they strive to entangle the workers in a party organisation in which general social-democratic phrases predominate, behind which their special interests are concealed and in which the particular demands of the proletariat may not be brought forward for the sake of beloved peace. Such a union would turn out solely to their advantage and altogether to the disadvantage of the proletariat. The proletariat would lose its whole independent, laboriously achieved position and once more sink down to being an appendage of official bourgeois democracy. This union must, therefore, be most decisively

rejected. Instead of once again stooping to serve as the applauding chorus of the bourgeois democrats, the workers, and above all the League, must exert themselves to establish an independent, secret and public organisation of the workers' party alongside of the official democrats and make each section the central point and nucleus of workers' societies in which the attitude and interests of the proletariat will be discussed independently of bourgeois influences. How far the bourgeois democrats are from seriously considering an alliance in which the proletarians would stand side by side with them with equal power and equal rights is shown, for example, by the Breslau democrats who, in their organ, the *Neue Oder-Zeitung*, most furiously attack the independently organised workers, whom they style Socialists. In the case of a struggle against a common adversary no special union is required. As soon as such an adversary has to be fought directly, the interests of both parties, for the moment, coincide, and, as previously, so also in the future, this connection, calculated to last only for the moment, will arise of itself. It is self-evident that in the impending bloody conflicts, as in all earlier ones, it is the workers who, in the main, will have to win the victory by their courage, determination and self-sacrifice. As previously, so also in this struggle, the mass of the petty bourgeois will as long as possible remain hesitant, undecided and inactive, and then, as soon as the issue has been decided, will seize the victory for themselves, will call upon the workers to maintain tranquillity and return to their work, will guard against so-called excesses and bar the proletariat from the fruits of victory. It is not in the power of the workers to prevent the petty-bourgeois democrats from doing this, but it is in their power to make it difficult for them to gain the upper hand as against the armed proletariat, and to dictate such conditions to them that the rule of the bourgeois democrats will from the outset bear within it the seeds of their downfall, and that their subsequent extrusion by the rule of the proletariat will be considerably facilitated. Above all things, the workers must counteract, as much as is at all possible, during the conflict and immediately after the struggle, the bourgeois endeavours to allay the storm, and must compel the democrats to carry out their present terrorist phrases. Their actions must be so aimed as to prevent the direct revolutionary excitement from being suppressed again immediately after the victory. On the contrary, they must keep it alive as long as possible. Far from opposing so-called excesses, instances of popular revenge against hated individuals or public buildings that are associated only with hateful recollections, such instances must not only be tolerated but the leadership of them taken in hand. During the struggle and after the struggle, the workers must, at every opportunity, put forward their own demands alongside of the demands of the bourgeois democrats. They must demand guarantees for the workers as soon as the democratic bourgeois set about taking over the government. If necessary they must obtain these guarantees by force and in general they must see to it that the new rulers pledge themselves to all possible concessions and promises—the surest way to compromise them. In general, they must in every way restrain as far as possible the intoxication of victory and the enthusiasm for the new state of things, which make their appearance after every victorious street battle, by a calm and dispassionate estimate of the situation and by unconcealed mistrust in the new government. Alongside of the new official governments they must establish simultaneously their own revolutionary workers' governments, whether in the form of municipal committees and municipal councils or in the form of workers' clubs or workers' committees, so that the bourgeois-democratic governments not only immediately lose the support of the workers but from the outset see themselves supervised and threatened by authorities which are backed by the whole mass of the workers. In a word, from the first moment of victory, mistrust must be directed no longer against the conquered reactionary party, but against the workers' previous allies, against the party that wishes to exploit the common victory for itself alone.

2. But in order to be able energetically and threateningly to oppose this party, whose treachery to the workers will begin from the first hour of victory, the workers must be armed and organised. The arming of the whole proletariat with rifles, muskets, cannon and munitions must be put through at once, the revival of the old Citizens' Guard directed against the workers must be resisted. However, where the latter is not feasible the workers must attempt to organise themselves independently as a proletarian guard with commanders elected by themselves and with a general staff of their own choosing, and to put themselves at the command not of the state authority but of the revolutionary community councils which the workers will have managed to get adopted. Where workers are employed at the expense of the state they must see that they are armed and organised in a separate corps with commanders of their own choosing or as part of the proletarian guard. Arms and ammunition must not be surrendered on any pretext; any attempt at disarming must be frustrated, if necessary by force. Destruction of the influence of the bourgeois democrats upon the workers, immediate independent and armed organisation of the workers and the enforcement of conditions as difficult and compromising as possible upon the inevitable momentary rule of the bourgeois democracy—these are the main points which the proletariat and hence the League must keep in view during and after the impending insurrection.

3. As soon as the new governments have consolidated their positions to some extent, their struggle against the workers will begin. Here, in order to be able to offer energetic opposition to the democratic petty bourgeois, it is above all necessary that the workers shall be independently organised and centralised in clubs. After the overthrow of the existing governments, the Central Committee will, as soon as it is at all possible, betake itself to Germany, immediately convene a congress and put before the latter the necessary proposals for the centralisation of the workers' clubs under a leadership established in the chief seat of the movement. The speedy organisation of at least a provincial inter-

linking of the worker's clubs is one of the most important points for the strengthening and development of the workers' party; the immediate consequence of the overthrow of the existing governments will be the election of a national representative assembly. Here the proletariat must see to it:

I. That no groups of workers are barred on any pretext or by any kind of trickery on the part of local authorities or government commissioners.

II. That everywhere workers' candidates are put up alongside of the bourgeois-democratic candidates, that they should consist as far as possible of members of the League, and that their election is promoted by all possible means. Even where there is no prospect whatsoever of their being elected, the workers must put up their own candidates in order to preserve their independence, to count their forces and to bring before the public their revolutionary attitude and party standpoint. In this connection they must not allow themselves to be seduced by such arguments of the democrats as, for example, that by so doing they are splitting the democratic party and making it possible for the reactionaries to win. The ultimate intention of all such phrases is to dupe the proletariat. The advance which the proletarian party is bound to make by such independent action is infinitely more important than the disadvantage that might be incurred by the presence of a few reactionaries in the representative body. If the democracy from the outset comes out resolutely and terroristically against the reaction, the influence of the latter in the elections will be destroyed in advance.

The first point on which the bourgeois democrats will come into conflict with the workers will be the abolition of feudalism. As in the first French Revolution, the petty bourgeois will give the feudal lands to the peasants as free property, that is to say, try to leave the rural proletariat in existence and form a petty-bourgeois peasant class which will go through the same cycle of impoverishment and indebtedness which the French peasant is now still going through.

The workers must oppose this plan in the interest of the rural proletariat and in their own interest. They must demand that the confiscated feudal property remain state property and be converted into workers' colonies cultivated by the associated rural proletariat with all the advantages of large-scale agriculture, through which the principle of common property immediately obtains a firm basis in the midst of the tottering bourgeois property relations. Just as the democrats combine with the peasants so must the workers combine with the rural proletariat. Further, the democrats will work either directly for a federative republic or, if they cannot avoid a single and indivisible republic, they will at least attempt to cripple the central government by the utmost possible autonomy and independence for the communities and provinces. The workers, in opposition to this plan, must not only strive for a single and indivisible German republic, but also within this republic for the most determined centralisation of power in the hands of the state authority. They must not allow themselves to be misguided by the democratic talk of freedom for the communities, or self-government, etc. In a country like Germany where there are still so many relics of the Middle Ages to be abolished, where there is so much local and provincial obstinacy to be broken, it must under no circumstances be permitted that every village, every town and every province should put a new obstacle in the path of revolutionary activity, which can proceed with full force only from the centre. It is not to be tolerated that the present state of affairs should be renewed, that Germans must fight separately in every town and in every province for one and the same advance. Least of all is it to be tolerated that a form of property, namely, communal property, which still lags behind modern private property and which everywhere is necessarily passing into the latter, together with the quarrels resulting from it between poor and rich communities, as well as communal civil law, with its trickery against the workers, that exists alongside of state civil law, should be perpetuated by a so-called free communal constitution. As in France in 1793 so today in Germany it is the task of the really revolutionary party to carry through the strictest centralisation.

We have seen how the democrats will come to power with the next movement, how they will be compelled to propose more or less socialistic measures. It will be asked what measures the workers ought to propose in reply. At the beginning of the movement, of course, the workers cannot yet propose any directly communistic measures. But they can:

1. Compel the democrats to interfere in as many spheres as possible of the hitherto existing social order, to disturb its regular course and to compromise themselves as well as to concentrate the utmost possible productive forces, means of transport, factories, railways, etc., in the hands of the state;

2. They must drive the proposals of the democrats, who in any case will not act in a revolutionary but in a merely reformist manner, to the extreme and transform them into direct attacks upon private property; thus, for example, if the petty bourgeois propose purchase of the railways and factories, the workers must demand that these railways and factories shall be simply confiscated by the state without compensation as being the property of reactionaries. If the democrats propose proportional taxes, the workers must demand progressive taxes; if the democrats themselves put forward a moderately progressive tax, the workers must insist on a tax with rates that rise so steeply that big capital will be ruined by it; if the democrats demand the regulation of state debts, the workers must demand state bankruptcy. Thus, the demands of the workers must everywhere be governed by the concessions and measures of the democrats.

If the German workers are not able to attain power and achieve their own class interests without completely going through a lengthy revolutionary development, they at least know for a certainty this time that the first act of this approaching revolutionary drama will coincide with the direct victory of their own class in France and will be very much accelerated by it.

But they themselves must do the utmost for their final victory by clarifying their minds as to what their class interests are, by taking up their position as an independent party as soon as possible and by not allowing themselves to be seduced for a single moment by the hypocritical phrases of the democratic petty bourgeois into refraining from the independent organisation of the party of the proletariat. Their battle cry must be: The Revolution in Permanence.

II

ADDRESS OF THE CENTRAL COMMITTEE TO THE COMMUNIST LEAGUE
June, 1850

Brothers!

In our last report, brought to you by the emissary we gave you an account of the position of the workers' party and, in particular, the League, both in the present situation and in the event of a revolution.

The chief purpose of this circular is to report on the present state of the League.

The defeats of the revolutionary party last summer succeeded for a moment in bringing the League to the point of almost total dissolution. The most active members had taken part in the various movements and were now scattered; many lost contact with each other and this fact, together with the censorship of the post made correspondence impossible for a time. So until towards the end of last year the central committee was condemned to complete inactivity.

As the first effects of the defeat wore off the need for a strong secret organisation of the revolutionary party throughout Germany made itself felt. In the Central Committee this need matured into the decision to send an emissary to Germany and Switzerland. Independently of the central committee a new clandestine group formed in Switzerland and the Cologne commune attempted to reorganise the League in Germany.

In Switzerland, early in the year, a number of refugees who had made a more or less distinguished name for themselves in the various movements formed themselves into a group. Their aim was to wait for a suitable moment in which to bring about the collapse of the governments and to keep men in readiness to lead the movement and even the government. The group did not belong to any particular party—the motley character of its adherents did not permit this. For they represented every political shade and ranged from resolute communists and even former League members to the most timorous petty-bourgeois democrats and ex-members of the Palatinate government.

At the time a large number of people from Baden and the Palatinate were roaming around Switzerland in search of places and other lesser ambitions. For them this party offered good opportunities for self-advancement.

Nor were the instructions which the party sent to its agents (and to which the Central Committee has access) of a kind to inspire much confidence. They are marked by the absence of a definite point of view as well as by the attempt to bring all the available oppositional elements into a specious unity. These failings were poorly concealed under a mass of detail about industrial, agricultural, political and military conditions in the different localities. The real strength of this party was likewise very insignificant. According to the complete list of members in our possession the whole affair at its zenith could count on no more than 30 members. It is noteworthy that among these there were hardly any workers. It was an army consisting exclusively of officers and N.C.O.s They included people like A. Fries and Greiner from the Palatinate, Körner from Elberfeld, Sigel, etc.

They sent two agents to Germany. The first, Bruhn, was a League member from Holstein. He contrived by false pretences to induce a number of League members and communes to join the new party for a time, in the belief that it was the resurrected League. At the same time he sent a report on the League to the Swiss central committee in Zürich and another on the Swiss party to us. Not content with acting as intermediary he wrote to the people in Frankfurt whom he had won for the new cause, and, at a time when he was still in correspondence with us, he made directly libellous remarks and instructed them to have nothing to do with London. Because of this he was at once expelled from the League. The situation in Frankfurt was cleared up by the League emissary. For the rest Bruhn's labours on behalf of the Swiss central committee remained without effect. The second agent was a student called Schurz. He too achieved nothing because, as he wrote to Zürich "he found that the League had full control over all potential members". He then left Germany suddenly and is now drifting around Brussels and Paris where the League keeps an eye on him.

That the Central Committee did not regard the new party as a serious problem was due also to the fact that a trusted League member (Wilhelm Wolff) belonged to their central committee and had instructions to keep us informed about the plans and measures resolved upon by these people. The Central Committee has also sent an emissary to Switzerland to assist the above-mentioned League member to attract useful people to the League and in general to organise the League in Switzerland. All this information is based on reliable evidence.

Another attempt of the same sort was made by Struve and Sigel, etc., who were in Geneva at the time. These people were impertinent enough to dress their party up as the League and to misuse the names of League members for this purpose. Of course, their lies deceived no-one. Their efforts were so futile that the few members of this abortive movement were finally forced to join the group already discussed. The more impotent their coterie became the more imposing were the titles they gave to themselves—like "Central Committee for European Democracy", etc. Here in London, too, Struve continued his efforts in this direction together with other disillusioned heroes. Manifestos and invitations to join the "Central Committee of the United German Emigration" and the "Central Committee for European Democracy" were sent all over Germany, but without the slightest response.

The alleged connections between this coterie and French and other non-German revolutionaries simply did not exist. Their total activities were confined to a number of petty intrigues among the local German refugees. They have no direct effect on the League and represent no threat. It is easy to keep an eye on them.

All undertakings of this sort will either have the same goal as the League, i.e. they will aim at revolutionising the organisation of the workers' party. In this case they will destroy the centralisation and strength of the party by fragmenting it and so they are definitely to be regarded as dangerous separatists. The only other possible goal is to misuse the workers' party for purposes alien or directly opposed to its own. The workers' party can use other parties for its own purposes on occasion but must never subordinate itself to any other party. But those people who were in the government during the last movement and who used their position to betray it and to suppress the workers' party wherever it appeared must be kept at a distance whatever the situation

We have the following to report about the present state of the League.

1. Belgium

The organisation of the League as it existed among the Belgian workers in 1846 and 1847 has, of course, disappeared since 1848, when the chief members were arrested, condemned to death and had their sentences commuted to imprisonment for life. The League in Belgium has lost much of its strength since the February Revolution and the expulsion of almost all the members of the German Workers' Society from Brussels. The present policy of the police has not permitted it to reorganise. Despite this a commune has managed to survive in Brussels to this day and it functions to the best of its ability.

2. Germany

It had been the intention of the Central Committee to deliver a special report on the situation of the League in Germany. But this is not possible at the present time as the Prussian police is conducting an extensive investigation into the revolutionary party. This circular will be sent to Germany by a safe route but a few copies may possibly fall into the hands of the police in the course of distribution within Germany. It must therefore be so formulated that its content will not give the police any evidence that could be used against the League. For the moment then the League confines itself to the following remarks.

The chief German centres of the League are Cologne, Frankfurt/Main,

Hanau, Mainz, Wiesbaden, Hamburg, Schwerin, Berlin, Breslau, Liegnitz, Glogau, Leipzig, Nuremberg, Munich, Bamberg, Wurzburg, Stuttgart and Baden.

The following are appointed Regional Branches: Hamburg for Schleswig-Holstein; Schwerin for Mecklenburg; Breslau for Silesia; Leipzig for Saxony and Berlin; Nuremberg for Bavaria; Cologne for the Rhineland and Westphalia.

For the time being the communes in Göttingen, Stuttgart and Brussels shall remain in direct communication with the Central Committee until they have extended their influence to the point where new regional branches can be formed.

The position of the League in Baden shall be determined on receipt of the report from the emissary sent there and to Switzerland.

Where, as in Schleswig-Holstein and Mecklenburg, there are Peasant and Labourers' Clubs, League members have been able directly to influence them and in part to gain complete control. The Workers' and Labourers' Clubs in Saxony, Franconia, Nassau and Hesse are also for the most part in the hands of the League. The most influential members of the Workers' Brotherhood also belong to the League. The Central Committee would point out to all communes and League members that such influence on the workers' sport, labourers' and peasant clubs is of the very greatest importance and should be increased wherever possible. The Central Committee requests the regional branches and communes in direct contact with them to make special mention of all progress in this area in their next reports.

The emissary to Germany, who has received a unanimous commendation from the Central Committee for his efforts, has everywhere admitted only the most reliable people as members to the League and has left the further expansion of the League in their hands, relying on their greater knowledge of local conditions. Whether it will be possible to recruit definite revolutionaries to the League will depend on the actual situation in the various localities. Where this is not possible a second class of League members should be formed from among people who do not understand the communist consequences of the movement but who are reliable and useful. This second class must be told that the party is local or provincial and must constantly be under the supervision of the actual League members and authorities. For with the aid of these additional contacts it will be possible to gain a firm grip on the sport and peasants' clubs. The detailed organisation can be left to the Regional Branches and the Central Committee looks forward to their reports on these matters.

One commune has proposed that a League congress be convened on German soil. The communes and regional branches will realise themselves that in the present circumstances it is not even advisable to convene provincial congresses of the leading regions everywhere. A general League congress is quite out of the question at the present time. But as soon as circumstances permit the Central

Committee will arrange a congress of the League in a suitable place.—The Prussian Rhineland and Westphalia have recently been visited by an emissary of the Cologne region. The report on this tour has not yet been received in Cologne. We request all regions likewise to send out emissaries to tour their provinces as soon as possible and to report back on the results. Lastly, we report that in Schleswig-Holstein contacts have been established with the army; we are still awaiting an account of what the League may hope for in this direction.

3. *Switzerland*

We are still awaiting the report of our emissaries and so we shall return to this in greater detail in our next circular.

4. *France*

Conracts with the German workers in Besançon and other places in the Jura will be re-established from Switzerland. In Paris, Ewerbeck, the League member who has been the leader of the commune there, has announced his resignation from the League as he thinks that his literary activities are more important. In consequence, contact has been disrupted for the time being and must be re-established with extreme caution as the Parisians have admitted a number of people who are quite useless and who in the past have even been actively hostile to the League.

5. *England*

The London Regional Branch is the strongest in the whole League. It has distinguished itself above all by the fact that for some years now it has financed the League and in particular the emissaries' journeys almost unaided. It recently strengthened itself still further by admitting new elements and it provides all the leadership for the local German Workers' Society as well as the most energetic section of the German *émigrés* here.

Contact is maintained with the resolutely revolutionary parties among the French, English and Hungarians by means of members delegated for the purpose.

Of the French revolutionaries the authentically proletarian party, led by Blanqui, has joined forces with us. The delegates of the Blanqui secret societies are in regular official communication with the League representatives whom they have entrusted with important tasks in preparation for the next French revolution.

The leaders of the revolutionary Chartist Party are also in close contact with the delegates of the Central Committee. Their journals are at our disposal. The breach between this independent revolutionary workers' party and the more conciliatory party led by O'Connor was materially hastened thanks to League delegates.

Similarly the Central Committee is in contact with the most progressive party of the Hungarian *émigrés*. This party is important as it boasts a number of excellent military leaders whose services would be available to the League in a revolution.

The Central Committee requests the Regional Branches to distribute this circular among their members and to prepare their reports as quickly as possible. All members are urged to make the greatest possible efforts; these are especially vital at this moment when the situation is so critical that the outbreak of a revolution can no longer be very far away.

III

MINUTES OF THE MEETING OF THE CENTRAL COMMITTEE OF THE COMMUNIST LEAGUE OF SEPTEMBER 15, 1850

Present: Marx, Engels, Schramm, Pfänder, Bauer, Eccarius, Schapper, Willich, Lehmann. Apologies from Fränkel.

As this is an extraordinary meeting the minutes of the last meeting are not here and will therefore not be read.

Marx: The Friday meeting had to be cancelled because of a clash with a meeting of the Society commission. As Willich has called a meeting of the Regional branches, a meeting whose legality I will not go into, this meeting must be held today. I wish to move the following resolution which is in three parts:

1. The Central Committee shall be transferred from London to Cologne and the Regional Branch there will undertake to form a new Central Committee with effect from the close of this meeting. This decision shall be reported to League members in Paris, Belgium and Switzerland. The new Central Committee will itself notify members throughout Germany.

Explanation: I was opposed to Schapper's motion to set up a Regional Branch in Cologne for the whole of Germany because this might disrupt the unity of the central authority. Our motion does away with this objection. There is a whole host of new reasons which support the motion. There is a minority in the Central Committee in open rebellion against the majority both in the motion of censure during the last meeting, in the general meeting called by the Region, in the Society and among the *émigrés*. The conclusion is that the Central Committee cannot possibly survive here. Its unity cannot be maintained, there would be a split and there would then be two Leagues. As the Party must come first I propose this way out.

2. The existing League statutes shall be declared null and void. The new Central Committee shall be responsible for drawing up new statutes.

Explanation: The Statutes of the Congress in 1847 were amended by the London Central Committee in 1848. Circumstances have now changed yet again. The latest London statutes weakened the principal articles of the original statutes. Both statutes are in force in different places, in some places there are no statutes at all or there are even unauthorised ones, so that anarchy is complete. Moreover the latest statutes have become public and so can no longer be used. My proposal, therefore, is to introduce statutes and to bring order into the present statuteless confusion.

3. Two Regional branches shall be formed in London to be entirely independent of each other joined only by the common bond with the League and their correspondence with the same Central Committee.

Explanation: It is necessary to form two branches here for the very reason that the unity of the League must at all cost be preserved. Quite apart from personal disagreements we have witnessed also differences of principle even in the Society. In the last debate "the position of the German proletariat in the next revolution" was discussed and views were expressed by members of the minority on the Central Committee which directly oppose those in the last circular but one and even the "Manifesto". A German nationalist point of view was substituted for the universal outlook of the "Manifesto" and the patriotic feelings of the German artisans were pandered to. The materialist standpoint of the "Manifesto" has given way to idealism. The revolution is seen not as the product of realities of the situation but as the result of a mere effort of will. What we say to the workers is: You have 15, 20, 50 years of civil war to go through in order to change society and to train yourselves for the exercise of political power, whereas they say, we must take over *at once*, or else we may as well take to our beds. Just as the Democrats abused the word "people" so now the word "proletariat" has been degraded to a mere phrase. To make this phrase effective it was necessary to describe the petty bourgeois as proletarians so that in practice it was the petty bourgeois and not the proletarians who were represented. The actual revolutionary process had to be replaced by revolutionary catchwords. This debate has finally laid bare the differences in principle which lay behind the clash of personalities, and the time for action has now arrived. For it is personal antagonism that has furnished both parties with their battle-cries and some members of the League have called the defenders of the "Manifesto" reactionaries, hoping thereby to make them unpopular, a vain endeavour, as they do not seek popularity. The majority would be justified in dissolving the London branch and expelling the minority as being in conflict with the principles of the League. I do not wish to put a motion to that effect as it would cause a pointless scandal and because these people are still communists in their own view even though the opinions they are now expressing are anti-communist and could at best be described as social-democratic. It is obvious, however, that it would be a mere waste of time, and a dangerous one at that, for us to remain together any longer. Schapper has often spoken of separation—very well, then, let us go ahead with it. I think that I have found the way to do so without destroying the Party.

I wish to state that, for my own part, I should like to have at most twelve people in our branch, as few as possible, and gladly leave the minority in possession of the great throng. If this proposal is accepted we shall obviously be unable to remain in the Great Windmill Street Society. Lastly, I should like to point out that I am not proposing that we make the hostile relationship permanent, but that, on the contrary, we eliminate the tension and so end the relationship. We remain together in the League and in the Party but we escape from a relationship that harms us both.

Schapper: Just as in France the proletariat parted company with the "Montagne" and "La Presse" so it is here also: the people who represent the party on the theoretical side have parted company from those who organise the proletariat. I am in favour of moving the Central Committee and also of making alterations in the statutes. The Cologne members are familiar with the situation in Germany. I also think that the new revolution will produce people who will know how to lead themselves and will do so with greater success than all those who made a name for themselves in 1848. As far as disagreements of principle are concerned, it was Eccarius who raised the question that made this debate necessary. I have defended the opinions attacked here because I am in general enthusiastic about the whole business. The question at issue is whether we are to chop a few heads off right at the start or whether it is our own heads that will fall. In France the workers will come to power and when this happens the same thing will take place in Germany. Were this not the case I would indeed take to my bed; in that event I would certainly be able to enjoy a different material position. If we come to power we can take all the measures necessary to ensure the rule of the proletariat. I am a fanatical supporter of this point of view but the Central Committee favours the very opposite. You want nothing more to do with us—very well, let us part company. I shall certainly be guillotined in the next revolution but this will still not stop me from going to Germany. You want two Regional Branches—very well, but that will be the end of the League. We shall meet again in Germany and perhaps join forces again. Marx is a personal friend of mine but you are in favour of separation—very well, we shall each go our separate ways. But in that case there should be two Leagues, one for those who work with the pen and one for those who work in other ways. I do not share the view that the bourgeoisie will come to power and on this point I am quite unshakeable—if I weren't I wouldn't give a brass farthing for the whole movement. But if there are two Regional Branches here in London, two societies and two refugee committees then we should also have two Leagues and complete separation.

Marx: Schapper has misunderstood my proposal. If the resolution is adopted we shall separate, the two Regional Branches shall separate and the people concerned will have no contact with each other. However, they will belong to the same League and share the same Central Committee. You can even retain the greater part of the League membership. As for personal sacrifice, I have given up as much as anyone; but for the class and not for individuals. And as for enthusiasm, not much enthusiasm is needed to belong to a party when you believe cnati ti s on the point of seizing power. I have always defied the momentary opinions of the proletariat. If the best a party can do is to just fail to seize power, then we repudiate it. If the proletariat could gain control of the government the measures it would introduce would be those of the petty bourgeoisie and not those appropriate to the proletariat. Our party can only gain power when the situation allows it to put *its own* measures into practice. Louis Blanc is the best instance of what happens when you come to power prematurely. In France, moreover, it wasn't just the proletariat that gained power but the peasants and the petty bourgeois as well, and it is their demands that will necessarily prevail. The Paris Commune shows what can be accomplished without being in the government. And incidentally why do we hear nothing from Willich and the other members of the minority who approved the circular unanimously at the time? We cannot and will not split the League; we wish merely to divide the London Region into two branches.

Eccarius: I did indeed raise the question and it certainly was my intention to have the whole matter discussed. I have explained why I think that Schapper's view is based on an illusion and why I do think that our party can come to power right from the start in the next revolution. When the revolution breaks out our party will be more important in the Clubs than in the government.

At this point Citizen Lehmann walked out without comment. Citizen Willich did likewise.

First part of the motion: all in favour, Schapper abstained.

Second part: all in favour, Schapper abstained.

Third part: all in favour, Schapper abstained.

Schapper made a general protest against us all: We are now completely separated. I have my own friends in Cologne and more will follow me than you.

Marx: We have acted in strict accordance with the statutes. The resolutions of the Central Committee are completely valid.

After the minutes were read out both Marx and Schapper declared that they had not already discussed the matter with Cologne.

Schapper was asked whether he had any objection to the minutes. He said he had no objection as he thought all objections were superfluous.

Eccarius proposed that everyone should sign the minutes. Accepted. Schapper declared that he would not sign.

Dated, London, September 15, 1850.

Read, approved and signed:

> K. Marx, Chairman of the Central Committee
> F. Engels, Secretary
> Henry Bauer, K. Schramm, J. G. Eccarius, K. Pfänder.

IV

ADDRESS OF THE COLOGNE CENTRAL COMMITTEE TO THE COMMUNIST LEAGUE

Brothers! Although the changes which have taken place in the League in recent months have already been communicated to the Regions and most of the communities we must refer to them yet again in this circular. This is partly so as to present the picture in full and thus to supplement various incomplete accounts that are circulating, and partly as preparation for the measures that have become necessary in consequence of these developments.

The Cologne regional branch first learned of the events in London which culminated in the split among League members from the minutes we received from the former central committee of their meeting on September 15th. At this meeting the following resolutions were approved by a majority of 4 out of 10 (7–3):

1. The central committee shall be transferred from London to Cologne and the regional branch there will undertake to form a new central committee.

2. The existing League statutes shall be declared null and void. The new central committee shall be responsible for drafting new statutes.

3. Two regional branches shall be formed from the existing London Region. They shall be independent of each other and joined only by the common bond with the central committee.

From the arguments in support of these motions and from the report of the Majority accompanying the minutes it became apparent than an incurable breach had developed among the members of the League and that the proposed separation was the only way to avert the danger of complete dissolution. Just how great the danger was became clear to us from the detailed report of the Minority which arrived shortly afterwards. According to this report the Minority, strengthened by members of the London Region, the majority in fact, had constituted itself into the new central committee and had expelled the members of the former central committee from the League, together with a number of their friends. Furthermore, they sent out invitations to a previously announced congress on October 20th in London. It was intended that this congress would ratify their resolutions (whose obvious illegality they did not venture to deny), and regard them as part of a rescue action.

However, the content of this document convinced us that these resolutions were not only illegal but also that they were based on principles diametrically opposed to the principles of the League and to the policy the League has pursued hitherto. Thus the attempt to expel the Majority of the central committee was based (in addition to its complaints against individual members) partly on the general principle that the League should expel all writers. It was argued that the

League was exclusively intended for factory workers and artisans and that if these groups only had the will they would be able to seize the reins of power as soon as revolution should break out again and so would be able to carry out the communist reorganisation of society without further ado. This meant that the proletarian party should return to the old policy of universal asceticism (see "Manifesto", III, 3) and a crude egalitarianism —policies which were justified at the time of the first proletarian movements when it was a matter of being able to oppose to the various political and economic doctrines of bourgeois society the general principle of proletarian class struggle. But this negative attitude was no longer directed at some version of bourgeois socialism: it excommunicated the authors of the "Communist Manifesto" of 1848 and of the "First Address of the Central Committee" of this year in which the policy of the party was set out in great detail. Indeed, it even condemned the "Manifesto" and the policy of the party itself. For according to the "Manifesto" and the "Address" the proletarian movement will advance only by first becoming aware of its own class-situation and then by absorbing all the cultural elements of the old society from within this situation. In this way it will acquire a theoretical understanding of the movements of a communist revolution; while, in practice, it will act as developments dictate and seek to make use of the conflicts between the various national parties to seize political and economic power for itself. In contrast with this programme the Minority declares all theoretical work to be over and done with; it adopts a hostile attitude to all intellectual activity and believes that it can realize the ultimate goal of the movement on the basis of actual conditions and, above all, of a new German revolution. It is, therefore, quite natural that these same people should appear to represent the proletariat to the exclusion of all else and yet that in their latest proclamation, sent into the world in the company of the French, Poles, and Hungarians under the heading of a "democratic-socialist committee" they should have trumpeted forth the single concept "revolution" and posed as the champions of the petty-bourgeois social-democratic republic. In this programme, then, the proletariat is once again thrown back into its old unpolitical stance; once again it is summoned into battle to defend the interests of another class; and once again it would afterwards be cheated of the fruits of its victory.

Confronted with such a dubious fact as the circular of the new Minority central committee the Cologne regional branch was forced to drop any objections that could have been urged against the resolutions of the Majority central committee. It was neither possible, nor was it morally permissible to form a judgment on the personal conflicts and hostilities which, incidentally, were couched in the most malicious vituperation in the document of the Minority. As for the question of formal legality it was clear that both parties had abandoned the procedure laid down in the statutes—for according to these they should have appealed to the Congress. But further reflection convinced us that in a sense both parties had acted rightly, for even if a congress had been physically feasible in London at that time, it would inevitably have brought about the complete disintegration of the League. Our task was above all to rescue the principles, the policy and the very existence of the League. We therefore had but one course open to us: to adopt the resolutions of the Majority central committee, for, in the circumstances, they were the only reasonable and appropriate ones. Accordingly the Cologne regional branch established the new central committee by nominating the three members who now send you this report.

To implement the third resolution we instructed Citizens Schapper and Eccarius each to form an autonomous regional branch. The instructions to Schapper, the chief delegate of the Minority, were sent to the former London regional branch in a letter in which we explained our decisions in detail. We also declared all resolutions adopted by the London regional branch to be null and void in so far as they conflicted with our own. In response to our letter an emissary from London appeared in our midst and asked us to negotiate with him. When his request was refused he read out a rambling document from his superiors in which the latter attempted to justify their previous decisions. Their justifications consisted partly of new personal attacks of the most malicious and senseless kind, partly of a defence of the principles they had already stated and, lastly, of the somewhat disingenuous claim that all their actions conformed to the requirements of the statutes. We then made a last attempt to dispel the melancholy aberrations into which these people had lapsed; but, of course, in vain. But when the emissary set about expelling us from the League we replied that it was mutual but with the difference that in that case the old London regional branch together with its central committee would be automatically excluded from the League—an exclusion we would not hesitate to reinforce with our own resolution to that effect.

We did not inform the whole League of this expulsion immediately as we had intended to make it the subject of this circular which we had hoped to distribute earlier than has in fact been possible. After this resolution had been adopted we received a formal proposal from the London regional branch newly formed by Eccarius "to expel all members of the separatist League and in particular, Schapper, Willich, Schärttner, Lehmann, Dietz (Oswald), Gebert, Fränkel (the last seven by name) and to inform all League regions and communities of this decision as well as the separatist League in London and its leaders". This proposal was based on the following extremely cogent arguments and we repeat them here for the information of the whole League.

"1. They have made reports, and false reports at that, concerning the split in London and communicated them to persons outside the League, to the leaders of secret societies and to émigrés of various nationalities.

2. They are in a state of open rebellion against the legally constituted central committee in Cologne; they act in defiance of the latter's decisions and have caused an emissary to travel around Germany to enlist support for the separatist League.

3. They have violated, and still do violate, all the obligations binding on the members of secret societies, above all in their relations with the members of the London regional branch.

4. They have, since the separation, broken all the laws of secret societies and to permit them to remain in the League any longer would only hasten its collapse."

Brothers, we have become convinced that these reasons, some of them new ones, are valid. Above all, we have been swayed by the activities of Haude, the emissary who has appeared on the Rhine (and who, as he had no success in Germany, had now returned to London). Therefore, on the basis of our earlier declaration and the resolution adopted by our London regional branch, we solemnly declare: All members of the separatist League, especially its leaders and plenipotentiaries, Citizens Schapper, Willich, Schärttner (A), Oswald Dietz, A. Gebert, Adolph Maier (who is a member of the aforementioned democratic socialist committee and so in all probability a member of the committee of the separatist League), Fränkel and Haude are hereby expelled from the League. All League members are required to terminate all friendly relations with members of this League. A close watch is to be kept on all separatist League authorities and all attempts by them to obtain a foothold in Germany or other League territories where they have hitherto not penetrated. All developments are to be reported to the central committee without delay....

Cologne, December 1, 1850.

V

STATUTES OF THE COMMUNIST LEAGUE

1. The *aim* of the Communist League is to bring about the destruction of the old order of society and the downfall of the bourgeoisie—the intellectual, political and economic emancipation of the proletariat, and the communist revolution, using all the resources of propaganda and political struggle towards this goal. In all the various stages of the struggle of the proletariat the League shall represent at all times the interest of the movement as a whole, just as it shall seek at all times to concentrate and organise all the revolutionary forces of the proletariat within itself; as long as the proletariat has not attained its ultimate goal the League shall remain secret and indissoluble.

2. *Membership* shall be open only to those who can satisfy the following conditions. A member must

   a. be emancipated from every religion and he must sever his connections with every church organisation; he may not participate in any ceremony not required by civil law;

b. understand the conditions, the history and the goal of the proletarian movement;

c. stand aloof from all organisations and parties that oppose or obstruct the progress of the League towards its ultimate goal;

d. show ability and zeal in making propaganda, he must be unswerving in his loyalty to his convictions and vigorous in promoting the cause of revolution;

e. maintain the strictest secrecy in all matters concerning the League.

3. *Admission* shall be granted by the unanimous vote of the commune. A new member will normally be admitted by the chairman in the presence of the whole commune. Members will swear to abide unconditionally by the decisions of the League.

4. Any member who contravenes the regulations shall be expelled. A majority decision of the commune is required for the expulsion of individuals. The central committee is empowered to expel whole communes where expulsion has been proposed by a Regional Branch [Kreis]. The whole League shall be notified of expulsions and shall keep those expelled under surveillance just like other suspect individuals.

5. The League shall be organised into communes, regions, a central committee and a congress.

6. A commune shall consist of at least three members of the same locality. It shall elect a chairman who will conduct the meetings and a deputy who will act as treasurer.

7. Above the communes of a country or a province there shall be a chief commune, the regional branch, to be nominated by the central committee. The communes shall deal directly only with their regional commune, the regions in turn deal with the central committee.

8. The communes shall meet regularly, not less than once a fortnight, they shall correspond at least once a month with their regional branch; the latter shall communicate with the central committee at least once every two months; every three months the central committee shall report on the state of the League.

9. The chairman and deputy of the communes and regions shall be elected for one year and can be deposed at any time by their electorate; the members of the central committee can only be deposed by the congress.

10. Every League member shall pay a monthly contribution whose minimum shall be determined by the congress. Half of the sums so raised will go to the regional branches and half to the central committee; they will be used to cover administration costs, the distribution of propaganda material and the dispatching of emissaries. The regions shall bear the cost of the correspondence with the communes. Contributions shall be sent every three months

to the regional branches who will forward half of the total income to the central committee and, at the same time, give an account of their income and expenditure to the communes. The central committee shall account to the congress for monies it has received. Extraordinary expenses will be met by special levies.

11. The *central committee* is the executive organ of the whole League. It shall consist of at least three members and shall be elected and augmented by the regional branch to which it has been assigned by the congress. It shall be responsible only to the congress.

12. The *congress* is the legislative arm of the whole League. It shall consist of the delegates of the regional assemblies which will elect *one* deputy for every five communes.

13. The *regional assembly* is the representative body of the region. It shall be convened in the regional headquarters regularly at every quarter by the committee of the chief commune to debate the affairs of the region. To this assembly each commune shall send one delegate. The regional assembly shall invariably be convened in the middle of July each year for the election of the League delegates.

> [Article 5 Commune
> Article 6 Region
> Article 7 Central Committee
> Article 8 The Congress
> Article 9 Admission to the League
> Article 10 Expulsion from the League/money . . .]

14. Fourteen days after the close of the regional district assemblies the congress shall meet at the seat of the central committee unless the latter decides upon another venue.

15. The congress shall receive from the central committee, which has a seat in it but no vote, a report on all its activities and on the state of the League; it shall lay down the principles governing the future policies of the League, decide upon amendments to the Statutes and determine the headquarters of the central committee for the coming year.

16. In case of emergencies the central committee can summon an extraordinary meeting of the congress which will consist in that event of the delegates last elected by the regions.

17. Disputes between individual members of a commune are to be settled by that commune; disputes between members of the same region should be settled by the regional assembly; those between members of different regions by the central committee; personal complaints about members of the central committee should be brought before the congress. Disputes among communes belonging to the same region are to be resolved by the regional commune, those between communes and their regional branch

or between regions, by the central committee; but in the first case an appeal may be made to the regional assemblies and, in the second, to the congress. The congress shall also resolve any conflicts between the central committee and the sub-committees of the League.

1. *Note:* These statutes accompanied the Address of the Cologne Central Committee.
2. *Note:* The section in brackets appears to be a marginal addition by Marx.

APPENDIX B

I

PRUSSIAN SPIES IN LONDON

LETTER TO THE *SPECTATOR*
64, Dean Street, Soho Square, June 14 1850.

Sir, — For some time past, we, the undersigned German refugees residing in this country, have had occasion to admire the attention paid to us by the British Government. We were accustomed to meet, from time to time, some obscure servant of the Prussian Ambassador, not being "registered as such according to law"; we were accustomed to the ferocious spouting and to the rabid proposals of such *agents provocateurs*, and we knew how to treat them. What we admire, is, not the attention the Prussian Embassy pay us—we are proud to have merited it; it is the entente cordiale which seems to be established, as far as we are concerned, between Prussian spies and English informers.

Really, Sir, we should have never thought that there existed in this country so many police-spies as we have had the good fortune of making the acquaintance of in the short space of a week. Not only that the doors of the houses where we live are closely watched by individuals of a more than doubtful look, who take down their notes very coolly every time one enters the house or leaves it; we cannot make a single step without being followed by them wherever we go. We cannot get into an omnibus or enter a coffeehouse without being favoured with the company of at least one of these unknown friends. We do not know whether the gentlemen engaged in this grateful occupation are so "on her Majesty's service"; but we know this, that the majority of them look anything but clean and respectable.

Now, of what use can be, to any one, the scanty information thus scratched together at our doors by a lot of miserable spies, male prostitutes of the lowest order, who mostly seem to be drawn from the class of common informers, and paid by the job? Will this, no doubt exceedingly trustworthy information, be of such value as to entitle any one to sacrifice, for its sake, the old-established boast of Englishmen, that in their country there is no chance of introducing that spy system from which not one country of the Continent is free?

Besides, we always have been, and are now, ready to give any information respecting ourselves the Government may desire, as far as this will be in our power.

We know, however, very well what is at the bottom of all this. The Prussian Government have taken occasion of the the late attempt on the life of Frederic William IV, to open another campaign against their political enemies in Prussia and out of Prussia. And because a notorious madman has fired a shot at the King of Prussia, the English Government are to be entrapped into enforcing the Alien Bill against us; although we are at a loss to conceive in what respect our presence in London can possibly come into collision with "the preservation of the peace and tranquillity of these realms".

Some eight years ago, when we, in Prussia, attacked the existing system of government, the official functionaries and press replied, why, if these gentlemen do not like the Prussian system, they are perfectly at liberty to leave the country. We left the country, and we knew the reason why. But after leaving it, we found Prussia everywhere; in France, in Belgium, in Switzerland, we felt the influence of the Prussian Ambassador. If, through his influences, we are to be made to leave this last refuge left to us in Europe, why then Prussia will think herself the ruling power of the world.

England has hitherto been the only obstacle in the way of the Holy Alliance, now reconstructing under the protection of Russia; and the Holy Alliance, of which Prussia forms part and parcel, aim at nothing more than at entrapping Anti-Russian England into a home policy of a more or less Russian cast. What, indeed, would Europe think of the late diplomatic notes and Parliamentary assertions of the British Government, if commented by an enforcement of the Alien Bill called forth by nothing but the revengeful instances of foreign reactionary Governments?

The Prussian Government declare the shot fired at their King to be the result of widespread revolutionary conspiracies, the centre of which is to be sought in London. In accordance with this, they firstly destroy the liberty of the press at home, and secondly demand the English Government to remove from this country the pretended chiefs of the pretended conspiracy.

Considering the personal character and qualities of the present King of Prussia, and those of his brother, the heir to the throne, which party has a greater interest in the speedy succession of the latter—the Revolutionary party or the Ultra-Royalists?

Allow us to state, that a fortnight before the attempt was made at Berlin, persons whom we have every reason to consider as agents either of the Prussian Government or the Ultra-Royalists, presented themselves to us, and almost directly engaged us to enter into conspiracies for organising regicide in Berlin and elsewhere. We need not add, that these persons found no chance of making their dupes of us.

Allow us to state, that, after the attempt, other persons of a similar character have tried to force themselves upon us, and spoken in a similar manner.

Allow us to state, that Sefeloge, the sergeant who shot at the King, was not a Revolutionist, but an Ultra-Royalist. He belonged to section No. 2 of the Ultra-Royalist society, the Treubund. He is registered under number 133 on the list of members. He has been for a time supported with money by this society: his papers were deposited at the house of an Ultra-Royalist Major employed at the War Office.

If ever this affair should come to be tried in open court, which we doubt, the public will see clear enough whether there have been any instigators to the attempt, and who they have been.

The Ultra-Royalist *Neue Preussische Zeitung* was the first to denounce the refugees in London as the real authors of the attempt. It even named one of the undersigned, whom already before it had stated to have been in Berlin during a fortnight, while, as scores of witnesses can prove, he never for a moment left London. We wrote to M. Bunsen, the Prussian Ambassador, requesting him to furnish us with the numbers in question of that paper. The attention paid to us by that gentleman did not go so far as to cause him to comply with what we had expected from the *courtoisie* of the Chevalier.

We believe, Sir, that under these circumstances, we cannot do better than bring the whole case before the public. We believe that Englishmen are interested in anything by which the old-established reputation of England, as the safest asylum for refugees of all parties and of all countries, may be more or less affected.

We are, Sir, your most obedient servants,

CHARLES MARX, ⎫   Editors of the *Neue Rheinische Zeitung*, of
FREDC. ENGELS, ⎭   Cologne.
AUG. WILLICH,   Colonel in the Insurrectionary Army of
              Baden.

This letter appeared in the *Spectator* on June 15, 1850.

II

PRUSSIAN SPIES IN LONDON

A PRESS REPORT

The trial of several persons in Cologne for an alleged conspiracy, has brought to light an abominable spy system employed in London by the Prussian Police during the Great Exhibition. It appears that at the invitation of the British Government, numerous continental policemen were brought to London for the purpose of detecting foreign pickpockets and thieves. Abusing the confidence of that Government the Prussian one instructed its police agents to act as spies over the German refugees in the British metropolis. Accordingly those unscrupulous agents had recourse to all the arts that have rendered them so odious in their own country. Under the falsest pretences some of them wormed themselves into the confidence of those refugees, others set to work at bribery, the utmost treachery was applied, and the result was that some of the documents in the possession of the leading refugees were stolen from their residences; a crime which would have lodged the perpetrators in an English prison if they had not been enabled—thanks to the ample funds with which they were provided—to escape to the Continent. Upon the strength of those documents acquired in defiance of all English law, several persons in Germany were arrested and thrown into unhealthy prisons, where they remained for more than eighteen months without a trial, until dragged the other day before the Cologne Assizes. There are, at this moment, some Prussian police agents in London, and it is to be hoped that if they be detected stealing the property of German refugees, the latter will immediately give the delinquents into custody.

This report appeared in The *Morning Advertiser*, October 26, 1852.

III

THE COLOGNE TRIALS

(To the Editor of the *People's Paper*)

Sir, — The undersigned call your attention to the attitude of the Prussian Press, including even the most reactionary papers, such as the *Neue Preussische Zeitung* during the pending trial of the Communists at Cologne, and to the honourable discretion they observe, at a moment where scarcely a third part of the witnesses have been examined, when none of the produced documents have been verified, and not a word has fallen yet from the defence. While those papers, at the worst, represent the Cologne prisoners and the undersigned, their London friends, in accordance with the public accuser, as "dangerous conspirators who alone are responsible for the whole history of Europe of the latter four years, and for all the revolutionary commotions of 1848 and 1849"—there are in London two public organs, The *Times* and the *Daily News* which really have not hesitated to represent the Cologne prisoners and the undersigned as a "gang of sturdy beggars", swindlers, etc. The undersigned address to the English public the same demand which the defensors of the accused have addressed to the public in Germany—to suspend their judgment, and to wait for the end of the trials. Were they to give further explanations at the present time, the Prussian government might obtain the means of baffling a revelation of police-tricks, perjury, forgery of documents, falsification of documents, thefts, etc., unprecedented even in the records of Prussian political justice. When that revelation shall have been made in the course of the present proceedings, public opinion in England will know how to qualify the anonymous scribes of The *Times* and *Daily News*, who constitute themselves the advocates and mouthpieces of the most infamous and subaltern of government spies.

We are, Sir, yours fraternally,

F. ENGELS
F. FREILIGRATH
K. MARX.

London, October 28th.

This letter appeared in the *People's Paper* on October 30, 1852.

IV

REPORT ON THE COMMUNIST TRIAL IN *THE TIMES*

PRUSSIA

(From our own Correspondent)

Berlin, October 9

The trial of the members of the Secret Democratic Societies, commenced on the 4th, at Cologne, proceeds day by day; on the 5th the indictment was read; on the 6th the public prosecutor delivered his address; on the 7th the examination of the prisoners was commenced; various parts of the indictment were proved, as far as it charged the prisoners with belonging to a body of which the Statutes and rules were in the hands of the Court. But the statutes themselves are drawn up in such vague phrases that what the Bund intended to effect cannot be clearly understood, except promoting a general confusion, and keeping it up, in the hope something might grow out of it. The London section of "world improvers", as the Germans call them, were very advanced indeed, rejecting the aid of the *Bourgeoisie*, however democratic, as that class has been found after a certain point to object to plunder and arson, and even to insist on putting a stop to them. This treachery the Bund is warned against; "next time" there must be no rescuing public buildings or the houses of public enemies from the flames, or any so-called restoration of order, the rock on which all revolutions have miscarried. This insane section of philanthropists, according to one of the witnesses, has its seat among the London exiles; the Cologne branch of the Bund is described as opposed to all violence, and working only by conviction and teaching. Perhaps the difference is in the fact that the Cologne committee has fallen into the power of the law, and has had time to meditate on its doctrines. Altogether there is a weakness of brain and a general infirmity of plan and design in all the manifests that looks unreal, as if the papers were concocted for a trading purpose; if sentimental begging-letter writers found it would pay to appear political conspirators we should have such documents going about by the hundred. There is a similar fluency of phrase and absence of real feeling, but calculated to stimulate contributions from political dupes in Germany and France, where unfortunately phrases have much power; that is nearly the whole of their object. All the documents lack reality; the only parts where the writers become earnest and clear are the appeals for money; the rest is a sickly verbiage. If the whole gang were treated as "sturdy beggars" instead of conspirators, they would be dealt with more according to their true characters.

This report, typical of those of which Marx and Engels had occasion to complain, appeared in *The Times* on October 12, 1852.

V

THE TRIAL OF COLOGNE

(To the Editor of the *Morning Advertiser*)

Sir, — I beg to offer you my best thanks for the generous protection you have afforded to the cause of my friends, the prisoners at Cologne. While the defence will bring to light the series of unscrupulous acts committed by the agents of the Prussian police, even during the progress of this trial, I wish to inform you of the last trick that has been had recourse to, in order to prove a criminal correspondence between myself and the Cologne prisoners. According to the report of the *Kölnische Zeitung* of October 29th, Mr. Stieber, the councillor of police, has produced another of his documents—a ridiculous letter, purporting to be in my handwriting, in which I am made to recommend one of my pretended agents "to push under the doors of acknowledged democrats, at Crefeld, 30 copies of the *Red Catechism*, and to choose for the execution of commission the midnight-hour of June 5, 1852".

For the sake of my accused friends, I herby declare —

1. That the letter in question is not written by myself.

2. That I learned its existence only from the *Kölnische Zeitung* of 29th inst.

3. That I never saw the so-called *Red Catechism*.

4. That I never caused any copies of the "Red" to be circulated, in whatever manner.

This declaration, made also before the magistrate in Marlborough Street, and consequently as valid as an oath, I have sent by post to Cologne. By your inserting it in the columns of your paper, you will the more oblige me, as that would be the most effective means of preventing the Prussian police from intercepting the document.

I am, Sir, your obedient servant,

Dr. CHARLES MARX.

London, October 30, 1852 — 28, Dean Street, Soho.

This letter appeared in the *Morning Advertiser* on November 2, 1852.

VI

A FINAL DECLARATION ON THE LATE COLOGNE TRIALS

To the Editor of the *Morning Advertiser*.

Sir, — The undersigned discharge a duty to themselves and towards their now condemned friends at Cologne, by laying before the English public a statement of facts connected with the recent monster trial in that city, which have not been made sufficiently known by the London press.

Eighteen months have been wasted on the mere getting up of the evidence for this trial. During the whole of that time our friends have been kept in solitary confinement, deprived of all means of occupation and even of books; those who became ill were refused proper medical treatment, or if they obtained it, the condition in which they were placed prevented them from benefiting thereby. Even after the "act of accusation" had been communicated to them, they were prohibited, in direct violation of the law, from conferring with their lawyers. And what were the pretexts for this protracted cruel imprisonment? After the lapse of the first nine months the "Chamber of Accusation" declared that there were no grounds on which a charge could be maintained, and that, therefore, the instruction had to be recommenced. It was recommenced. Three months later, at the opening of the assizes, the public accuser pleaded that the mass of the evidence had grown into a larger bulk than he had as yet been able to digest. And after three further months the trial was again adjourned, on the ground of the illness of one of the chief government witnesses.

The real cause of all this delay was the fear of the Prussian Government to confront the meagre substance of the facts with the pompously announced "unheard-of-revelations". At last, the Government succeeded in selecting a jury, such as the Rhenish provinces had never yet beheld, composed of six reactionary nobles, four members of the *haute finance*, and two members of the bureaucracy.

Now, what was the evidence laid before this jury? Merely the absurd proclamations and correspondence of a set of ignorant phantasts, importance-seeking conspirators, the tools and associates at once of one Cherval, an avowed agent of the police. The greater part of those papers were formerly in the possession of a certain Oswald Diez in London. During the Great Exhibition the Prussian police, while Diez was absent from his home, had his drawers broken open, and thus obtained the desired documents by a common theft. These papers, in the first instance, furnished the means of discovering the so-called Franco-German plot at Paris. Now, the proceedings at Cologne proved, that those conspirators, and Cherval, their Paris agent, were the very political opponents of the defendants and their undersigned London friends. But the public accuser pleaded, that a mere personal quarrel had prevented the latter from taking part in the plot of Cherval and his associates. By such an argumentation it was intended to prove the moral complicity of the Cologne defendants in the Paris plot; and while the accused of Cologne were thus made responsible for the acts of their very enemies, the professed friends of Cherval and his associates were produced by the Government in court, not at the bar like the defendants—nay, in the witness-box, to depose against them. This, however, appeared too bad. Public opinion forced the Government to look out for less equivocal evidence. The whole of the police machinery was set to work under the direction of one Stieber, the principal Government witness at Cologne, royal councillor of police, and chief of the Berlin criminal police. In the sitting of October 23rd, Stieber announced, that an extraordinary courier from London had delivered to him most important documents, proving, undeniably, the complicity of the accused in an alleged conspiracy with the undersigned. "Amongst other documents, the courier had brought him the original minute-book of the sittings of the secret society, presided over by Dr. Marx, and with whom the defendants had been in correspondence." Stieber, however, entangled himself in discordant statements as to the date on which his courier was to have reached him. Dr. Schneider, the leading counsel for the defence, charged him directly with perjury, upon which Stieber ventured no other reply than to fall back upon his dignity of the representative of the Crown, entrusted with a most important mission from the very highest authority of the state. As to the minute-book, Stieber declared twice on oath, that it was the "genuine minute-book of the London Communist Society", but later on, closely pressed by the defence, he admitted that it might be a mere book of notes, taken by one of his spies. At length, from his own evidence, the book was proved to be a deliberate forgery, and its origin traced back to three of Stieber's London agents, Greiff, Fleury and Hirsch. The latter has since admitted that he composed the book under the guidance of Fleury and Greiff. So decisive was the evidence at Cologne on this point, that even the public accuser declared Stieber's important document a "most unfortunate book" a mere forgery. The same personage refused to take notice of a letter forming part of the Government evidence, in which the handwriting of Dr. Marx had been imitated; that document, too, having turned out a gross and palpable forgery. In the same manner every other document brought forward in order to prove, not the revolutionary tendencies, but the actual participation of the accused in some distant plot, turned out a forgery of the police. So great were the Government's fears of an exposure, that it not only caused the post to retain all documents addressed to the counsel for the defence, but the latter to be intimidated by Stieber, with a threatened prosecution for his "criminal correspondence" with the undersigned.

If now, in spite of the absence of all convincing proof, a verdict has, nevertheless, been obtained, that result has only become possible, at the hands even of such a jury, by the retroactive application of the new criminal code, under which *The Times* and the Peace Society themselves might at any time be tried on the formidable charge of high treason. Moreover, the trial at Cologne had assumed, by its duration, and by the extraordinary means employed on the part of the prosecution, such vast dimensions, that an acquittal would have equalled a condemnation of the Government; and a conviction prevailed generally in the Rhenish provinces, that the immediate consequence of an acquittal would be the suppression of the entire institution of the jury.

We are, Sir, your most obedient servants,

F. ENGELS.
F. FREILIGRATH.
K. MARX.
W. WOLFF.

London, November 20, 1852.

This letter appeared in the *Morning Advertiser* on November 20, 1852.

VII

THE BERLIN CONSPIRACY

CORRESPONDENCE OF THE *NEW YORK TRIBUNE*

London, Friday, April 1, 1853

At length, the fifth of the "Great Powers", Prussia, enjoys the good fortune of having added of her own to the great discoveries made by the Austrian Police, with respect to the "demagogical machinations" of the revolutionists. "The Government," we are assured by its official organs, "having obtained proof that the chiefs of the Democratic party held continued relations with the revolutionary *propaganda*, ordered domiciliary visits to be made, on the 29th of March, at Berlin, and succeeded in arresting 40 individuals, among whom were Streckfuss, and the ex-members of the Prussian N. Assembly, Behrens, Waldeck, etc. Domiciliary visits were made in the houses of eighty persons, suspected of participation in a conspiracy. Arms and ammunition were found." Not content with publishing these "startling facts" in its official papers, the Prussian Government thought proper to forward them by telegraph to the British Foreign Office.

In order to lay bare the mystery of this new police farce, it is necessary to go somewhat back. Two months after the *coup d'état* of Bonaparte, Mr. Hinckeldey the *Polizei Praesident* of Berlin and his inferior, Mr. Stieber, the *Polizei-Rath*, conspired together, the one to become a Prussian *Maupas*. and the other to become a Prussian *Piétre*. The glorious omnipotence of the French police, perhaps, disturbed their slumbers. Hinckeldey addressed himself to Herr von Westphalen, the Minister of the Interior, making unjust representation to that weak-minded and fanatical reactionist (Herr von Westphalen being my brother-in-law I had ample opportunity of becoming acquainted with the mental powers of the man), on the necessity of concentrating the whole police force of the Prussian State in the hands of the *Polizei Praesident* of Berlin. He stated, that in order to accelerate the action of the police, it must be made independent of the Minister of the Interior and entrusted exclusively to himself. The minister von Westphalen, represents the ultra Prussian aristocracy and the President of the ministry, Herr von Manteuffel, represents the old bureaucracy; the two are rivals, and the former beheld in the suggestion of Hinckeldey, although it apparently narrowed the circle of his own department, a means of inflicting a blow on his rival, whose brother, M. von Manteuffel, was the director in the ministry of the Interior, and especially charged with the control of the entire police. Herr von Westphalen therefore submitted his proposition to a council of State, presided over by the King himself.

The discussion was very angry. Manteuffel, supported by the Prince of Prussia, opposed the plan of establishing an independent ministry of police. The King inclined to the proposition of Herr von Westphalen, and concluded with the Solomonian sentence, that he would follow the example of Bonaparte and create a ministry of police, "if the necessity of that step were proved to him by facts". Now, the affair of the Cologne Communists was chosen by Hinckeldey and Stieber to furnish these facts. You are aware of the heroic performances of those men in the Cologne trials. After their conclusion the Prussian Government resolved to elevate the openly perjured Stieber, the man who had been hissed wherever he showed himself in the streets of Cologne to the dignity of a *Polizei Director* of Cologne. But M. de Behtmann-Hollweg and other well-meaning conservative deputies of Rhenish Prussia, intervened, representing to the ministers that such an open insult to the public opinion of that province might have very ominous consequences at a moment when Bonaparte coveted the *natural limits* of France. The Government yielded, contenting itself with the nomination of Stieber as *Polizei-Director* of Berlin, in reward for his perjuries committed at Cologne and his thefts committed at London. There, however, the affair stopped. It was impossible to accomplish the wishes of Mr. Hinckeldey and to create for him an independent ministry of police on the ground of the Cologne trial. Hinckeldey and Stieber watched their time. Happily there came the Milan insurrection. Stieber at once made twenty arrests at Berlin. But the thing was too ridiculous to be proceeded with. But then came Libeny, and now the King was ripe. Overwhelemed with fearful apprehensions he saw at once the necessity of having an independent ministry of police, and Hinckeldey saw his dreams realised. A royal ordinance created him the Prussian Maupas, while the brother of Herr von Manteuffel tendered his resignation. The most astounding part of the comedy, however, was yet to come. Scarcely had Mr. Hinckeldey rushed into his new dignity when the "great Berlin conspiracy" was discovered directly. This conspiracy, then, was made for the express purpose of proving the necessity of Mr. Hinckeldey. It was the present Mr. Hinckeldey made over to the imbecile King in exchange for his newly-gained police-autocracy. Hinckeldey's adjunct, the ingenious Stieber, who had discovered at Cologne that whenever letters were found terminating with the words "Gruss" and "Bruderschaft", there was unquestionably a Communist conspiracy, now made the discovery that there appeared at Berlin for some time since an ominous quantity of "Calabrese hats", and that the Calabrese hat was unquestionably the "rallying sign" of the revolutionists. Strong upon this important discovery, Stieber made on the 18th of March several arrests, chiefly of workmen and foreigners, the charge against whom was the wearing of Calabrese hats. On the 23d *ejusdem* domiciliary visits were made in the house of Karl Delius, a merchant at Magdeburg and brother of a member of the Second Chamber, who had also an unhappy taste for Calabrese hats. Finally, as I informed you at the beginning of this letter, on the 29th ultimo the great *coup d'état* against the Calabrese hats was struck at Berlin. All those who know anything of the milk-and-water opposition of Waldeck, Behreus, &c., will laugh at the "arms of munition" found in the possession of these most inoffensive Brutusses.

But futile as this police comedy may appear to be got up, as it were, by mere personal motives of Messrs. Hinckeldey and Stieber, it is not without significance. The Prussian government is exasperated at the passive resistance it meets with in every direction. It smells the breath of Revolution in midst of the apparent apathy. It despairs at the want of a tangible form of that spectre, and feels alleviated, as it were, from the nightmare every time the police affords bodily shapes to its ubiquitous but invisible antagonist. It attacks, it will go on attacking, and it will successfully convert the passive resistance of the people into an active one.

KARL MARX

This article appeared in the *New York Tribune* on April 18, 1853.

VIII

THE BERLIN CONSPIRACY

CORRESPONDENCE OF *THE NEW YORK TRIBUNE*

London, Friday, April 8, 1853

At the time of writing my last letter concerning the great conspiracy discovered by Mr. Stieber, I could not anticipate, that my views on that affair would be more or less confirmed by two Conservative Berlin papers. The

Preussiche Wochenblatt the organ of the Conservative faction headed by Mr. von Bethmann-Hollweg, was confiscated on April 2 for recommending its readers "not to believe too hastily in the tales of the police respecting 'the late arrests'". But of far greater importance is an article in the *Zeit*, the semi-official journal belonging to the section of the Prussian Ministry headed by M. von Manteuffel. The *Zeit* is compelled to make the following admission:

"Whosoever is not struck with blindness, cannot but be aware that the numerous and inextricable complications presented by the general situation of Europe must lead in a given time, to a violent explosion, which the sincere endeavours of the Great Powers of Europe may postpone for a while, but to prevent which in a permanent way they are utterly unable, notwithstanding all human exertions. It is for us the accomplishment of a duty not to dissimulate any longer, that discontent is spreading wider and wider and *is the more dangerous and the more deserving of serious attention, as it appears not at the surface but conceals itself more and more in the depth of men's minds*. This discontent, we must say without paraphrase, is created by the efforts to bring about a counter-revolution in Prussia latterly paraded with an incredible *étourderie*."

The *Zeit* is only mistaken in its conclusion. The Prussian counter-revolution is not now about to be commenced, it is to be ended. It is not a thing of recent growth, but began on March 20, 1848, and has been steadily advancing ever since that day. At this very moment the Prussian Government is hatching two very dangerous projects, the one of limiting the free sub-division of real property, the other subjecting public instruction to the Church. They could not have selected two objects more appropriate to alienate the peasantry of Rhenish Prussia and the middle classes throughout the monarchy. As a curious incident, I may also mention the forced dissolution of the Berlin Hygienic Society (a Mutual Benefit Sick Club), in consequence of the "great discovery". This society was composed of nearly 10,000 members, all belonging to the working classes. The Government, it appears, are convinced, that the present constitution of the Prussian State is incompatible with "hygienics".

The London press, till now unconscious of the doings of the London police, are surprised by statements in the Vienna *Presse* and the *Emancipation*, the leading reactionary journal of Belgium, that the police of London have drawn up a list of all the political refugees in that city, with a variety of details relating to their private circumstances and conduct. "Once such a system is 'tolerated with regard to foreigners'", exclaims the *Morning Advertiser*, "it will be employed whenever deemed advisable by the Government, or any member of it, in order to become acquainted with the details of the private lives of our own countrymen. Is it not saddening to think that the London police should be called upon to play the infamous part assigned to their continental colleagues?" Besides these statements in Belgian and other papers, the London press is this day informed by telegraphic dispatch from Vienna, "that the Refugee question is settled: the British Government has promised to keep a strict guard on the refugees, and to visit them with the full severity of the law whenever it should be proved that they have taken part in revolutionary intrigues.

"Never before," remarks the *Morning Advertiser*, "did England appear in so humiliating a situation as she does now, in having prostrated herself to the feet of Austria. No degradation could equal this. It was reserved for the Coalition Cabinet."

This report appeared in the *New York Daily Tribune* on April 24, 1853.

IX

HIRSCH'S CONFESSIONS

Hirsch's *Confessions* only have value, it appears to me, in so far as they receive confirmation from other sources. If only because they are self-contradictory. On his return from his mission to Cologne he declared openly in a workers' meeting that Willich was his accomplice. Of course, this was too contemptible for anyone to think it worth recording in the minutes. After this a number of people approached me, with or without instructions from Hirsch, saying that Hirsch was willing to make a full confession. I refused. I heard later on that he was living in the utmost penury. I have not the slightest doubt, therefore, that his "very latest" confessions have been written in the interest of the party that happens to be *paying* him at the moment. Strangely enough, there are people who find it necessary to shelter behind this Hirsch.

I shall confine myself to a number of marginal comments for the time being. A number of spies have now presented us with their confessions: Vidocq, Chenu, de la Hodde, etc. They all agree on one point: they are not just ordinary spies; they are spies in a higher sense, in fact they are neither more nor less than reincarnations of Cooper's "Spy". Their Confessions are inevitably a collection of Apologias.

Thus Hirsch hints strongly that it was not he, but Colonel Bangya who informed Greif, and through Greif, Fleury, of the day on which my Party comrades held their meetings. These took place on a Thursday on the few occasions when Hirsch was present, but we met on Wednesday after his expulsion. The false minutes dating from before and after Hirsch's expulsion all give Thursday as the day on which the meetings took place. Who but for Hirsch could have brought about this "misunderstanding"?

On another matter Hirsch is more fortunate. He claims that Bangya has repeatedly disclosed dates referring to my correspondence with Germany. As all the data contained in the Cologne trial-documents in connection with this matter are false it is not possible to decide who invented them. Now to Bangya.

Spy or no spy, Bangya could never become a threat to me and my Party comrades as I *never* discussed *my* Party affairs with him, and Bangya himself—

as he reminds me in one of his apologias—took good care not to broach any of these matters. Hence, spy or no spy, he could reveal nothing because he knew nothing. The Cologne trial-documents have confirmed this. They have confirmed that apart from the confessions obtained in Germany itself and the documents seized there, the Prussian police knew nothing of the Party to which I belong and they were therefore compelled to invent the most infantile fairytales.

But did not Bangya sell to the a police pamphlet by Marx "about the *émigrés*"?

Bangya learned from me that Ernst Dronke, Friedrich Engels and I intended a serial publication in several instalments about the German *émigrés* in London. He assured me that he could find a bookseller in Berlin for it. I asked him to see about it without delay. A week or so later he told me that a Berlin bookseller called Eisermann was prepared to publish the *first* instalment on condition that it appeared without the names of the authors, as otherwise he would be exposed to the risk of confiscation. I agreed but stipulated for my part that I should be paid my fee on receipt of the MS. as I had no desire to repeat my experiences with the *Revue of the Neue Rheinische Zeitung*. I insisted also that the MS. should be printed on receipt. I then went up to see Engels in Manchester where the MS. was being prepared. In the interval Bangya brought my wife a letter from Berlin in which Eisermann agreed to my conditions with the proviso that the publication of the second instalment would depend upon sales of the first. On my return Bangya received the MS. and I my fee.

But the printing was delayed on a series of plausible pretexts. I became suspicious. Not of the fact that the MS. might have been given to the police to print. I am fully prepared to this day to hand my MSS. over to the Emperor of Russia, if he for his part is prepared to print them. But the very opposite: what I feared was the suppression of the MS.

In it I had attacked the charlatans of the moment, of course, not as revolutionaries dangerous to the state, but as straws in the wind of counter-revolution.

My suspicions were confirmed. Georg Weerth whom I had asked to check up on Eisermann in Berlin wrote to say that no Eisermann could be discovered. Together with Dronke I went to see Bangya. Eisermann it now appeared was only the manager in the firm of Jacob Collmann. As I was anxious to obtain Bangya's statements in writing, I insisted that he should repeat them in my presence in a letter to Engels in Manchester, giving Collmann's address. I also wrote a few lines to Bruno Bauer asking him to discover who lived in the house that Bangya alleged to belong to Collman, but received no answer. The pretended bookseller replied to my reminders that the *contract* said nothing about printing dates. He was the best judge of the most suitable moment for publication. In a later letter he waxed indignant. Finally, Bangya told me that the bookseller refused to print the MS. and would return it. He himself disappeared to Paris.

The Berlin letters and Bangya's letters which report the whole transaction together with a number of self-justificatory writings of Bangya are in my possession.

But why was I not misled by the suspicions of Bangya put about by the *émigrés?* Precisely because I knew the origins of these suspicions. But this is a story which I propose to leave in the obscurity it merits.

I could afford to neglect them because I *knew* that, as an officer of the revolution in the Hungarian war, Bangya had performed similar actions. Because he was in correspondence with Szemere whom I respect and on friendly terms with General Perczel. Because I have seen with my own eyes a diploma in which Kossuth appointed him to the post of Police Chief in partibus, a document that had been countersigned by Count Szirmay, Kossuth's confidant, who lived in the same house as Bangya. If I am not mistaken Bangya is still Kossuth's agent in Paris at this very time.

The Hungarian leaders must have known with whom they had to deal. What was I risking compared to them? Nothing worse than the suppression of a copy to which I had retained the original.

Later on I approached Lizius, a bookseller in Frankfurt, as well as other booksellers in Germany with the request to publish the MS. They declared that it was not possible at the present time. More recently there seems to be some prospect of seeing it printed outside Germany.

To conclude these remarks which, of course, are not directed at Mr. Hirsch but are meant for my fellow countrymen in America, it remains only to put the "open question": how can the suppression of a pamphlet against Kinkel, Willich and the other "Heroes of the Exile" have served the interests of the Prussian police?

> Löse mir, Oerindur,
> Diesen Zwiespalt der Natur!
> (Solve for me, o Oerindur,
> This riddle of Nature!)

London, April 9, 1853.   KARL MARX

X

GOTTFRIED KINKEL
A LIFE IN THREE PICTURES
by
CHARLES DICKENS

PICTURE THE FIRST

The winter of 1844 was a severe one in Germany. Both sides of the Rhine, for many miles between Coblenz and Cologne, were frozen hard enough to bear a horse and cart; and even the centre, save and except a thin stream where the current persisted in displaying its urgent vitality, was covered over with thin ice, or a broken film that was constantly endeavouring to unite and consolidate its quivering flakes and particles. We were staying in Bonn at this time. All the Englishmen in the town, who were skaters issued forth in pilot-coats or dread-nought pea jackets, and red worsted comforters, with their skates dangling over their shoulders. Holding their aching noses in their left hands, they ran and hobbled through the slippery streets, and made their way out at the town gates near the University. They were on the way to Popplesdorf—a little village about a mile distant from Bonn. We were among them;—red comforter round neck—skates over shoulder.

The one great object in this little village is a somewhat capacious and not unpicturesque edifice called the Schloss, or Castle, of Popplesdorf. The outer works of its fortifications are a long avenue of trees, some pretty fir groves and wooded hills, numerous vineyards, and a trim series of botanic gardens. The embrasures on its walls are armed with batteries of learned tomes; its soldiers are erudite professors and doctors who have chambers there; students discourse on philosophy and art, and swords and beer, and smoke forever on its peaceful drawbridge; and, on the wide moat which surrounds it, Englishmen in red comforters—at the time whereof we know speak—are vigorously skating with their accustomed gravity. This scene was repeated daily for several weeks, in the winter of 1844.

One morning, issuing forth on the same serious business of life, we perceived that the peasantry of Popplesdorf, who have occasion to come to Bonn every market-day, had contrived to enliven the way and facilitate the journey by the gradual construction of a series of capital long slides. We stood and contem-plated these lengthy curves, and sweeps, and strange twisting stripes of silver, all gleaming in the morning sun, and soon arrived at the conviction that it was no doubt the pleasantest market-pathway we had ever seen. No one was com-ing or going at this moment; for Popples is but a little *dorf*, and the traffic is far from numerous, even at the busiest hours. Now, there was a peculiar charm in the clear shining solitude of the scene, which gave us, at once, an impression of loneliness combined with the brightest paths of life and activity.

And yet we gradually began to feel we should like to see somebody—student or peasant—come sliding his way from Popplesdorf. It was evidently the best, and indeed the correct mode for our own course to the frozen moat of the castle. But before we had reached the beginning of the first slide (for they are not allowed to be made quite up to the town gates), we descried a figure in the distance, which, from the course it was taking, had manifestly issued from the walls of the castle. It was not a peasant—it was not one of our countrymen; be it whom it might, he at least took the slides in first-rate style. As he advanced, we discerned the figure of a tall man, dressed in a dark, long-skirted frock coat, buttoned up to the throat, with a low-crowned hat, from beneath the broad brim of which a great mass of thick black hair fall heavily over his shoulders. Under one arm he held a great book and two smaller ones closely pressed to his side, while the other hand held a roll of paper, which he waved now and then in the air, to balance himself in his sliding. Some of the slides required a good deal of skill; they had awkward twirls half round a stone, with here and there a sudden downward sweep. Onward he came, and we presently recognised him. It was Dr. Gottfried Kinkel, lecturer on Archaelogy; one of the most able and estimable of the learned men in Bonn.

Gottfried Kinkel was born in a village near Bonn, where his father was a clergyman. He was educated at the Gymnasium of Bonn, and during the whole of that period, he was especially remarkable, among companions by no means famous for staid and orderly habits, as a very quiet, industrious, young man, of a sincerely religious bent of mind, which gained for him the notice and regard of all the clergy and the most devout among the inhabitants of the town. His political opinions were liberal; but never went beyond those which were commonly entertained at the time by nearly all men of education. He studied divinity at the University, where he greatly distinguished himself in various branches of learning, and obtained the degree of Doctor in Philosophy.

He first preached at Cologne, and with great success, his oratory being considered as brilliant as his reasonings were convincing. His sermons were subsequently published, and became very popular, and he was chosen as a teacher of Theology in the University of Bonn.

He next turned his attention to the study of the Arts. On this subject he wrote and published a History, and lectured on "Ancient and Mediaeval Art", both in the University and other public institutions, with unparalleled success and applause.

His labours at this period, and for a long time after, were very arduous, generally occupying thirteen hours a day. Being only what is called a "privat-docent", he did not as yet receive any salary at the University; he was therefore compelled to work hard in various ways, in order to make a small income. However, he did this very cheerfully.

But his abandonment of Theology for these new studies, caused him the loss of most of his devout friends. They shook their heads, and feared that the change denoted a step awry from the true and severely marked line of orthodox opinions. They were right; for he soon after said that he thought the purity of religion would be best attained by a separation of Church and State!

Dr. Kinkel suffers no small odium for this; but he can endure it. He has uttered an honest sentiment, resulting from his past studies; he has become a highly applauded and deservedly esteemed lecturer on another subject; he is, moreover, one of the best sliders in Bonn, and is now balancing his tall figure (as just described) with books under one arm, on his way to the University.

Happy Gottfried Kinkel!—may you have health and strength to slide for many a good winter to come!—rare Doctor of Philosophy, to feel so much boyish vitality after twenty years of hard study and seclusion!—fortunate lecturer on Archaeology, to live in a country where the simplicity of manners will allow a Professor to slide his way to his class, without danger of being reproved by his grave and potent seniors, or of shocking the respectable inhabitants of his town !

PICTURE THE SECOND

The Castle of Popplesdorf commands the most beautiful views of some of the most beautiful parts of Rhenish Prussia; and the very best point from which to look at them, is the window of the room that used to be the study of Dr. Gottfried Kinkel. That used to be—and is not now—alas, the day! But we must not anticipate evils; they will come only too soon in their natural course.

In this room, his library and study, we called to see Dr. Kinkel. There he sat—dressing-gown, slippers, and cloud-compelling pipe. The walls were all shelves, the shelves all books,—some bound, some in boards, "some in rags, and some in jags",—together with papers, maps, and scientific instruments of brass and of steel. There stood the Hebrew, Greek, and Roman authors; in another division, the Italian and French: on the other side, in long irregular ranges, the old German and the modern German; and near at hand, the Anglo-Saxon and English. What else, and there was much, we had not time to note, being called to look out at the window. What a window it was!—a simple wooden frame to what exquisite and various scenery! Let the reader bear in mind, that it is not winter now—but a bright morning in May.

Close beneath the window lay the Botanic Gardens, with their numerous parterres of flowers, their lines and divisions of shrubs and herbs. Within a range of a few miles round, we looked out upon the peaceful little villages of Popplesdorf and Kessenich, and the fertile plain extending from Bonn to Godesberg—with gentle hills, vales, and ridges, all covered with vineyards, whose young leaves gave a tender greenness and fresh look of bright and joyous childhood to the scenery. Beyond them we saw the Kessenicher Höhe, the blue slate roofs and steeples of many a little church and chapel, and the broad, clear, serpent windings of the Rhine, with the grey and purple range, in the distance, of the Seven Mountains, terminating with the Drachenfels. Over the whole of this, with the exception only of such soft, delicate, shades and shadows as were needful to display the rest, there lay a clear expanse of level sunshine, so tender, bright, and moveless, as to convey an impression of bright enchantment, which grew upon your gaze, and out of which rapture you awoke as from a dream of fairy land, or from the contemplation of a scene in some ideal sphere.

Fortunate Dr. Kinkel, to have such a window as this! It was no wonder that, besides his studies in Theology, in ancient and mediaeval art, and in ancient and modern languages—besides writing his History of the Arts, and contributing learned papers to various periodicals—besides preaching, lecturing, and public and private teaching, his soul was obliged to compose a volume of poems

—and again displease the severely orthodox, by the absence of all prayers in verse, and the presence of a devout love of nature.

> For, here, in their placidity,
>   Learning and Poesy abide;
> Not slumbering on the unfathomed sea,
>   Yet all unconscious of the tide
> That urges on mortality
>   In eddies, and in circles wide.

> Ah, here, the soul can look abroad
>   Beyond each cold and narrow stream,
> Enrich'd with gold from mines and ford,
>   Brought sparkling to the solar beam;
> Yet be no miser with its hoard,—
>   No dreamer of the common dream.

Thus sang Dr. Kinkel, in our imperfect translation thus inadequately echoed; and here he wrought hard in his vocation, amidst the smiles of some of the loveliest of Nature's scenes.

But besides the possession of all these books, and of this wonderful window, Dr. Kinkel was yet more fortunate in his domestic relations. He was married to an amiable, highly educated, and accomplished lady, who endeavoured, and by all the means in her power, to assist his labours, and render them less onerous by her own exertions. She was a very fine musician, and a superior pianoforte player—one of the favourite pupils of Moscheles, and afterwards, we believe, of Mendelssohn. She divided her time equally between assisting her husband, educating their child, and giving private lessons in music; and because this accomplished hard-working couple did not find their energies quite worn out by toiling for thirteen hours a day, they gave a private concert at the Castle once a month, at which a whole opera of Mozart or Weber was often gone through—both the instrumental and vocal parts being by amateurs, or pupils of Madam Kinkel.

So, once again, we say, notwithstanding all these labours, Dr. Kinkel's life in the Castle of Popplesdorf, was that of a fortunate and happy man. At this period he was about two and thirty years of age. He could not have been more; probably he was less.

PICTURE THE THIRD

It is the year 1848, and the Continental Revolutions are shaking all the foreign thrones. Everybody, not directly or indirectly in the pay of a Court, feels that the lot of the people should be ameliorated. The populations of all nations have borne enormous burdens, with extraordinary patience, for a very long time—say a thousand years—and at last they have no more patience left.

But what is all this to abstract thought, to learning and science, to poetic raptures and picturesque ease? It has hitherto been regarded as too grossly material, or of too coarse and common a practicality for the great majority of those whose lives were passed in abstract studies and refinements. Ay—but this must not continue. The world has come to a pass at which *every* soul must awake, and should be "up and doing".

Dr. Gottfried Kinkel, now, besides his other honours and emoluments, and private earnings, is installed as a salaried Professor in the University of Bonn. It cannot be but such a man must awake, and take an interest in these Continental revolutions which are boiling up all round him. Still, it is not likely he will step into the vortex, or approach it. His wordly position is strong against it —all his interests are against it; moreover, he has a wife, and besides he has now three children.

Howbeit, Dr. Kinkel does rise with these events, and his wife, so far from restraining him, feels the same enthusiastic patriotism, and exhorts him to step forward, and swell the torrent of the time. He feels strongly that Prussia should have a constitution; that her intellect and sober character deserves a constitutional monarchy, like ours in England, with such improvements as ours manifestly needs, and he places himself at the head of the popular party in Bonn, where he delivers public orations, the truthful eloquence and boldness of which startle, delight, and encourage his audiences.

He is soon afterwards elected a member of the Berlin parliament. He sides with the Left, or democratic party; he advocates the cause of the oppressed people and the poor; he argues manfully and perseveringly the real interests of all governments, in granting a rational amount of liberty, showing that in the present stage of the moral world, it is the only thing to prevent violence, and to secure good order. His speeches breathe a prophetic spirit.

The revolution gathers fuel, more rapidly than can be well disposed, and it takes fire at Baden. The flames reach near and far—many are irresistibly attracted. They have seen, and too well remember, the faithlessness and treachery of governments—they believe the moment has come to strike a blow which shall gain and establish the constitutional liberty they seek. Dr. Kinkel immediately leaves his Professorship; he believes he ought now to join those who wield the sword, and peril their lives in support of their principles. He proposes to hasten to Baden, to defend the Constitution framed by the Frankfort parliament. His patriotic wife consents, and in the evening he takes leave of her, and of his sleeping children.

It must not be concealed that with this strong feeling in favour of a constitutional monarchy, there was an infusion of principles of a more sweeping character; nor would it be going too far to say that amidst the insurgents of Baden were some who entertained opinions not far removed from red republicanism. Be this as it may, we are persuaded that Dr. Kinkel's political principles and aims were purely of a constitutional character, however he may have been drawn into the fierce vortex of men and circumstances which surrounded him.

Dr. Kinkel serves for eleven days in a free corps in Baden, where the army of the insurgents have assembled. At the commencement of the battle, he is wounded, and taken prisoner with arms in his hands. The sequel of these struggles is well enough known; but the fate of the prisoners who survived their wounds, must be noticed.

According to the Prussian law, Dr. Kinkel should have been sentenced to six years' confinement as a state prisoner. This sentence is accordingly passed upon the other prisoners; and with a wise and commendable clemency many are set free after a short time. But as Dr. Kinkel is a man of high education and celebrity, it is thought best to give him a very severe punishment, according to the old ignorance of what is called "making an example",—as if this sort of example did not provoke and stimulate, rather than deter others; and, as if clemency were not only one of the noblest attributes of royalty, but one of its best safeguards in its effect on the feelings of a people.

Dr. Kinkel is, accordingly, sentenced to be imprisoned for life in a fortress, as a state criminal; and away he is carried.

But now comes into play the anger and resentment of many of those who had once so admired Kinkel, and held him up as a religious champion, until the woeful day when he left preaching for the study of the arts; and the yet more woeful, not to call it diabolical hour, when he announced his opinion that a separation of Church and State might be the best course for both. After a series of intrigues, the enemies of Kinkel induce the King to alter the sentence; but in order to avoid the appearance of unusual severity, it is announced that his sentence of imprisonment in the fortress shall be *alleviated*, by transferring him to an ordinary prison. In pursuance, therefore, of these suggestions of his enemies, he is ordered to be imprisoned for life in one of the prisons appropriated to the vilest malefactors—viz., to the prison of Naugard, on the Baltic.

Dr. Kinkel is dressed in sackcloth, and his head is shaved. His wedding-ring is taken from him, and every little memento of his wife and children which might afford him consolation. His bed is a sack of straw laid upon a board. He has to scour and clean his cell, and perform every other menial office. Light is allowed him only so long as he toils; and, as soon as the requisite work is done, the light is taken away. Such is his melancholy lot at the present moment!

He who used to toil for thirteen hours a day amidst the learned languages and the works of antiquity, in the study of Theology, and of the arts—the eloquent preacher, lecturer, and tutor—is now compelled to waste his life, with all its acquirements, in spinning. For thirteen hours every day, he is doomed to spin. By this labour he earns, every day, threepence for the state, and a halfpenny for himself! This latter sum, amounting to threepence a week, is allowed him in mercy, and with it he is permitted to purchase a dried herring and a small loaf of coarse brown bread,—which, furthermore, he is allowed to eat as a Sunday dinner,—his ordinary food consisting of a sort of odious pap in the morning (after having spun for four hours), some vegetables at noon, and some bread and water at night.

For months he has not enjoyed a breath of fresh air. He is allowed to walk daily for half-an-hour in a covered passage; but even this is refused whenever the gaoler is occupied with other matters, and cannot attend to trifles.

Dr. Kinkel has no books nor papers;—there is nothing for him but spinning—spinning—spinning! Once a month he is, by great clemency, allowed to write one letter to his wife, which has to pass through the hands of his gaoler, who, being empowered to act as censor, judiciously strikes out whatever he does not choose Madam Kinkel to know. All sympathising letters are strictly withheld from him, while all those which severely take him to task, and censure his political opinions and conduct, are carefully placed in his hands, when he stops to take his breath for a minute from his eternal spinning.

Relatives are not, by the law, allowed to see a criminal during the first three months; after that time, they may. But after having been imprisoned at Naugard three months—short of a day—Dr. Kinkel is suddenly removed to another prison at Spandau, there to re-commence a period of three months. By this device he is prevented from seeing his wife, or any friend—all in a perfectly legal way.

The gaoler is strictly enjoined not to afford Dr. Kinkel any sort of opportunity, either by writing or by any other means, of making intercession with the King to obtain pardon, or the commutation of his sentence into banishment. All these injunctions are fully obeyed by the gaoler—indeed the present one is more severe than any of the others.

Nevertheless, the melancholy truth has oozed out—the picture has worn its tearful way through the dense stone walls—and here it is for all to see—and, we doubt not, for many to feel.

Gottfried Kinkel, so recently one of the most admired professors of the University of Bonn, one of the ornaments of the scholarship and literature of modern Germany, now clothed in sackcloth, with shaven head, and attenuated frame, sits spinning his last threads. He utters no reproaches, no complaints; but bears his sufferings with a sweet resignation that savours already of the angelic abodes to which his contemplations are ever directed. He has entreated his wife to have his heart buried amidst those lovely scenes on which he so often gazed with serene rapture, from his study-window in the Castle of Popplesdorf.

Those who behold this last picture, and revert to the one where the professor came happily sliding his way to his class at the University, may perchance share the emotion which makes us pass our hands across our eyes, to put aside the irrepressible tribute of sorrow which dims and confuses the page before us. His worst enemies could never have contemplated anything so sad as this. Many, indeed, have already relented,—but let their interceding voices be heard before it is too late.

The literary men of no country are united, or they might move the whole kingdom. Still less are the literary men of different countries united, or they might move the world. But are they, therefore, without a common sympathy for one another? We are sure this is not the case; and making this appeal to the literary men of England, we believe it will not be in vain. Nor are we without hope, that a strong sympathy of this kind, being duly and respectfully made known to the King of Prussia, or to Baron Manteufel, the Minister of the Interior, may induce His Majesty to consider that, the revolution being at an end, clemency is not only the "brightest jewel in a crown," but its noblest strength, and that, while royal power can lose nothing, it must gain honour by remitting all further punishment of one who has only shared in the political offence of thousands who are now at liberty. All that the friends, at home and abroad, of Gottfried Kinkel ask is—his liberation from prison, and a permission to emigrate to England or America.

This article by Charles Dickens was published in *Household Words*, a weekly journal conducted by Charles Dickens, on November 2, 1850.

SELECT BIBLIOGRAPHY

A. PRIMARY SOURCES

1. The translations are based on the text in *Karl Marx and Friedrich Engels. Werke*, Vol. 7–9, Berlin, 1960, etc. The letters and declarations, etc., in Appendix B are reprinted from the original English versions.
2. *Enthüllungen*, etc., Mehring's edition, 1914.
3. Karl Bittel, *Der Kommunistenprozess zu Köln* (1852) *im Spiegel der zeitgenössischen Presse*. Berlin, 1955.
4. Wermuth und Stieber, *Die Communisten-Verschwörungen des 19. Jahrhunderts*, Berlin, 1853–1854.
5. Gerhard Winkler, *Dokumente zur Geschichte des Bundes der Kommunisten*, Berlin, 1957.

B. SECONDARY SOURCES

6. Frolinde Balser, *Sozialdemokratie 1848/9–63*, Stuttgart, 1963.
7. G. Becker, *Karl Marx und Friedrich Engels in Köln 1848–1849*, Berlin, 1963.
8. Ludwig Bergsträsser, *Geschichte der politischen Parteien in Deutschland*, München Wien, 1965.
9. Aron Bernstein, *Revolutions- und Reaktionsgeschichte Preussens und Deutschlands von den Märztagen bis zur neuesten Zeit*, Berlin, 1882.
10. Stephan Born, *Erinnerungen eines Achtundvierzigers*, Leipzig, 1898.
11. Julius Braunthal, *History of the International, 1864–1914*, London, 1966.
12. T. S. Hamerow, *Restoration, Revolution and Reaction*, 1958.
13. Rudolf Herrnstadt, *Die erste Verschwörung gegen das internationale Proletariat*, Berlin, 1952.
14. Wilhelm Hirsch, 'Die Opfer der Moucharderie, *New-Yorker Criminal-Zeitung*, April 1, 8, 15 and 22, 1853.
15. E. R. Huber, *Deutsche Verfassungsgeschichte seit 1789*, 4 vols., 1963.
16. F. Lessner, *Vor 1848 und nachher. Erinnerungen eines alten Kommunisten*, 1898.
17. F. Mehring, *Karl Marx, The Story of his Life*.
18. F. Mehring, *Geschichte der deutschen Sozialdemokratie*, 4 vols., Stuttgart, 1919.
19. B. Nicolaevsky and O. Maenchen-Helfen, *Karl Marx: Man and Fighter*, London, 1934 and 1936.
20. Karl Obermann, *Zur Geschichte des Bundes der Kommunisten, 1849 bis 1852*, Berlin, 1955.
21. Joseph von Radowitz, *Schriften und Reden* (ed. R. Meinicke), Munich, 1921.
22. R. Rosdolsky, 'K. Marx und der Polizeispitzel Bangya', *International Review for Social History*, Vol. II, pp. 229–44, Leiden, 1936.
23. Arnold Ruge, *Geschichte unserer Zeit von den Freiheitskriegen bis zum Ausbruch des deutsch-französischen Krieges*, Leipzig, 1881.
24. Carl Schurz, *Aus den Lebenserinnerungen eines Achtundvierzigers*, Berlin, 1948.
25. Veit Valentin, *1848 Chapters of German History*, London, 1940.
26. Wilhelm Weitling, *Schlussbemerkung zum Kölner Kommunistenprozess, Republik der Arbeiter*, December 23, 1852.
27. August Willich, 'Dr. Karl Marx und seine Enthüllungen, *Belletristisches Journal und New-Yorker Criminal-Zeitung*, October 28 and November, 4, 1853.

INDEX OF NAMES

Abraham a Sancta Clara (1644–1709). Court preacher in Vienna; satirist. 221–3

Anneke, Friedrich (Fritz) (*c.* 1817—*c.* 1872). Prussian artillery officer, later member of the Cologne Commune of the Communist League; 1848 founder-member and secretary of the Cologne Workers' Club in which he was a supporter of Gottschalk; editor of the *Neue Kölnische Zeitung*, member of the regional committee of the Rhenish Democrats; July–December 1848 under arrest; 1849 member of the military commission in the Baden-Palatinate uprising; later participated in the American Civil War on the Northern side. 161

Arnim, Bettina von (1785–1859). German Romantic writer, sister of Clemens Brentano; friendship with Goethe; later, a supporter of liberal ideas in the 1840s. 150, 231–2

Arnim, Graf Harry von (1824–81). Conservative Prussian diplomat, 1871–74 ambassador in Paris; opponent of Bismarck who recalled him and ruined his career. 122

Auerswald, Rudolf von (1795–1866). Prussian statesman, member of the liberal nobility; Prime Minister and Foreign Minister (June–September 1848). 96

Bangya, Johann (1817–68). Austrian officer. Active in the Hungarian Revolutionary army; later exiled and played an active part in emigré organisations as a police informer. 33–5, 275–7.

Barbes, Armand (1809–70). Revolutionary, one of the leaders of the Society of the Seasons under the July monarchy; in 1848 he became a deputy in the Assembly where he supported Ledru-Rollin; after the revolution collapsed he was sentenced to life-imprisonment but was amnestied in 1854 after which he emigrated. 40, 199.

Barthélemy, Emmanuel (*c.* 1820–55). French worker, follower of Blanqui, member of revolutionary secret societies under the July monarchy; took part in the June uprising in Paris; exile in England, charged with criminal offences and executed in 1855. 199–200.

Bauer, Bruno (1809–82). Young Hegelian philosopher. 151, 173, 175, 176, 181, 189–90, 232, 276.

Bauer, Heinrich. Shoemaker from Franconia, one of the leaders of the League of the Just and the German Workers' Educational Association in London; member of the Central Committee of the Communist League; travelled around Germany as an emissary of the League (April–May 1850); 1851 he emigrated to Australia. 18, 40, 52, 53, 118, 250, 253.

Becker, August (1814–71). Journalist, worked on the *Rheinische Zeitung* and the Paris *Vorwärts*; supporter of Weitling and after the latter's arrest (1842) Becker led the communist artisan movement in Switzerland. 41

Becker, Hermann Heinrich (1820–85) known as "Red Becker", defendant in the Communist Trial in Cologne; lawyer and journalist, member of various democratic organisations, editor of the *Westdeutsche Zeitung* (May 1849–July 1850); member of the Communist League from 1850; in later years he became a National Liberal, Mayor of Dortmund and Cologne and a member of the Prussian Upper House. 20–1, 29, 54–5, 59, 85, 109, 112.

Beckerath, Hermann von (1801–70). Crefeld banker, one of the leaders of the liberal bourgeoisie in the Rhineland; member of the Frankfurt Assembly (right-centre); Finance Minister in the Imperial government (August and September 1848). 207.

Beckmann,? Prussian spy in Paris in the early 1850s; Paris correspondent of the *Kölnische Zeitung.* 75, 122.

Bermbach, Adolph (1822–75). Cologne lawyer, democrat, member of the Frankfurt Assembly; defence witness in the Cologne Trial in which he also acted as a contact between Marx and the defendants; in later years a Liberal. 83, 85–6, 89.

Birnbaum, Wilhelm. Secretary of the organisation for the relief of the poor in Cologne; witness for the defence in the Communist Trial. 88–9.

Bismarck, Otto von (1815–98). 11–12, 19, 32, 55, 132, 134.

Blanc, Jean-Joseph-Louis (1811–82). French socialist, journalist and historian; member of the provisional government and president of the Luxembourg Commission in 1848; in favour of a pact with the bourgeoisie; emigrated to London in August 1848 where he was one of the leaders of the petty-bourgeois emigration. 51, 54, 199–201, 253.

Blanqui, Louis Auguste (1805–81). French revolutionary, utopian communist; believed that the proletariat could come to power only as the result of a conspiracy but also acknowledged the need for a revolutionary dictatorship; organised a number of secret societies as well as the uprising of May 12, 1839; in 1848 he was one of the leaders of the revolutionaries; spent altogether 36 years of his life in gaol. 39, 199, 200, 219.

Blind, Karl (1826–1907). Democratic writer and journalist; active in the revolutionary movement in Baden 1848–49; 1849 member of the provisional government of Baden; one of the leaders of the petty-bourgeois emigration in London, later on a National Liberal. 180.

Blum, Robert (1807–48). German politician, leader of the Left in the Frankfurt Assembly; took part in the Viennese uprising in October 1848 and was executed after the fall of the city. 199.

Boiardo, Matteo Maria (1434–94). Italian poet of the Renaissance; his chief work was the romance *L'Orlando inamorato*. 32, 182, 214, 218–9, 230, 232–3.

Born, Stephan (1824–98). Member of the Communist League; one of the important founders of the German working-class movement, concentrating however on the guilds; after 1848 he emigrated first to Switzerland and then to England. 51, 52.

Börne, Ludwig (1786–1837). Radical journalist and critic, friend and later antagonist of Heine. 32, 184, 233.

Brentano, Lorenz Peter (1813–91). Lawyer in Mannheim, democratic; 1848 member of the Frankfurt Assembly; 1849 head of the Baden provisional government; emigrated after Rastatt first to Switzerland and then to America. 172, 180, 182, 211, 212, 228.

Brüggemann, Karl Heinrich (1810–c. 1877). Economist and liberal journalist, editor of the *Kölnische Zeitung* (1846–55). 181.

Brunswick and Lüneburg, Karl Friedrich August Wilhelm, Duke of (1804–73). In 1823 succeeded to the Duchy; 1830 overthrow and exile; persistent attempts to recover his possessions; in the 1840s and 1850s he was in contact with democratic movements and gave financial support to the *Deutsche Londoner Zeitung*. 172, 186, 205.

Bucher, Lothar (1817–92). Member of the Prussian justiciary, journalist; left-centre member of the Prussian National Assembly in 1848; *émigré* in London; later a National Liberal active in Bismarck's Foreign Ministry; friend of Lassalle. 198, 201, 222.

Büchner, Georg (1813–37). German dramatist and revolutionary; forced into exile after attempting to provoke an uprising in 1834. 39.

Bürgers, Heinrich (1820–78). Defendant in the Communist Trial in Cologne; radical journalist in Cologne; 1842–43 worked on the *Rheinische Zeitung*; member of the Cologne commune of the Communist League; 1848–49 on the editorial board of the *Neue Rheinische Zeitung*; 1850 Central Committee of the Communist League; author of the Address of December 1850; arrested in Dresden after Nothjung; sentenced to 6 years gaol at Cologne; later a progressive member of the Reichstag. 20, 21, 29, 54, 55, 59, 60, 108, 117.

Burritt, Elihu (1810–79). American linguist, philanthropist and pacifist; organised a number of international pacifist congresses. 190.

Carlier, Pierre-Charles-Joseph (1799–1858). Prefect of Police in Paris (1849–51), Bonapartist. 67–9.

Cherval, Julien (i.e. Joseph Crämer). Prussian spy and agent provocateur who had gained entry into the Communist League; after the split of September 1850 he joined the Willich–Schapper faction and led one of the Paris Communes; accused of complicity in the so-called Franco-German plot in Paris in February 1852; escaped with the connivance of the police and went to England. 25, 34, 67–81, 98–9, 109, 113, 115, 118, 122, 124, 128, 131, 269, 270.

Chianella. A Crefeld waiter and police spy; witness in the Cologne Trial. 105–6.

Clausewitz, Karl von (1780–1831). Prussian general and military theorist. 186.

Clement, Knut Jungbohn (1810–73). Historian and philologist, professor at Kiel University. 191.

Cobden, Richard (1804–65). English calico manufacturer in Manchester; liberal, freetrader, one of the founders of the Anti-Corn Law League. 190.

Cromwell, Oliver (1559–1698). 217.

Damm. Petty-bourgeois democrat, Chairman of the Baden Constituent Assembly; emigrated later to England. 223.

Daniels, Dr. Roland (1819–55). Doctor in Cologne, member of the Communist League from 1850, close friend of Marx and Engels, according to Mehring he was "probably the true intellectual leader of the Cologne Central Committee"; acquitted by the Cologne jury. 20–1, 26, 29, 54–5, 59.

Darasz, Albert (1808–52). One of the leaders of the Polish National Liberation movement, active in the uprising of 1830–31, played a leading part in the Polish *émigré* organisations and was a member of the Central Committee for European Democracy. 188, 202.

Dickens, Charles (1812–70). 18, 166–7, 277–85.

Dietz, Oswald (c. 1824–64). Architect from Wiesbaden, active in the revolution 1848–9, then secretary of the German Workers' Educational Association in London, member of the central committee of the Communist League; when the League split in 1850 he joined the Central Committee of the Willich–Schapper League; in later years he took part in the American Civil War. 21, 63, 65–6, 70–89, 109, 122, 198, 256–7, 269.

Dronke, Ernst (1822–91). Writer and journalist; at first a "True" Socialist, later a member of the Communist League; one of the editors of the *Neue Rheinische Zeitung* in 1848–9; after the defeat of the revolution he emigrated to Switzerland and then to England; supported Marx and Engels after the split in the League but later withdrew from all political activity. 91, 100–3, 276.

Duchâtel, Charles-Marie-Tanneguy, Comte (1803–67). French statesman, Orleanist; Minister of Trade (1834–6), and Minister of the Interior (1839 and 1840–48); Malthusian. 178.

Dulon, Rudolph (1807–70). Parson, associated with the Illuminati; emigrated to America in 1853. 178, 188–9.

Eccarius, Johann Georg (1818–89). Member of the Communist League, after 1851 an emigrant in London; remained on the side of Marx and Engels after the split in 1850. 24, 47, 250, 252–3, 256.

E(h)rhard, Johann Ludwig Albert (b. 1820). Shop assistant in Cologne, member of the Communist League; defendant in the Communist Trial 1852 but acquitted. 20, 29, 55.

Ewerbeck, August Hermann (1816–60). Doctor and writer; led the Paris commune of the League of the Just; later a member of the Communist League which he left in 1850. 45, 54, 249.

K

Faucher, Julius (1820–78). German journalist, Young Hegelian, advocate of Free Trade, in the early 1850s he propagated individualistic, anarchist views; exile in England 1850–61, later in Germany as a member of the Progressives. 209–11.

Fazy, Jean-Jacques (*James*) (1794–1878) Swiss statesman and publicist, radical, leader of the Cantonal government in Geneva (1846–1853 and 1855–61). 172.

Feuerbach, Ludwig (1804–72). 156, 173, 178, 181.

Fickler, Joseph (1808–65). Journalist, democrat; one of the leaders of the radical and democratic movement in Baden in 1848–9; member of the Baden provisional government in 1849, afterwards he emigrated to Switzerland, England and America. 209–13, 221, 224–7.

Fleury, Charles (also *Schmidt*, i.e. *Carl Friedrich August Krause*) (b. 1824). London business-man, Prussian spy and police agent. 21, 25, 72–4, 80, 89–93, 98–104, 110–13, 120–9, 270, 275.

Flocon, Ferdinand (1800–66). Democratic French politician and journalist; edited *La Réforme;* member of the provisional government in 1848. 50.

Follen, August Adolf Ludwig (1794–1855). Poet, journalist and politician; volunteer in the War of Liberation against France 1814; after 1815 he became a member of the Burschen-schaft, in opposition at the time; emigrated to Switzerland in 1821. 189.

Freiligrath, Ferdinand (1810–76). Revolutionary poet, one of the editors of the *Neue Rheinische Zeitung* 1848–49; member of the Communist League, there was a warrant for his arrest along with the other Cologne defendants but he had escaped to England; withdrew from politics in the 1850s. 20, 54, 94, 157, 266, 271.

Friedrich Wilhelm IV (1795–1861), King of Prussia (1840–1861). 10–13, 18, 64, 152, 263.

Garibaldi, Giuseppe (1807–82). 32, 195, 199.

Gebert, August. Carpenter from Mecklenburg, member of the Communist League in Switzerland and later in London; after the split he joined Willich–Schapper and sat on their Central Committee. 198, 256, 257.

Geiger, Wilhelm Arnold. Prussian police official; in 1848 examining magistrate and then Police Director in Cologne. 82.

Gipperich, Joseph. Tailor, member of the Paris Communes of the Communist League, joined the Willich–Schapper faction after the split; defendant in the trial following the so-called Franco–German plot in February 1852; later emigrated to England. 70–2, 78–9.

Girardin, Emile de (1806–81). French journalist and politician; editor of *La Presse* (1836–57 with interruptions); in politics he was distinguished by his extreme indifference to principles: in opposition to Guizot before the revolution, bourgeois republican during the revolution, deputy of the Legislative Assembly (1850–51), later on a Bonapartist. 190.

Göbel. Judge of the Court of Appeal, President of the Assizes Court in the Cologne Trial. 98, 114.

Goegg, Amand (1820–97). Democratic journalist, member of the Baden provisional government in 1849; emigrated after the defeat of the revolution; in the 1870s he returned and joined the Social Democrats. 54, 172, 209, 211, 213–4, 219, 221–27.

Goethe, Johann Wolfgang von (1749–1832). 137–8, 145–8, 154, 209–10, 231, 232, 234.

Goldheim. Police officer, one of the secret Prussian agents in London in the 1850s. 61, 83, 84, 89–96, 98–102, 126–9.

Gö(h)ringer, Karl (b. *c.* 1808). Innkeeper from Baden, took part in the Baden revolutionary movement 1848–49; emigrated to London, member of the Communist League; after the split he joined Willich–Schapper; owned a public house in London which became the meeting-place of the petty bourgeois German *émigrés.* 204–9.

Greif(f). Prussian police officer, one of the leaders of the Prussian agency in London in the early 1850s. 21, 61, 78–80, 83–4, 90–3, 100–2, 104, 110, 120–7, 131, 270, 275.

Haacke (Hake), Johann Carl (b. *c.* 1820). Tailor's apprentice from Brunswick, member of the Communist League, emigrated to London, joined the Willich-Schapper faction after the League split up in 1850. 109.

Hansemann, David Justus (1790–1864). Businessman, one of the leaders of the liberal bourgeoisie; member of the United Diet in 1847; in 1848 he was a deputy in the Prussian Assembly and from May to September he was Prussian Finance Minister. 14, 198.

Harring, Harro Paul (1798–1870). Democratic writer; from 1825 he lived mainly in exile in various European countries. 46, 190–6.

Hätzel, Karl Joseph August (b. *c.* 1815). Shoemaker, member of the Communist League, tried with a group of League members in Berlin in 1850 but acquitted; after the League split up he joined Willich-Schapper; appeared for the prosecution in the Cologne Communist Trial. 85, 109.

Hatzfeldt zu Trachenberg–Schönstein, Maximilian Friedrich Franz Karl, Graf von (1813–59). Prussian diplomat and ambassador in Paris. 122.

Haug, Ernst. Austrian officer, democrat, active in the revolution in Italy (1848–49); emigrated later to England became one of the editors of the weekly magazine *Der Kosmos*. 188, 201–7, 224.

Hauk, Ludwig (1799–1850). Austrian officer, took part in the uprising in Vienna and in the revolution in Hungary 1848–49; on the defeat of the revolution he was shot. 204.

Haupt, Hermann Wilhelm (b. *c.* 1831). Shop assistant member of the Communist League in Hamburg, arrested before the Cologne Trial, turned King's evidence and was released; fled to Brazil. 20, 23, 54, 125.

Heck, Ludwig (b. *c.* 1822). Tailor from Brunswick, member of the Communist League, joined up with Willich-Schapper after the League split up in 1850. 74.

Hecker, Friedrich Franz Karl (1811–81). Lawyer in Mannheim, radical republican; member of the Vorparlament in 1848, one of the leaders of the Baden uprising of April 1848; emigration in Switzerland and later in the U.S.A. where he became a colonel on the Northern side in the Civil War. 171.

Hegel, Georg Wilhelm Friedrich (1770–1831). 64, 137, 141, 148, 151–2, 173–4, 176, 184, 190, 203, 217, 231.

Heine, Heinrich (1798–1856). 32, 118, 176–7, 231.

Heinzen, Karl (1809–80). Radical journalist, opposed to Marx and Engels, took part briefly in the uprising in Baden and the Palatinate, then emigrated to Switzerland, England and finally to the U.S.A. in 1850. 178, 182–7, 197, 205–6, 213, 227.

Hentze, A. Former officer, member of the Communist League, joined Willich-Schapper after the League split in 1850; witness for the prosecution in the Cologne Communist Trial. 85, 109, 112.

Herder, Johann Gottfried (1744–1803). 178.

Hertle, Daniel (b. 1824). Democratic journalist, took part in the uprising in Baden and the Palatinate in 1849; emigrated to the U.S.A. in 1850. 224.

Herwegh, Georg Friedrich (1817–75). Revolutionary poet, in 1848 he was one of the leaders of the German Democratic Society in Paris that organised a battalion of volunteers to assist the revolution in Germany. 50, 173.

Hess, Moses (1812–75). Journalist, one of the founders of the *Rheinische Zeitung*, one of the chief advocates of True Socialism in the 1840s; after the split in the Communist League he supported Willich-Schapper; later, he became a follower of Lassalle. 25, 109, 131, 134.

Hinckeldey, Karl Ludwig Friedrich von (1805–56). Lawyer, Police President of Berlin from 1848 with responsibility of protecting the constitution throughout Prussia. This gave him immense power which he used to suppress the Left (although he spied also on the extreme Right). Killed in a duel. 12, 19–25, 105, 125, 131–2, 271–3.

Hirsch, Wilhelm. Shop assistant from Hamburg, Prussian police agent in London in the 1850s. 25, 35, 86–91, 98, 100, 104, 110–12, 120, 124–9, 131, 270, 275, 277.

Hodde, Lucien de la (1808–65). French journalist, member of secret revolutionary societies during the restoration and the July monarchy; police agent. 122, 123, 275.

Hoffmann, Ernst Theodor Amadeus (1776–1822). 32, 142.

Hontheim, Richard von (d. 1857). Lawyer in Cologne, defence counsel in the Cologne Communist Trial. 27, 89, 94, 95, 97.

Imandt, Peter. Teacher in Crefeld, democrat, chairman of the Crefeld Workingmen's Club; active in Cologne and Trier during the revolution (1848–49); later emigrated, member of the Communist League, in contact with Marx and Engels. 91, 100–3.

Itzstein, Johann Adam von (1775–1855). Baden politician, leader of the liberal opposition in the Baden Diet; in 1848–49 member of the extreme Left in the Frankfurt Assembly; emigrated to Switzerland after the collapse of the revolution. 185.

Jacobi, Dr. Abraham (b. 1832). Defendant in the Communist Trial in Cologne; doctor in Berlin, member of the Communist League; acquitted at Cologne, emigrated to the U.S.A. 20, 29, 54, 55.

Jacoby, Johann (1805–77). Doctor in Königsberg; journalist and politician; member of the Vorparlament, the Prussian National Assembly and the Frankfurt Assembly, always on the extreme left; he later became a resolute opponent of Bismarck's policies and a member of the S.P.D. 199.

Jaup, Heinrich Karl (1781–1860). Liberal jurist, Prime Minister of Hesse-Darmstadt (1848–50), President of the Peace Congress in Frankfurt (August 1850). 190.

Junkermann. Police inspector in Crefeld; witness for the prosecution in the Cologne Communist Trial. 105.

Kant, Immanuel (1724–1804). 156.

Kinkel, Gottfried (1815–82). Poet, and journalist; took part in the uprising in Baden and the Palatinate, wounded and taken prisoner by the Prussians who sentenced him to life imprisonment in a fortress; escaped November 1850 with the aid of his disciple Carl Schurz and went to England; there he became one of the leaders of the petty-bourgeois *émigrés* opposed to Marx and Engels. 9, 17–18, 31, 33–4, 54, 107–10, 137–68 passim, 181, 191, 196–208, 210, 211, 215–6, 219–230, 277–85 passim.

Klein, Dr. Johann Jacob (b. c. 1818). Doctor in Cologne, member of the Communist League, defendant in the Communist Trial 1852 but acquitted by the jury. 20, 29, 54–5.

Kock, Paul de (c. 1794–1871). French writer of frivolous popular novels. 178.

Kossuth, Lajos (1802–94). Leader of the movement for Hungarian national liberation, head of the Hungarian revolutionary government 1848–9; after the revolution was defeated he fled at first to Turkey and later to England and America. 34–5, 54, 118, 182, 183, 199, 230, 277.

Kothes, D. Businessman in Cologne; witness for the defence in the Communist Trial. 82–4, 90.

Kotzebue, August Friedrich Ferdinand von (1761–1819). Popular dramatist, suspected of being an agent of the Russian Czar he was murdered by a student; his death gave rise to the repressive laws of the Metternich era known as the Karlsbad Decrees. 147, 253.

Kriege, Hermann (1820–50). "True" Socialist; during the latter half of the 1840's he was the leader of the German "True" Socialists in New York. 46.

Ladendorf, Dr. phil. August. Son of a senator from Prenzlau, a bourgeois democrat; in the revolution he was president of a popular Club in Berlin, became involved in a plot provoked by the Prussian government and sentenced to 5 years imprisonment in 1853. 127, 130.

Lamartine, Alphonse-Merie-Louis de (1790–1869). Poet, historian and politician; a republican during the 1840's he became Foreign Minister and effective head of the provisional government in 1848; deputy of the Assembly and member of the Executive Commission. 50, 166, 185.

Landolphe. French socialist, *émigré* in London; joined Willich–Schapper after the split in the Communist League (1850). 200.

Lassalle, Ferdinand (1825–64). 30, 125.

Laube, Samuel. Tailor, member of the Communist League; went over to Willich–Schapper after the League split up in 1850. 74.

Ledru-Rollin, Alexandre-Auguste (1807–74). French journalist and politician, one of the leaders of the petty-bourgeois democrats, editor of *La Réforme*; in 1848 he was Minister of the Interior and member of the Executive Commission, he was also a member of the Constituent and Legislative Assemblies, as part of the Montagne; after June 1849 he emigrated to England. 54, 180, 188, 196–201, 205, 215, 228, 232.

Leibniz, Gottfried Wilhelm (1646–1716) 64.

Leo, Heinrich (1799–1878). Historian and journalist, the advocate of conservative political and religious views, he became one of the ideologists of the Prussian Junkers. 189.

Lessner, Friedrich (1825–1910). Journeyman tailor from Weimar, member of the Communist League, active in the Rhineland in 1848–49, member of the Cologne Workers' Club and of the Cologne militia; emissary of the Communist League in Mainz and Wiesbaden in 1850; defendant in the Communist Trial of 1852 at which he was sentenced to three years imprisonment in a fortress; he later emigrated to England; member of the General Council of the First International; friendly with Marx and Engels. 20–1, 26, 29, 47, 55.

Lewald, Fanny (1811–89). Writer associated with the group known as Young Germany who were influenced by Heine and Börne. 178.

Lichnowski, Felix Maria, Prince von (1814–48). Silesian landowner and Prussian officer; in 1848 he was a member of the Frankfurt Assembly (right-wing); killed during the September uprising. 96.

Liebknecht, Wilhelm (1826–1900). 27, 88–95, 98–103, 125–7.

Lochner, Georg (born *c.* 1824). Carpenter, member of the Communist League and of the General Council of the First International. 47.

Majer, Adolph (b. *c.* 1820). Member of the Communist League, joining forces with Willich–Schapper after the split in 1850; as their emissary he worked in France and Switzerland from the end of 1850 to 1851; defendant in the trial following the so-called Franco-German Plot in February 1852. 67, 75, 198, 257.

Manteuffel, Otto Theodor, Freiherr von (1805–1882). Conservative Prussian statesman; Minister of the Interior (Nov. 1848–Dec. 1850), Prime Minister and Foreign Minister (1850–58). 18–19, 180, 232, 272, 274, 285.

Marheinicke, Philipp Konrad (1780–1846). Protestant theologian and historian of Christianity, influenced by Hegel. 137.

Maupas, Charlemagne-Emile de (1818–88). French lawyer, Bonapartist, Prefect of the Paris police (1851) and one of the organisers of the *coup d'état* of December 2, 1851; Minister of Police (1852–53). 105, 123, 271–2.

Mazzini, Giuseppe (1805–72). Italian revolutionary, one of the leaders of the national liberation movement in Italy; Head of the Provisional government of the Roman Republic (1849); in 1850 he was one of the organisers of the Central Committee of European Democracy in London; in the early 1850s he sought support in Bonapartist circles. 30, 40, 43, 54, 188, 94, 196–99, 201–2, 204–7, 214, 225, 228, 233.

Meyen, Eduard (1812–70). Young Hegelian journalist, democrat; emigrated to England after 1848–49; in later years he became a National Liberal. 124, 209–11, 216, 228–8.

Mockel, Johanna (i.e. Frau Johanna Kinkel). 32–3, 140, 150–68 passim, 206–8, 281–5.

Moll, Joseph (1812–49). Watchmaker from Cologne, one of the leaders of the League of the Just and the German Workers' Educational Association in London, member of the Central Committee of the Communist League; from July to September 1848 he was President of the Cologne Workers' Club; member of various revolutionary organisations in Cologne, took part in the Baden uprising and was killed in a skirmish on the River Murg. 40, 47, 50, 52, 118, 237.

Mügge, Theodor (1806–61). Writer and journalist of the Young Hegelian school. 210.

Müller, Franz Joseph. Legal Counsellor in Cologne, the father-in-law of Dr. Roland Daniels, one of the defendants in the Cologne Trial (1852). 88.

Nette, Ludwig Heinrich (b. *c.* 1819). Tailor from Hanover, member of one of the Paris Communes of the Communist League, went over to Willich–Schapper after the split in 1850; defendant in the trial following the discovery of the so-called Franco–German plot of February 1852. 79, 117.

Nicolai, Christoph Friedrich (1733–1811). Writer, publisher and bookseller, adherent of absolutist Enlightenment, frequently satirised by Goethe. 174, 179.

Nothjung, Peter (1821–80). Tailor, member of the Cologne Commune of the Communist League, the Workingmen's Club; in 1848 he became a member of the Committee of Public Safety and took part in the Elberfeld uprising in May 1849; his arrest in May 1851 in Leipzig because he had no identity papers triggered off the Cologne Communist Trial; the propaganda material in his possession led to the arrest of the other League members; at Cologne he was sentenced to 6 years imprisonment; in later years he became a supporter of Lassalle. 20–1, 29, 54–5, 59, 60, 65.

Novalis (1772–1801). German Romantic poet, author of *Heinrich von Ofterdingen*. 145, 231.

Oppenheim, Heinrich Bernhard (1819–80). Politician, political scientist and journalist; democrat; in 1848 he was one of the editors of the Berlin paper *Die Reform*; emigrated 1849–50; later he became a National Liberal. 197, 210–11, 216, 224, 227–8.

Otto, Karl Wunibald (b. 1810). Chemist, member of the Cologne Worker's Club and the Communist League (1848–49); defendant in the Cologne Trial and sentenced to 5 years detention in a fortress. 18, 20, 29, 54, 55.

Pfänder, Karl (*c.* 1818–76). Painter, member of the League of the Just, of the Central Committee of the Communist League and the General Council of the First International. 47, 250, 253.

Proudhon, Pierre-Joseph (1809–65). 51.

Prutz, Robert Eduard (1816–72). Political poet and literary historian; bourgeois democrat in the revolution of 1848–49; associated with the Young Hegelians. 176.

Radowitz, Joseph Maria von (1797–1853). Prussian general and politician, closely associated with the extreme right–wing court camarilla; one of the leaders of the Right in the Frankfurt Assembly. 11, 12, 15, 205.

Reichenbach, Oskar, Count (b. 1815). Silesian landowner, member of the Frankfurt Assembly (1848–49), *émigré* in England (1850) and later in America. 110, 201, 216, 220, 223, 229, 230.

Reiff, Wilhelm Joseph (b. *c.* 1824). Member of the Communist League and the Cologne Workers' Club, later secretary of the Workers' Educational Association; expelled from the Communist League in 1850 but was nevertheless tried at Cologne in 1852 and sentenced to 5 years imprisonment. 18, 20, 28, 29, 54, 55.

Reininger, Johann Georg. Tailor, chairman of one of the Paris communes of the Communist League; after the split in 1850 he joined the Willich–Schapper faction; emissary in Mainz in September 1851, arrested but acquitted by a court in May 1853. 74.

Renard. Writing teacher in Cologne, expert witness in the Communist Trial of 1852. 105.

Reuchlin, Johann (1455–1522). Philologist and lawyer, one of the great figures of the German Renaissance. 178.

Reuter, Max. Prussian police agent in London in the early 1850s. 66, 109, 122.

Rings, L. W. Member of the Communist League, *émigré* in London in the early 1850s, a supporter of Marx and Engels. 27, 88–90, 95, 100, 125.

Robespierre, Maximilien-Marie-Isidore de (1758–94). 199.

Ronge, Johannes (1813–87). Priest, founder and leader of the German–Catholic movement; became a petty-bourgeois democrat, took part in the revolution of 1848–49; *émigré* in England 1849–61. 178, 201–3, 206, 221, 224.

Röser, Peter Gerhard (1814–65). Worked in a cigar factory; president of the Workers' Educational Association in Cologne and member of the Communist League; only joined after convincing himself that it was hostile to every kind of conspiracy; defendant in the Cologne Trial and sentenced to 6 years imprisonment; regarded by the prosecution as "perhaps the wickedest of all"; in later years he became a supporter of Lassalle. 18, 20, 21, 26, 29, 54, 55, 59, 109, 117.

Rotteck, Karl Wenzeslaus Rodecker von (1775–1840). Historian, one of the leaders of the Baden Liberals. 171, 188, 205.

Ruge, Arnold (1802–80). Radical journalist, one of the most prominent Young Hegelians; in 1844 he published the *Deutsch-französische Jahrbücher* with Marx; in 1848 he became a member of the left-wing of the Frankfurt National Assembly; in the 1850s he was one of the leaders of the petty-bougeois *émigrés* in England; National Liberal after 1866. 31, 54, 62, 124, 169, 173–81 passim, 184, 188, 189–91, 196–206, 211, 215, 220, 221, 224, 227–8, 234.

Saedt, Otto Joseph Arnold (1816–86). Prussian legal official, from 1848 he was State prosecutor in Cologne; chief prosecutor in the Cologne Communist Trial. 27, 59, 61–2, 75, 79, 90, 104, 113–6.

Schabelitz, Jacob (1827–99). Swiss publisher and bookseller. 29.

Schapper, Karl (*c.* 1812–70). One of the leaders of the League of the Just and the German Workers' Educational Association in London, member of the Central Committee of the Communist League; in 1848 he was proof-reader for the *Neue Rheinische Zeitung*, and president of the Cologne Workers' Club (February–May 1849); became the leader with Willich of the anti-Marx party of the Communist League from September 1850 but was reconciled with Marx in 1856; later he became a member of the General Council of the First International. 10, 21–5, 34, 40, 45, 50, 52, 54–5, 62–7, 70, 73–5, 80, 107–11, 118, 122, 131, 198, 200, 250–7.

Schärttner, August. Cooper in Hanau, active in the revolution of 1848–49 as well as in the Baden uprising of 1849; emigrated to England and opened a restaurant which became a meeting place for the petty-bourgeois *émigrés*; joined the Communist League and after the split in 1850 he became a member of the Central Committee of the Willich–Schapper party. 110, 111, 198, 209, 256–7.

Schiller, Friedrich von (1859–1905). 148, 231.

Schimmelpfennig, Alexander (1824–65). Former Prussian officer, then a democrat active in the uprising in Baden and the Palatinate; as an *émigré* he joined the Willich–Schapper party and later went America where he fought in the Civil War. 34, 197, 216, 220, 223.

Schmitz, Th. Private secretary in Cologne, witness for the defence in the Communist Trial of 1852. 88, 90.

Schneider II, Karl. Democratic lawyer in Cologne; member of various committees during the revolution of 1848–9; defended Marx and Engels in the case against the *Neue Rheinische Zeitung* of 1849 and was the chief counsel for the defence in the Communist Trial at Cologne in 1852. 27, 78, 83, 88, 89, 92, 94–8, 103, 106, 270.

Schramm, Konrad (c. 1822–58). Member of the Communist League, *émigré* in London after 1849, responsible editor of the *Neue Rheinische Zeitung. Politisch-Ökonomische Revue;* in the split of the League he remained on the side of Marx and Engels. 75, 76, 250.

Schramm, Rudolph (1813–82). Democratic journalist, left-wing member of the Prussian National Assembly in 1848; after the defeat of the revolution he emigrated to England where he joined the opponents of Marx; in the 1860s he became a supporter of Bismarck. 169, 181, 198, 201, 225, 226, 228.

Schulz (d. 1852). Police director in Cologne, one of the principal organisers of the Communist Trial of 1852. 21, 60, 81, 87, 113.

Schurz, Karl (1829–1906). Democrat, active in the uprising in Baden and the Palatinate of 1849, organised Kinkel's escape from Spandau in 1850, emigrated to Switzerland in 1850 and later to the U.S.A. (1852); took part in the Civil War and later became an American Ambassador to Spain, a senator and Minister of the Interior. 152, 166, 197–8, 216, 220, 222–5, 229–30, 246.

Schütz. Democrat, took part in the uprising in Baden and the Palatinate, representative of the Baden Provisional government in Paris, later emigrated to England. 180.

Seckendorf, August Heinrich Eduard Friedrich, Freiherr von (1807–85). Prussian jurist and legal official, member of the Prussian Lower House (1849–51), assistant prosecutor in the Cologne Communist Trial (1852). 59, 61–2, 79, 90, 94, 114, 116.

Sigel, Franz (1824–1902). Baden Officer, democrat; took part in the revolution of 1848–49 in Baden as one of the outstanding leaders of the Campaign for the Imperial Constitution; emigrated to the U.S.A. in 1852 and later fought on the Northern side in the Civil War. 209, 211–12, 214–15, 220–9, 246.

Stahr, Adolf Wilhelm Theodor (1805–76). Writer of historical novels and works dealing with aesthetic and literary problems. 165.

Stechan, Gottlieb Ludwig (b. *c.* 1814). Carpenter from Hanover, member of the Communist League, on the side of Willich–Schapper in 1850 but in December 1851 he went over to Marx and Engels; from January 1852 he stood at the head of the Workers' Club in London. 88.

Stein, Lorenz von (1815–90). Hegelian, professor of philosophy and constitutional law at Kiel, secret agent of the Prussian government, author of *Socialism and Communism in contemporary France.* 115, 116, 119, 178.

Steingens, Luitbert (Suitbert) Heinrich Hermann (b. *c.* 1817). Painter from Crefeld, member of the Communist League, adherent of Willich–Schapper after the split in the League (1850), witness for the prosecution in the Cologne Communist Trial of 1852. 85, 110.

Stieber, Dr. Wilhelm (1818–82). Jurist, entered the Prussian police in 1844, disciplined because of his dubious procedures in 1845; defence counsel in criminal and political cases (1848–50); in 1851 he became head of Security police in Berlin under Hinckeldey; chief witness in the Cologne Communist Trial of 1852; his methods again came under attack in 1857 and he was put on trial in 1860 and again in 1861 but acquitted; he was forced into retirement; worked as an agent for the Czarist government 1861–5, then recalled by Bismarck and made head of the Central Information Office i.e. the political police; instrumental in assembling the information that led to the ban on the S.P.D. in 1874, although Stieber had been dismissed in 1873. The author of *Communist Conspiracies in the Nineteenth Century* together with Wermuth. 18, 19, 21, 24, 25, 39, 48, 60–1, 64–100 passim, 106, 109, 112–14, 118, 120, 122–3, 125–32, 268, 270–3.

Stirner, Max (i.e. Johann Caspar Schmidt) (1806–56). Philosopher of the Young Hegelian school who arrived at an extreme individualistic and anarchistic position in his principal book *The Ego and its Own*, a work attacked at some length by Marx in *The German Ideology*. 178.

Strauss, David Friedrich (1808–74). Philosopher of the Young Hegelian school. 155, 173, 232.

Strodtmann, Adolf (1829–79). Writer, took part in the revolutionary movement of 1848–49 in Schleswig-Holstein, emigrated in 1850. 137, 150, 152, 165, 197–8, 216.

Struve, Gustav (1805–70). Lawyer and journalist, republican democrat; one of the most radical members of the Frankfurt Vorparlament and one of the leaders of the Baden uprisings in April and September 1848 and the Baden and Palatinate campaigns in 1849; emigrated to London where he became one of the leaders of the petty-bourgeois *émigrés* and later to the U.S.A. where he fought in the Civil War on the Northern side. 31, 169, 170–3, 181, 186–91, 198, 201–8, 216, 246.

Szemere, Bartholomäus (1812–69). Revolutionary Hungarian politician. 34, 277.

Tausenau, Karl (1808–73). Austrian politician on the left-wing of the democratic movement, head of the Central Committee of the Democratic Societies of Vienna (1848), after 1849 he lived as an *émigré* in London. 201, 221, 223–4, 226–8.

Techow, Gustav Adolf (1813–93). Former Prussian officer, then a democrat; active in Berlin during the revolution; chief of the general staff in the campaign in Baden and the Palatinate; after the defeat of the revolutionary armies he went to Switzerland (1849) and in 1852 emigrated to Australia. 197, 216, 220.

Tietz, Friedrich Wilhelm (b. c. 1823). Tailor, member of the Communist League, joined the Willich-Schapper party when the League split in 1850. 74.

Treitschke, Heinrich Gotthard von (1834–96). Historian and National Liberal Deputy; anti-semitic and violently opposed to the workers' movement. 133.

Ulmer, Johann. Member of the Communist League, émigre in London in the early 1850s, supporter of Marx and Engels. 99, 100, 125.

Venedey, Jacob (1805–71). Radical politician, left-wing member of the Vorparlament and the Frankfurt National Assembly. 39, 184, 233.

Vidil, Jules. Former French officer, socialist, member of the committee of the Blanquist Emigrant Union in London, in contact with the Willich–Schapper party. 200.

Waldeck, Benedikt Franz Leo (1802–70). One of the leaders of the Left and Vice-President of the Prussian National Assembly in 1848; member of the Second Chamber in 1849, later a Progressive. 199.

Weerth, Georg (1822–1856). Journalist, edited the 'Feuilleton' in the *Neue Rheinische Zeitung;* sentenced to three months imprisonment in 1849; lived in exile after 1850. 28, 276.

Weitling, Christian Wilhelm (1808–71). Tailor, one of the founders of socialism in Germany. 41–6, 52, 54.

Wermuth. Police director in Hanover, witness for the prosecution in the Communist Trial in Cologne; together with Wilhelm Stieber he wrote *Communist Conspiracies in the Nineteenth Century.* 39, 48, 61, 84, 98, 118.

Westphalen, Ferdinand Otto Wilhelm von (1799–1876). Reactionary Prussian statesman; Minister of the Interior (1850–58); Marx's brother-in-law. 12, 19, 21, 272.

Weydemeyer, Joseph (1818–66). Member of the Communist League; took part in the Revolution of 1848–9 and then emigrated to the U.S.A. (1851). 28.

Wigand, Otto (1795–1870). Leipzig bookseller and publisher of a number of works by radical writers. 180.

Willich, August (1810–78). Former Prussian lieutenant who left the service on political grounds, member of the Communist League, leader of a volunteer corps in the campaign in Baden and the Palatinate; leader together with Schapper of the section of the League hostile to Marx and Engels; in 1853 he went to America and became a general in the Civil War on the Northern side. 10, 21–5, 32, 34, 52, 54–5, 62–81 passim, 107–2, 120, 122, 131, 198–205, 215–16, 219–20, 224–30, 250, 253, 256–7, 265, 277.

Windischgraetz, Alfred, Prince (1787–1862). Austrian Field Marshal; one of the leaders of the counter-revolution in Austria; crushed the uprisings in Prague and Vienna and later in Hungary. 10, 180.

Wolff, Wilhelm (1809–64). Teacher and journalist; active in the Burschenschaft movement; member of the Central Committee of the Communist League, editor of the *Neue Rheinische Zeitung;* after the revolution was defeated he emigrated first to Switzerland and then to England (after 1851); close friend of Marx and Engels. 47, 50, 51, 94, 246, 271.

Wrangel, Friedrich Heinrich Ernst, Count von (1784–1877). Prussian General; one of the leaders of the counter-revolution in Prussia in November 1848. 10, 179–80.

Zabel, Friedrich (1802–75). Liberal journalist, editor of the Berlin *National-Zeitung* (1848–75). 124, 210.

ST. MARY'S COLLEGE OF MARYLAND
ST. MARY'S CITY, MARYLAND

055342